AERIAL RECONNAISSANCE

The 10th Photo Recon Group

In World War II

Thomas G. Ivie

AERO PUBLISHERS, INC.
FALLBROOK

Published by Aero Publishers, Inc.
329 West Aviation Road, Fallbrook, CA 92028
Copyright © 1981 by Aero Publishers, Inc.
All rights reserved
International Standard Book Number: 0-8168-8900-7
Library of Congress Catalog Card Number: 80-68922
Printed and bound in the United States of America

Library of Congress Cataloging in Publication Data

Ivie, Thomas G.
  Aerial reconnaissance.

  Includes index.
  1. World War, 1939-1945—Aerial operations, American. 2. United States. Army Air Forces. Photo Reconnaissance Group, 10th—History. 3. Aerial reconnaissance—History. 4. World War, 1939-1945—Campaigns—Western. I. Title.
  D785.I84   940.54'4973   80-68922
  ISBN 0-8168-8900-7   AACR2

Table of Contents

Acknowledgments   v

Contributors   vii

INTRODUCTION   1

CHAPTER I   THE EARLY DAYS   9
September 1941–February 1944 - Activation as 73rd Observation Group and Training

CHAPTER II   PRELUDE TO INVASION   19
February 1944–D-Day - Assignment to the Ninth Air Force, Early Operational Missions

CHAPTER III   D-DAY AND AFTERMATH   35
June 6–July 31, 1944 - Battlefield Coverage of the Invasion Front and Group Reorganization

CHAPTER IV   THE BREAKOUT   53
August–Early September 1944 - Move to France to Cover Third Army's Drive

CHAPTER V   STALEMATE   71
September–November 8, 1944 - Patton Drive Stops, Photo and TAC R Missions Increase

CHAPTER VI   THE FALL OFFENSIVE   91
November 8–December 17, 1944 - Third Army Offensive Resumes, Aerial Combat Intensifies

CHAPTER VII	THE BATTLE OF THE BULGE	105
	December 17, 1944—January 1945 - The 10th Helps Turn Germany's Last Offensive	
CHAPTER VIII	THE MARCH TO THE RHINE	129
	February—March 1945 - Third Army Supported by the 10th's Battlefield Coverage	
CHAPTER IX	ACROSS THE RHINE TO VICTORY	143
	March—May 8, 1945 - Aerial Recon Aids Patton, TAC R Scores Its Final Victories	

Appendixes

    1. Aircraft and Tactics   171
    2. Low-Altitude Flights   182
    3. Organizational Changes   183
    4. Group Aces   186
    5. Aerial Victories   189
    6. Colors and Markings   191

Index   195

Acknowledgments

The author had the help and generous assistance of many people in the preparation of this history of the 10th Photo Reconnaissance Group. Without it this project could not have been undertaken, and to them a great debt of gratitude is owed.

The idea for such a history was born out of the author's friendship with John Hoefker, who served with distinction with the 15th Tactical Reconnaissance Squadron, and was developed in 1974 when the 10th Photo Reconnaissance Group had its first reunion.

A lion's share of the credit for this project must go to Newton E. Jarrard, who provided needed assistance in many ways. He introduced the author to many individuals who served in the Group, purchased microfilm of the Group's records for use in this project, provided numerous photos and documents from his personal files, and led the way in assisting my search for "lost" members of the 10th Photo Reconnaissance Group. In addition to his material help, his constant enthusiasm and encouragement went a long way in seeing the history through to completion.

Most of the narrative in this book is based on unit records and 9th Air Force records and publications. Much of the documentation pertaining to Group Headquarters came from Gen. Russell A. Berg (ret.), who commanded the 10th from June 20, 1944 to the end of the war, and Col. William B. Reed (ret.), who commanded the Group from September 1943 to June 20, 1944. Both were kind enough to send documents from their personal records and files and long letters covering their thoughts and recollections about the Group's activities and accomplishments. Additional valuable material pertaining to Group HQ came from Mr. E. A. Poe, who served as Assistant Operations Officer for many months before his transfer to the 363rd Reconnaissance Group.

The appeal for Squadron records was answered from numerous sources, and these came in surprising quantities. From Lyon Davis, former CO of the 15th Tactical Reconnaissance Squadron, came copies of most of the unit's records and the Squadron photo album. Lt. Col. J. E. Williams (ret.), who served with the 155th Night Photo Squadron, sent monthly historical reports and the Squadron photo album. Mr. William I. Williams provided the 162nd Tactical Reconnaissance Squadron's records and photos. Colonel Merritt Garner, who commanded the 31st Photo Squadron, sent unit historical records pertaining to his Squadron. Mr. John Florence, who commanded the 12th Tactical Reconnaissance Squadron, sent personal files and photos, and his material was supplemented by microfilm of the Squadron's records sent by Mr. William N. Hess. J. B. Woodson of the 33rd Photo Squadron Association sent Squadron records and photos, as did Mr. Harold Vaughn of the 34th Photo Squadron Association. Additional material pertaining to the 155th Night Photo Squadron was obtained from the Air Force Museum files, thanks to Mrs. Vivian White, Miss Katherine Cassity, and Tom Brewer.

Personal diaries and journals were made available by several former pilots, and these provided insight into what day-to-day life was like in the Group. Special thanks must go to Mr. Fred Trenner, Mr. John Miefert, Maj. Haylon R. Wood (ret.), Mr. John Hoefker, Lt. Col. Clyde East (ret.), Col. Edward Bishop (ret.), and Col. Rufus Woody (ret.) for allowing me to quote from these documents.

A special part of this book is its photographs, of which about 95 percent were provided by former members of the 10th Photo Reconnaissance Group who dug through their albums and old footlockers in order to help. Because of this effort on their part it is possible to provide an excellent pictorial history of the life and times of the Group in World War II.

Finally, I must express my appreciation to a number of people who helped in the production of this book through their technical assistance. Mr. J. Griffin Murphey spent many hours during the last five years copying photos for the history. Mr. William N. Hess proofread the manuscript and offered much help and assistance based on his many years of experience as a World War II aviation author. And Mrs. Betsy Barkley and Miss Donna Crowe typed numerous letters and other material for me. The unsung heroes of all this have been my wife Dottie and my children Karen, Kathy, and David for their patience and understanding during the preparation of this book.

Thomas G. Ivie

Contributors

Kinniard Allen
Eugene Balachowski
Dr. William Barone
Gen. Russell Berg (Ret.)
Col. Edward L. Bishop (Ret.)
Walter Campbell
Leon Canady
Amos Christianson
James Collins
Wendell Conard
Joe Conroy
James F. Cooper
Mrs. Mike Crevar
William O. Davenport
Lyon L. Davis
Robert Dawson
Eugene Demaris
Lang Dickinson
Jack Dingle
LTC. Clyde B. East (Ret.)
CMSGT. Hal Edwards (Ret.)
M. Leo Elliott
Jeff Ethell
William Enneis
Mrs. Alma Fette
John Florence

Albert O. Frick
William R. Gardner
Col. Merritt G. Garner (Ret.)
Raymond Gaudette
Carl Giesler
Dr. Fairfield Goodale
James E. Harvey
William N. Hess
LTC. Richard Hibbert (Ret.)
John H. Hoefker
A. Cliff Holm
Newton Jarrard
E. L. Kenny
Frank Khare
Victor Krasnickas
Edward Lamir
Henry Lewis
Mrs. James Lichtenwalner
Richard Linehan
Robert C. Little
William Long
Joseph Luplow
Donald Lynch
Cliff Mackie
Richard McFadden
Howard Martin

Edmund Maxwell
John F. Miefert
Ernest Schonard
Dale Shimon
Robert Shively
Col. R. T. Simpson (Ret.)
Thomas H. Milner
Earl Miner
Gen. Stanley Newman
Charles Ochs
Garry Pape
Wayne S. Patrick
Franklin Pfeiffer
E. A. Poe
Col. Wm. B. Reed (Ret.)
Fred H. Remian
Marvin Renner
Harold Robertson
Ben Rosen
Kenn Rust

John Stilla
William L. Swisher
John Tillett
E. B. Travis
Fred J. Trenner
Ted Trulson
Harry S. Utley
Harold Vaughn
Elmer Wagner
Merle Wallen
Byrne Warren
Arthur Wiedenbein
LTC. J. E. Williams (Ret.)
Wm. I. Williams
Stewart A. Wilson
Maj. Haylon Wood (Ret.)
Gordon H. Woodrow
J. B. Woodson
Col. Rufus Woody (Ret.)
Richard Youll

Introduction

Aerial reconnaissance was born in the French Army as far back as 1794, when on June 2, Colonel Jean-Marie Countelle, the commanding officer of the French "air force" made his initial balloon ascent at Maubeuge. From his vantage point he was able to observe the enemy's movements northeast of the city and enabled the French to win the battle. It was also the French who first began attempts to do aerial photography. The earliest attempts recorded are experiments by Colonel Aime' Lassudat, who attempted to make topographic maps for the French Corps of Engineers. Gaspard F. Tourchon was the first to recognize and demonstrate the military value of aerial photography. He had written to the General Staff about having a better "belfry" than the standard use of church steeples as observation posts and proved his idea would work when in 1858 he photographed a village from an altitude of 250 feet.

It was during the American Civil War that the military put aerial reconnaissance to work for them. After two balloonists, John Allen of the Rhode Island First Regiment and John Wise, failed in their attempts, another balloonist, John LaMountain, succeeded. In August of 1861 his captive balloon was operated from a ship anchored off Hampton Roads, Virginia and on his first aerial observation mission he observed heavy concentrations of Confederate batteries positioned to fire on Fort Monroe. As a result the surprised Rebels and their guns were quickly captured. He also was credited for providing a good estimate of enemy strength in the area by counting camp fires that could be observed from his balloon. In the fall of 1861 he made several free ascent flights over the Rebel lines and sketched their positions and brought back important information to the Union Army. His activities were finally halted in November when high winds broke his balloon away and it disappeared. Probably the most successful of the balloonists during the Civil War was Thaddeus S. C. Lowe. In over 3000 reconnaissance flights he provided the Union Army with much valuable information, developed aerial artillery adjustment by use of the telegraph, developed a signal system of phosphorescent balloons, and improved aerial photography by coming up with a photo enlarger that enabled the famous photographer Matthew Brady to enlarge aerial photos from three to twenty inches. Though Lowe was often misunderstood and mishandled, which resulted in his resignation in 1863, he rendered a tremendous service to the U.S. Army and set a pattern for things to come.

The Army's last use of the aerial balloon for reconnaissance was in the Spanish-American War. During the now famous Battle of San Juan Hill, the aerial reconnaissance made by Lt. Colonel Joseph E. Maxfield and Lt. Colonel George M. Derby probably was the deciding factor in the victory. By spotting a new route for General Shafter to send up reinforcements and adjusting artillery fire directed into the Spanish positions, a decisive victory was won.

The Wright brothers' airplane has changed the world in many ways, and the use of aircraft for reconnaissance was no exception. In spite of the Top Brass' usual reluctance to try any new and unheard of tactics, some forward looking aviators began looking into the use of aircraft for observation purposes. The first truly observation mission was flown by Lieutenant Benjamin Foulois during the 1911 maneuvers. Since he did not spot the "enemy" the Army considered it a failure, but the determined lieutenant did not give up. The next year he again was ordered to take part in the Connecticut maneuvers and this time he was able to provide excellent intelligence to the side he was observing for. In 1916 after Pancho Villa raided New Mexico, President Wilson ordered General John J. Pershing into Mexico to track him down. With him into Mexico, Pershing took the 1st Aero Squadron, and for the first time the U.S. Air Service was used in a foreign land. The significance of this Mexican expedition to aerial reconnaissance is that it was able to observe and photograph areas in which the infantry and cavalry could not effectively operate. This proved to the many skeptics that the airplane could be a very important addition to the nation's military strength and resulted in a high appropriation from Congress for aviation research.

By the time the United States entered World War I, both the Germans and the Allied forces had nearly three years to develop observation and photo reconnaissance tactics. It is not truly known who made the first successfuluse of photo reconnaissance in the war, but once its worth was discovered, both sides began widespread use of it.

Down through the years military aviators have been painted as gallant, romantic figure by writers and Hollywood alike. The chief character has been the dashing fighter pilot, and secondly the hard working bomber pilot. Both of these did an outstanding and heroic job and deserve much credit for their work. However there has been little said or written about the less glamorous job of the reconnaissance pilot and crew whose mission was to fly a certain route or line and report back. Why? It is just routine many believe, but if they gave it much thought they would realize that the reconnaissance pilot had one of the hardest, most dangerous, and in many cases the least appreciated job of all pilots.

The First World War provided a graphic illustration of this point, as during most of the entire war fronts were static, and trench warfare developed. The static trench warfare strategy became an artilleryman's war, and the observation and photographing of the enemy's positions and movements was of paramount importance. In those days the camera was still a quite primitive instrument and required a stable, slow-flying aircraft handled by an excellent pilot and crewed by a good cameraman to accomplish the mission. The very importance of these vital missions made these aircrews the target of every gun the enemy could bring to bear, both on the ground and in the air. Many a famous fighter pilot of that era built his reputation on the destruction of the enemy's observation planes and balloons. Probably the best two examples are Germany's Red Baron, Manfred von Richthofen who listed 45 observation planes among his 80 kills, and Lieutenant Frank Luke of the United States Air Service, who in a torrid 45 days destroyed four aircraft and 14 observation balloons before he himself was killed while trying to destroy another balloon. For his exploits Lt. Luke was posthumously awarded the Congressional Medal of Honor. As aerial tactics developed the fighter pilot was given two important tasks, i.e., protecting his own reconnaissance planes and destroying the enemy's. These pioneers of photo reconnaissance stuck doggedly to their tasks, and during the course of the war, U.S. reconnaissance units took 18,000 photos which were developed into 585,000 prints and distributed to all levels of command. The courage these men showed proved worthwhile as they developed a technique that is now used to insure the existence of nations. The Cuban missile crisis of 1962 is an excellent example of how a nuclear war was possibly averted through the use of aerial photo reconnaissance and photo interpretation.

At least two of the Squadrons which later became a portion of the 10th Photo Reconnaissance Group were activated during the First World War

Fairchild F-1A, the first Army aircraft designed for photo reconnaissance. (Air Force Museum)

French-built Salmson, used by the 12th Aero Squadron in World War I. (Air Force Museum)

and one, the 12th Aero (Observation) Squadron, served in France from December 1917 throughout the remainder of the war and with the Army of Occupation. The other, the 15th Aero Squadron, was based in New York and from January 1918 until the end of the war was charged with reconnaissance of the North Atlantic seaboard.

At the end of World War I interest in military aviation took a plunge and appropriations and progress both suffered. During the years between the wars little or nothing was initiated by the Air Force to improve the techniques of aerial reconnaissance. The old wartime idea of observation squadrons still prevailed and the aircraft used and designed for reconnaissance work were still slow and vulnerable. During this lull, however, some important steps were made in the development of aerial cameras. In 1919 Dr. George W. Goddard was assigned to McCook Field in Dayton, Ohio as Officer-in-Charge of aerial photographic research and developed several revolutionary new ideas to include infrared photography and long range photography, plans for aircraft especially designed for photo reconnaissance, special cameras for these aircraft, and one other most important aspect for battlefield units, the portable field laboratory unit. Probably one of the most significant developments during these years of his leadership at McCook was the long focal length lens which was later put to excellent use in World War II. Another important development he was to play a part in was the photographic mapping of various parts of the United States.

In 1926 the U.S. Air Service became the U.S. Army Air Corps and with the new prestige it gained by being given the status of a combat arm of the Army, new funds were allocated. The Army Air Corps was asked to photo-map the east and west coasts of Florida and did so quite successfully, which resulted in additional funding to photo-map another 35,000 square miles of territory. The additional funding allowed Goddard to experiment with the new Bagley K-3 triple lens camera, and to develop water proof paper, both of which were to play a big part later on. Strangely enough though, as these big steps were being made in aerial photography, limited funding for aircraft allowed the purchase of only one type of aircraft, the Fairchild F-1A, which was designed especially for photo use.

By 1931 some of the Army's and Navy's leaders were beginning to recognize the potential of aerial reconnaissance and the historic agreement between General MacArthur and Admiral William Pratt was real progress. This agreement was that the Army would be responsible for defense of the coast lines and overseas possessions, while the Navy would base its planes with the fleet. After the agreement three important missions, the 1935 B-10 flight to Alaska, the 1937 interception of the battleship Utah, and the 1938 interception of the Italian liner REX were flown. These missions proved the worth of long range reconnaissance work, and in the case of the Alaskan mission taught valuable lessons in extreme cold weather photography.

As war began to approach, it became obvious we would need people who were trained to take and interpret photos, and in 1939 such a course was developed. After the invasion of Poland took place the program expanded drastically, and a course to train aerial photographers to operate from bombers was begun. Another step in the right direction was the development of the S-2 strip camera which was designed by Fred Sonne and could be used for high speed-low altitude photography. As it looked more and more obvious that the United States might become involved, Captain Harvey C. Brown Jr. was sent for a photographic course from the British. During his stay he met the famous photo interpreter Constance Babbington-Smith who startled and amazed Brown with the information and facts she could glean from a photo. At the same time, Goddard was in England and was so impressed by the photo reconnaissance work done by the Royal Air Force that upon his return to the United States he demanded that our country develop faster and better aircraft for this purpose. However at this time Washington wasn't listening to either Brown or Goddard, and it wasn't until the British warned the United States that the Japanese were flying over the Gilbert Islands and photographing that official Washington was impressed enough to do something. By the time the decision to photograph Japanese installations was made, and the long-range aircraft were made ready, it was too late. One of the aircraft was in fact parked in Hawaii on December 7, 1941. Consequently no real aerial reconnaissance was carried out, and the apathy which was shown by our leaders after the British warning resulted in the disgrace of Pearl Harbor.

While the principles of long range reconnaissance were being developed during the mid and late 1930s, the observation squadrons still languished using outmoded equipment and tactics. For the most part they flew short range missions which were in support of or cooperation with the ground forces. The reconnaissance squadrons were attached to the bomber forces and flew modified bombers, and this practice was to prove ineffective and costly during the early stages of the war.

The Observation squadrons during the late 1930s and early war years flew aircraft that were too ponderous and obsolete for modern warfare.

It was outmoded thinking that had good pilots risking their lives flying observation or artillery adjustment missions in aircraft such as the O-47 and O-52. The 10th Photo Reconnaissance Group and its predecessor the 73rd Observation Group were involved in the transition from these outmoded concepts to the development of modern photo and tactical reconnaissance techniques, which played an invaluable part in the defeat of Nazi Germany. This is their story.

Top: Capt. Lloyd Warren's P-40N over the Tennessee Maneuvers area in September 1943, 15th TAC R Squadron. *(Jim Collins)* Bottom: An O-46 of the 91st Observation Squadron, early 1941. *(Air Force Museum)*

CHAPTER I

The Early Days

September 1941–February 1944 - Activation as 73rd Observation Group and Training

---

After a combat tour in North Africa that included a major part in the Ploesti raids, the 9th Air Force was being reborn in England. The time was October 1943 and the 9th's new role was to be tactical air support. Initial missions would find it attacking targets in occupied Europe with medium and light bombers as part of OPERATION POINTBLANK, the combined bomber offensive calling for the destruction of German aircraft, ball bearing, and munitions factories. At the same time all of its bomber, fighter, troop carrier, and reconnaissance groups were preparing for their new role, that of supporting the ground forces during the coming invasion of Europe.

In December 1943, the 9th Air Force became part of the Allied Expeditionary Air Force commanded by British Air Marshall Sir Trafford Leigh-Mallory, who controlled all British and American tactical air forces that would support OVERLORD, the invasion of Europe. At this time the 9th Fighter Command had only one reconnaissance group, the 67th Tactical Reconnaissance Group, to support its operations. The 67th, flying P-51 aircraft, could perform its tasks well, but with the invasion nearing, it was obvious that they could not provide the large demands for reconnaissance alone, and in February 1944, the 10th Photographic Group (Reconnaissance), under the command of Colonel William B. Reed, arrived in England and set up its headquarters at Chalgrove.

On paper, the 10th was a newly-formed unit; however its existence actually began on September 1, 1941, as the 73rd Observation Group in Harrisburg, Pennsylvania, with Major Edgar Scattergood as acting Commander and Technical Sergeant John Pettigrew as First Sergeant. These two men began the task of organizing the unit, but before much could be accomplished, the 73rd was reassigned to Godman Field, Fort Knox, Kentucky, and placed under the command of Lt. Colonel John C. Kennedy.

Headquarters, 73rd Observation Group moved to Godman Field on November 25, 1941, and was placed in command of the following squadrons: 12th Observation Squadron, Godman Field, Kentucky; 16th Observation Squadron, Lawson Field, Georgia; 22nd Observation Squadron, DeRidder Army Air Base, Louisiana; and 91st Observation Squadron, Wheeler-Sack Field, Pine Camp, New York.

While each of its squadrons was already an operational unit flying O-46, O-47, O-52, L-1 and L-4 aircraft at their respective bases, the 73rd Headquarters was still a skeleton unit composed of a small cadre directing most of its efforts toward recruiting. One of the first men attracted to the unit was Louis Stapp of Louisville, Kentucky, who recalls that he enlisted on an impulse one day while making a delivery to Fort Knox, and then after a few days began to wonder why he did. His enlistment had begun at the time the 73rd had no supplies, little equipment, and very little for the Headquarters personnel to do, so his main task was to just keep busy doing something and to keep out of trouble. In that assignment, Private Stapp excelled and used this time of relative inactivity to perform a service that was to have lasting significance to the Group, for it was he who designed and created the unit crest of Argus Watching Over the World, and gave the 73rd its motto: Ceaseless Watch.

It was the Japanese attack on Pearl Harbor, December 7, 1941, that provided the impetus to get the organization and training begun in earnest, and on December 11, nine officers and twenty enlisted men were transferred to Group Headquarters from the 12th Observation Squadron to form the Staff and Headquarters Squadron. An attempt at a coordinated training schedule was also begun at this time and although it was quite difficult to administer due to the widely scattered locations of the squadrons, what mattered was that the Group was now gearing itself to wartime conditions.

Early Operational Training Missions

For the 91st Observation Squadron at Pine Camp, New York, the training missions beginning after the attack on Pearl Harbor took on an operational flavor, for they were assigned to fly along the border between New York and Canada and photograph any possible landing sites for enemy aircraft. The attack on Pearl Harbor had smashed forever the idea that an ocean barrier would prevent an attack on the United States.

As the 91st undertook these missions in their O-46 and O-47 aircraft, they found that their worst enemy was the cold, snowy New York weather which cost them their first operational loss of aircraft. Newton E. Jarrard who was assigned as an aerial observer recalls that fateful mission. "We all thought someone was crazy because we knew of no German aircraft that could fly the ocean while laden with equipment necessary to land and set up operations from the North American continent. Nevertheless, we set about scheduling the mission, and on a cold overcast day, we took off to make our photo runs. Our crew was assigned to photograph the area around Lake Placid, and we were out of radio range when the recall to base signal was sent out from our field. We had just finished photographing several civilian fields and were heading toward Lake Placid when the snowstorm hit us and forced us down to about fifty feet altitude. At this time we were becoming hopelessly lost in the heavy snow and finally the pilot announced we were down to less than five minutes of fuel. We decided to belly it in on a big pasture when the pilot spotted a highway and tried a wheels down landing. The O-47 was rolling down the highway when we suddenly pulled up and passed over an oncoming automobile and a tree, then we lost power again and landed on the highway. The O-47 was still rolling at about fifty miles an hour when we came to a bend in the road, clipped about three feet off the left wing and then washed out the plane against a telephone pole. Needless to say our Commanding Officer was quite upset with us since we had reduced his O-47 inventory by 50%, and had no surviving photos to show for our efforts."

After these needless photo missions were completed, the 91st began flying training flights involving air-to-ground communication, photography, and navigation. In the summer of 1942 they were sent to Panama City, Florida, for flexible gunnery training, and then finally joined the rest of the Group at Godman Field in August 1942.

By the time the 91st joined the 73rd Observation Group at Fort Knox several organizational changes had already been made. The Group was now commanded by Colonel Robert M. Lee and consisted of Headquarters 73rd Group, the 15th Observation Squadron, which had been assigned in March 1942, the 28th Observation Squadron, which was formed after Headquarters Squadron was disbanded, and the 91st, all of which were now at Godman Field.

The training missions recorded in the 15th Observation Squadron's historical reports are typical of the type of training the Group undertook during the spring and summer of 1942. These missions were in support of the armored divisions stationed at Fort Knox and consisted of strafing, bombing, aerial reconnaissance, and photography. In July the 15th was

Above: A Douglas A-20 used by the 73rd Observation Group at Godman Field, Ft. Knox, Kentucky, July 1942. *(Jim Collins)* Below: A P-39 of the 152nd TAC R Squadron on display at Berry Field, Nashville, Tennessee, September 1943. *(N. Jarrard)*

Right: P-39D of the 15th TAC R Squadron at Bowling Green. Kentucky, during maneuvers in summer 1943. (Ray Gaudette) *Below:* Field maintenance on a P-39 at Bowling Green. (L. Davis)

sent to Louisiana to participate in the maneuvers, and returned to Godman in September 1942. The 15th continued to train its pilots in its support role, however as the year 1942 began drawing to a close something new was apparently in the air because the unit began to receive newer and more modern aircraft to include some examples of the P-51A.

Period of Transition

It was the reports that filtered back from the North African campaign during late 1942 and early 1943 that made the Army Air Force realize that its old theories about observation tactics and aircraft were no longer valid. The day of the lumbering observation planes, such as the O-46s, O-47s, and O-52s that flew leisurely along doing artillery spotting and general reconnaissance, was over. This modern war was calling for fast, maneuverable fighter aircraft flying photo reconnaissance, tactical reconnaissance, and photomapping missions. By March 1943 the 15th Observation Squadron was being reequipped with P-39 fighter aircraft, and on April 9, 1943, the 73rd Observation Group was redesignated as the 73rd Reconnaissance Group. Its squadrons were also redesignated as the 15th and 91st Reconnaissance Squadrons (Fighter), the 28th Reconnaissance Squadron (Bomber), and the 14th Liaison Squadron (assigned March 1943).

During April, May and June 1943, the 73rd worked in conjunction with the armored forces stationed at Fort Knox and flew what were termed "cooperative missions." These missions were flown against simulated enemy positions and signalled the beginning of the transition from traditional observation tactics to the tactical reconnaissance missions that later became so valuable in supporting the drive across Europe.

The Tennessee Maneuvers

In the summer and fall of 1943 the 73rd participated in the Tennessee maneuvers and its squadrons operated from fields in Bowling Green, Kentucky and at Camp Campbell, Kentucky. During these maneuvers many of the new concepts of tactical reconnaissance were tested while the 73rd supported the 101st Airborne Division, and its success was recognized by Letters of Commendation from the Commanding General of the 101st. The effort was not without loss however, and during the period of April through October 1943, several pilots lost their lives, including Captain James Kaden, the Commanding Officer of the 15th Reconnaissance Squadron.

By August 1943, the reorganization and refinement of reconnaissance responsibilities and tactics were well on their way and again the 73rd Reconnaissance Group was redesignated as the 73rd Tactical Reconnaissance Group. It now consisted of the 15th TAC R Squadron, 28th TAC R Squadron, and 152nd TAC R Squadron (assigned August 1943). The 91st Reconnaissance Squadron was reassigned in June and the 14th Liaison Squadron in August 1943. Coinciding with the unit's new designation, the first training manual for "ADVANCED FIGHTER RECONNAISSANCE TRAINING" was released and put into use. The manual was developed by Major William B. Reed, who assumed command of the 73rd in September, and got the opportunity to put his theories into practice. One of the prime points of emphasis placed in the introduction was the requirements demanded of a TAC R pilot. It stated:

"Fighter Reconnaissance Pilots must be thoroughly impressed with the fact that they are *fighter trained as well as reconnaissance trained* and must be capable of performing their duties in both roles in an excellent manner. Pilots must not only develop and perfect their reconnaissance skill, accuracy, speed in observing, but *they must also maintain at a high level the fighter tactics and techniques with which they were primarily indoctrinated* when they were graduated from the Fighter Command School. An *excellent* fighter reconnaissance crew by virtue of the additional training skill and technique will be, in general, equal to a *superior* fighter crew that had only fighter training."

In addition to the development of the tactical reconnaissance tactics, another technique which was also being tested during the Tennessee maneuvers was that of night photo reconnaissance. Dr. Harold Edgerton, the inventor of the flash unit, brought an example of the "Edgerton Lamp" to the maneuver area and the 73rd mounted it in an A-20. The experimental night missions demonstrated that good photos could be produced using this technique, but some major problems still had to be resolved. However, the tests did show sufficient promise to warrant a recommendation that these bugs be worked out as soon as possible so the night photo technique could be pressed into service.

A third experimentation performed by the 73rd was the testing of some of the early strip cameras and evaluating their potential, a concept which was later to play a big part in the Normandy missions.

At the end of the Tennessee maneuvers the 73rd Headquarters and its sole remaining squadron, the 15th TAC R Squadron, was reassigned to Key Field, Meridian, Mississippi for more training. During October 1943 the 15th TAC R Squadron received alert orders for overseas movement

A P-51A of the 15th TAC R Squadron after a hard landing at Fort Campbell Army Air Field, September 1943. (J. Collins)
The aircraft display at Berry Field held during the Tennessee Maneuvers. (N. Jarrard)

and reassignment to the 67th Tactical Reconnaissance Group in England, and after some additional training departed for their new assignment in December 1943.

After the departure of the 15th TAC R Squadron for its new assignment, Colonel Reed received notice that the 73rd Group Headquarters would be disbanded and its members reassigned to other commands. On the 30th of December 1943, an angry Colonel Bill Reed who was not about to see his well-trained and combat ready Headquarters deactivated stormed off to Washington, D.C. to rectify the situation. After two days of door pounding and sales efforts, he was given an audience with the Deputy Chief of Staff for Operations. At the outset of the meeting Colonel Reed was told that none of the Theatres had stated a need for anything other than squadron-sized units and that the 73rd was excess to the needs of the service. The discussion was getting nowhere, Colonel Reed recalled, until "I expounded on the super qualifications of the 73rd as an organization which, with minimum retraining, could effectively command anything from a heavy bomb group to a photo group, to which the Deputy Chief said, 'Did you say "photo group"?' I nodded and he said, 'I think we've got a request for a photo group headquarters which I'll check out and let you know tomorrow.' This request was verified and I rushed back to Key Field to let everyone know we were alive and well as the 10th Photo Reconnaissance Group."

Colonel Reed's briefing to the staff upon his return was recalled by Newton Jarrard: "Colonel Reed not only returned with orders keeping us in existence as the Headquarters, 10th Reconnaissance Group, but also with orders alerting us for overseas movement. He called us into his office and said, 'We are now the 10th Photo Reconnaissance Group Headquarters. Now Charley Allen over there is a good photo officer, he knows a lot about cameras and equipment and that kind of stuff; Jarrard over there has had three weeks of Photo Interpretation at Harrisburg, Pennsylvania, I can fly an airplane, Jim Smelley can fly an airplane, Jack Poe and Jack Dingle can fly an airplane, and that's enough. We are experts in aerial photography.' And do you know just because of that son-of-a-gun's attitude, we went ahead and won the damn war."

After a brief training program at Will Rogers Field, Oklahoma, the 10th Headquarters personnel packed up and departed on January 24, 1944 enroute to England and assignment to the 9th Air Force. Nearly one month later, on February 21, 1944, the 10th set up operations at Station 465, Chalgrove with the 30th Photo Squadron as its first assigned squadron.

Lt. Albert Lanker, who flew the first dicing mission on May 6, 1944. (R. Woody)

CHAPTER II

Prelude to Invasion

February 1944 – D-Day - Assignment to the Ninth
Air Force and Early Operational Missions

The situation in the Allied camp at the time of the 10th Photo Reconnaissance Group's arrival in England can best be described as a flurry of activity, both from planning and operational standpoints. General Dwight D. Eisenhower had returned in January from his duties in the Mediterranean to become the Supreme Commander of the Allied invasion force that would attempt to break through Hitler's Atlantic Wall and liberate the occupied countries of Europe during 1944, and was already heavily involved in the planning for this attack.

First and foremost, if the invasion was to be a success the Luftwaffe and the industrial complex that fed the German war machine would have to be destroyed, and to accomplish this the American Air Forces based in England had gone through a major reorganization. This reorganization which begun a few months before the 10th's arrival involved bringing the 9th Air Force back to England and retraining it as a tactical air force, establishing the 15th Air Force in Italy, and shaking up the command structures in the 8th Air Force which after a year of flying virtually unescorted bombing missions had suffered terrible losses and showed terribly discouraging results. Along with this reorganization came the implementation of the Combined Bomber Offensive involving all of these American Air Forces along with the Royal Air Force's Bomber Command. General H. H. Arnold emphasized the need to eliminate the Luftwaffe as a prerequisite to invasion by issuing this aggressive order to his field commanders, "This is a must, destroy the enemy air forces wherever you find them, in the air, on the ground, and in the factories." To add emphasis to his words he was insuring that the Fighter Commands were receiving the new long range escort fighter, the P-51, and that effort was being made to increase the range of the P-38 and the P-47.

By February 1944 the 8th Air Force was able to mass escorted raids of the enemy's aircraft factories deep in Germany, and on the very week of the 10th's arrival in England, General Doolittle launched a series of raids known as "Big Week" in which German aircraft factories were devastated and production was set back two months. While the 8th Air Force was hitting at these strategic targets, the 9th Air Force was deeply committed to attacking POINTBLANK and CROSSBOW (the code name given to attacks against V-1 targets in France) targets. Their POINTBLANK target responsibilities were the French railroads, rail facilities and bridges, industrial facilities and airfields in the occupied countries, as well as German coastal defenses and radar systems. During these pre-invasion air assaults, reconnaissance units were heavily employed and played an important role in the success of these operations. Of course photo reconnaissance missions of the 8th Air Force's attacks and TAC R missions over France were constantly flown, but of major importance was a need for exact information regarding the invasion area and it had to be carried out without obviously concentrating in one area. In February and March the 9th Air Force's 67th Tactical Reconnaissance Group won a Distinguished Unit Citation for providing Supreme Headquarters with excellent oblique photos of the proposed invasion beaches. However, even with these excellent results it was becoming quite obvious that the need for photographic intelligence was so great that the 67th could no longer support the effort alone, and Headquarters 9th Air Force was overjoyed when Colonel Reed and his headquarters personnel reported in and began setting up at their new base at Chalgrove.

The 10th Becomes Operational

Joining the Group Headquarters at Chalgrove was its first assigned squadron, the 30th Photo Squadron commanded by Captain Richard Leghorn and equipped with Lockheed F-5A and F-5C Lightnings. The 30th had arrived at Chalgrove on February 1, and therefore had the opportunity to get in some training flights so Colonel Reed, anxious to end the two and one half years of training, declared them combat ready and launched the Group's first operational sortie on February 25, 1944.

The first mission was flown by Captain Leghorn who took his F-5 over the Cherbourg Peninsula and through 9/10s cloud cover successfully photographed the German airfields at Querqueville and Maupertus, and then returned to receive the hearty congratulations of his buddies at Chalgrove. Four days later the 30th launched its second mission, but this

Above: Maj. Lloyd O. Warren flew the first operational mission of the 15th TAC R on March 26, 1944, with Capt. John Hoefker. Warren was commanding officer of the squadron from May 1943 to April 30, 1944 after Capt. James Kaden was killed in a P-39 crash. (J. Collins) *Below left:* Maj. Jack Dingle's damaged F-5 after his dicing mission over Anzio. (J. Dingle) *Below right:* Maj. Donn Hayes, commanding officer of the 34th Photo Squadron, after completing his first mission, April 19, 1944. (B. Rosen)

The F-5 flown by Lt. G. A. York of the 34th Photo Squadron on his May 19, 1944 dicing mission. The photo was taken at St. Dizier on September 22, 1944. (W. Swisher)

Bomb damage assessment photo taken on May 4, 1944 to assess damage to targets along the French coast. (E. A. Poe)

time it was unsuccessful as Captain William Mitchell found both of his target areas, the Le Havre and Octeville airdromes, completely socked in by 10/10s cloud cover.

In March 1944 the priorities for Ninth Bomber Command shifted and now German airfields, railroad marshalling yards and U-boat pens along the coast went to the top of the list, and almost overnight the importance of the 10th Photo Reconnaissance Group's missions increased.

During March 1944, their first full month of combat service, the Group began Bomb Damage Assessment missions in addition to airfield coverage and during the month flew 38 missions over northeastern France, 27 of which were successful. In carrying out these missions of bomb damage assessment the pilots of the 30th Photo Squadron would appear over the target area within thirty minutes after the attack and photograph the results for first phase interpretation.

The first six sorties of the month were flown on March 2 and 3 by Lieutenants Miller, Rudel, Thompson, Simpson, Bone, and Sarvik who successfully photographed port areas and airfields along the Channel from Calais to Cherbourg.

Weather aborted all missions on March 4, but luck returned on the sixth when Lt. Martin photographed the Port of Le Havre and nearby airfields, and again on the eighth when six of the 30th's pilots roared off in their F-5s to photograph Channel ports in France and Belgium, and numerous airfields in France. All returned with excellent photos of their assigned targets.

No missions were flown for another week, but on March 15, the 30th pilots began covering the devastating B-26 raids on marshalling yards, locomotive works and other targets along the French-Belgian border. On March 20 Lts. Thompson, Martin, and Wallaert accompanied the attacks of 124 B-26s of the 386th, 387th, 344th, and 391st Bomb Groups which heavily damaged the Criel marshalling yards, several factories, and a locomotive works. Lt. Thompson's attempt to photograph was unsuccessful due to cloud cover and heavy flak in his area, but Lt. Martin was able to expertly photograph the area, and Lt. Wallaert brought back some good photos of Le Havre.

The big news of March 23 was the Group's coverage of the return attacks on the Criel marshalling yards and the German air base at Beaumont-Le-Roger and the arrival at Chalgrove of the 31st Photo Squadron commanded by Major Rudolph Walters. Their arrival could not have been more timely as the demand for photographic information was increasing tremendously, and to illustrate the point, Major Walters was told to have his men and his F-5s ready for operations within three weeks.

While the 31st was readying itself for combat the 30th flew another series of successful sorties on the 26th and 27th, but weather again closed in and cancelled all missions between March 28 and March 30. Two missions were flown on March 31, one by Colonel Reed who mapped a portion of the Cherbourg Peninsula, and the other by Major Edgar A. Poe, the Group Assistant Operations Officer, who photographed the Port of Cherbourg and two airfields on the Peninsula.

By April 1944 the effects of OPERATION POINTBLANK were beginning to show as much of Germany's fighter strength was pulled out of France and the Low Countries and those that remained were pulled back to bases deeper in France. With the Luftwaffe gone from the Channel coast and vast areas behind it, the 9th Air Force's Bomber and Reconnaissance groups could proceed with their tasks of preparing the way for the invasion.

Mapping the Continent

During April the 10th's mission was still Bomb Damage Assessment, but the additional missions of mapping large portions of the continent and thirty-six new airfields to watch vastly increased their workload. From April 1 through the eighth, operations were hampered by weather and only two of six missions flown were successful, and three others had to be cancelled.

On April 10 the weather improved and 16 missions, including the 31st Photo Squadron's first mission flown by Major Walters, were dispatched and thirteen were successful. Major Walters' mission was to take him to the Cherbourg Peninsula to photograph the airfields at Maupertus and Querqueville, but a solid cloud cover blanketed these targets so he was forced to head for a secondary target and brought back some good photos of the LeHavre harbor facilities.

April 18 was a day of masterful accomplishment in the short operational history of the Group when five of its pilots from the 30th Photo Squadron performed an outstanding feat of aerial mapping. This historic mission was flown by Lts. Spencer, Rudel, Simpson, Wallaert, and Wright who took their F-5s up to 30,000 feet over Holland and mapped three-fourths of that country in just 45 minutes—a remarkable feat which showed the 10th was rapidly coming of age.

On April 19 the Group's third squadron, the 34th Photo Squadron which had arrived at Chalgrove on March 30, became operational when its Commanding Officer, Major Don Hayes, photographed the airfields at Maupertus and Querqueville on the Cherbourg Peninsula. With three squadrons now in service the 10th was able to send its planes far and wide over the continent and began covering targets in Normandy, Brittany, Loire, Belgium and even to Metz, a heavily defended communications center near the German border.

During the last week of April the Group's fourth and last F-5 Squadron, the 33rd Photo Squadron under the command of Major Leon McCurdy, arrived at Chalgrove, and instituted a new phase of photography work for the unit. Immediately after their arrival Flight "D" of the 33rd was put on detached service with the 423rd Night Fighter Squadron to begin training in night photo reconnaissance and thereby set in motion the activation of the 155th Night Photo Squadron.

With the 31st and 34th Squadrons becoming operational the 10th was able to dispatch 170 missions during April, of which 135 were successful, and in doing so was able to map large portions of France, Belgium, and Holland which provided valuable information to the men on General Eisenhower's staff who were planning the upcoming invasion.

In addition to the missions over the Continent, the 31st was assigned a list of targets in England to photograph for the Air Ministry to aid in the study of defense installations. During one of these missions the 31st Photo Squadron lost its first pilot, Lt. William Haywood, who crashed in bad weather near Shrewsbury. The 34th Photo Squadron also lost its first pilot on April 14, as Lt. Cameron was killed in a training accident.

The Dicing Missions

While the squadrons of the 10th Photo Reconnaissance Group flew these early operational and training missions over Europe, one very significant item that missed general notice was the trip that their Commanding Officer, Colonel Reed, Colonel Richard Hibbert, Group S-2, and Major Jack Dingle, Group S-3, made to the Italian Theatre to visit Photo Reconnaissance units. Here they were briefed by the "Old Master" of Reconnaissance, Colonel Karl Polifka, and what they saw was a far cry from the high altitude missions of 29,000 to 35,000 feet that they had been flying over France. He demonstrated the low-level and dicing* missions that they had been flying in Italy, and discussed the possibilities of ultra-

---

*See Appendix 1

low level missions where extra fine detail was required. While in Italy Colonel Reed and Major Dingle flew some of these low-level missions themselves, and Dingle was almost lost in the Anzio area flying what was actually the 10th's first dicing mission. His F-5 was hit several times by flak, one of which tore a gaping hole in his left rudder and sent him limping back to base.

With the seed implanted of how to get the much needed detail shots of the German beach defenses along the Normandy coast Colonel Reed and his party headed back to Chalgrove to report what they had learned and to set things in motion for the Group's indoctrination to "dicing." One can well imagine the surprise on the faces of the pilots who were told when they began operations back in February and March that at times they "might have to operate as low as 29,000 feet "—that they would now make photo runs over heavily defended Normandy at altitudes of 50 feet. However many lessons had been learned and it had become apparent that high altitude photos would supply only a part of the need for information concerning the enemy's beach defenses. Especially needed by the 21st Army Group were low-level photos showing the barriers, mines, and other beach obstacles in detail, and the 10th Photo Reconnaissance Group was now prepared to get these photos to them.

By early May all of the Group's plans and preparations were complete, and on May 6 Lt. Albert Lanker of the 31st Photo Squadron was chosen from several volunteers to fly the first dicing mission. To quote from the 31st Squadron History, "On the afternoon of May 6, he took off with the prayers and good wishes of every man in the squadron riding with him. This was his third mission, and Lt. Lanker was to photograph a strip of beach twenty miles long from LeTreport to Berck-sur-Mer. Because missions of this type had always been considered suicidal by most photo recce pilots Lt. Lanker was somewhat nervous and apprehensive as he lifted his F-5 off the runway at Chalgrove and headed toward the Channel. At Dungeness he was flying at fifty feet above the trees when he circled his aircraft and shot across the Channel ten to fifteen feet above the waves. Near Berck-sur-Mer Lt. Lanker turned around a sand dune to lessen his possibilities as a target (photos later revealed the sand dune to be an enemy gun emplacement), and then gaining speed in a short dive started his photo run. At this point Lt. Lanker said his nervousness left him and he began to enjoy himself immensely. During the four minutes his cameras were operating he encountered five groups of workmen building defenses on the beach, and later related, 'I headed straight for every group just to watch them scatter and roll. They were completely surprised—didn't see me until I was almost on top of them.' Near the end of the run he scaled a cliff with the wingtip six feet from the top, and a German soldier fired a rifle at him. This was the only opposition he encountered during the entire mission." When Lanker returned and landed his aircraft he was met, cheered and congratulated by members of the 10th Headquarters and the 31st Squadron alike. Their jubilance was certainly warranted because the excellent photos Lanker brought back showed the beach defenses in great detail, and workmen ducking to escape the plane which must have seemed heading straight for them.

So successful was Lieutenant Lanker's first "dicing" mission two more were laid on for the next day. On the seventh the Group dispatched 25 sorties, 10 of which were unsuccessful and cost two pilots. One of the pilots reported missing was Lt. Haslup of the 34th Photo Squadron who was lost on a conventional photo run over Chateaudun airfield, and the second was Lt. Fred Hayes of the 31st. Lt. Hayes was lost undertaking a "dicing" mission. After leaving the English coastline pilot and plane simply vanished and were never seen or heard from again. Captain William Mitchell of the 30th who took off at the same time as Lt. Hayes was able to successfully complete the second "dicing" mission over the coast from Dunkirk to Ostend, Belgium.

For the next several days stretching from May 8th through the 15th the pilots concentrated on photographing marshalling yards, airdromes, bridges, and mapping. During these missions Lt. Knickerbocker of the 34th was lost over Aerschot marshalling yards, and Lt. Alberty of the 30th bailed out successfully over England. No missions were flown from May 15 through the 18th, but on May 19th, the second series of "dicing" missions were flown, this time over the destined invasion beaches of Normandy, from Ouistreham to St. Vaast—La Hogue. Three were flown successfully by Lt. Donald F. Thompson of the 30th; Lt. Rufus Woody of the 31st; and Lt. Garland A. York of the 34th.

An excellent account of these missions is provided by Rufus Woody who flew one of the three successful missions that day. "Because of the success of Al Lanker's mission a requirement came in for four missions to be flown at the same time covering various portions of the French coast. I volunteered along with Bob Holbury, Gerry Garner, and Al York. These missions had to be flown at low-low tide, which only occurred during a certain phase of the moon. I believe this was on May 16th. We were briefed on the mission, maps prepared and we went out to our aircraft. We were all scheduled to fly at the same time for surprise, and to keep the enemy from alerting other areas that dicing missions were being flown.

Pilots of the 15th Tactical Reconnaissance Squadron, at Middle Wallop, England, May 1, 1944. Front row, kneeling l. to r.: Lt. R. Raymond, Lt. F.W. Ristau, Lt. T.E. Reger, Lt. R.E. Stelle, Lt. C.I. Read, Lt. T.H. Milner, Capt. J.H. Hoefker, Capt. R.T. Simpson, Major G.T. Walker (Sqdn. C.O.), Capt. L.L. Davis, Lt. J.E. Conklin, Lt. E.M. Schonard, Lt. F.J. Trenner, Lt. R.C. Youll, Lt. R.E. Knoebel. Back row, standing l. to r.: Lt. A.O. Frick, Lt. J.O. Warenskjold, Lt. R.E. Culbertson, Lt. J.F. McCormick, Lt. E.H. Cash Jr., Lt. G.H. Staup, Lt. H.W. Hansen, Lt. J.W. Waits, Lt. W.J. Boyle, Lt. F.J. Khare, Lt. J.L. Murtha, Lt. M.F. Johnson, Lt. R.E. Dawson, Lt. C.B. East, Lt. T.M. Trulson, Lt. J.F. Miefert. (R. Dawson)

Before engine start time, the weather officer came out and told us that fog had rolled in along the French coast.

"The next two days we prepared for our missions just as we had previously. Each day the weather was bad or too marginal to attempt the mission, but we had to go out to our aircraft just in case the weather would clear. Each day we became more apprehensive about our chances of being successful. If you know you have a mission to perform, you do it without thinking, however given a delay, you had time to think and worry. We were getting very edgy.

"On May 19 again we were told that the weater was marginal, but the tide was far enough beyond low-low tide as to preclude the needed photos if not taken that day. Again we were briefed, sent to our aircraft and told to stand by for late information on the weather. Finally we were told that the weather was breaking, and we were to attempt the mission. We were cautioned against fog over the Channel, but we were to remain as low as possible to avoid detection. I think we took off after 4:30 p.m.

"Al York and I flew in formation to mid-channel, and then he turned slightly right to make his landfall on the Cherbourg Peninsula. I gave him a good luck 'thumbs-up' and flew straight ahead. As I recall the flight was 45 minutes across the Channel (could have been from takeoff but I don't think so). We were barely above the waves and hit patches of fog flying across the Channel, however, as forecast the French coast was clear. I made landfall exactly where I expected at the base of the Cherbourg Peninsula and turned east. At the beginning of the run, as I turned on my cameras (nose and right side oblique), the land was flat as I crossed the mouth of a river, however within seconds there were high rolling hills followed by cliffs. The beach was wide initially and was covered with various obstacles, many with mines sitting on top. I observed some Germans working and several Frenchmen at various locations on the beach. I did not observe any flak but flew as low as I could. I saw a couple of depressions where valleys led down to the beach, and I observed some houses along the top of the hills. I barely missed several seagulls—I would duck as I flew past them. I saw a seawall ahead of me and just as I pulled up to go over it I saw one of our planes approaching me on a head-on collision course. I don't recall which went over the other, but we didn't miss by too many feet! We both turned to the north after passing each other. That part of the mission was complete, and the return flight to Chalgrove was uneventful. All four of us landed within minutes of each other—all relieved that each of us had made it back okay."

Lt. Merritt G. Garner of the 31st was unable to take off with the other

Above: V-1 site in France photographed by Lt. John Hickman, 67th Recon Group, during Operation Pointblank. (J. Hickman) Below: Pilots of the 34th Photo Squadron go over the map with briefing officer, Capt. Jarrell, on June 4, 1944. L. to r.: Lt. Siek, Lt. Spearman, Lt. Bosworth, Capt. Jarrell, Lt. York, and Lt. Peterson. (B. Rosen)

Photos from Lt. Albert Lanker's dicing mission over the Normandy beaches May 6, 1944. Above: The beach obstacles as seen through Lanker's nose camera. Note German workers fleeing as his F-5 approaches. (E.A. Poe) Below: Lanker's oblique camera picks up gun positions on the beach (with arrows). (E.A. Poe)

three aircraft because of brake trouble, and by the time he reached his assigned area the Germans had been alerted and put up such intense and accurate flak that he could not make his photo run. On May 20 three more "dicing" sorties were flown, this time by Lt. James M. Poole of the 31st, Lt. Robert Holbury of the 31st, Lt. Joseph H. Smith of the 30th, and a fourth "dicing" sortie flown by Lt. Allen R. Keith of the 34th was foiled by an "enemy" bird. Just prior to completing his assigned area of Fe Camp to Heuqueville, Lt. Keith hit a seagull which crashed through the plexiglass front of his canopy and was stopped by the bullet-proof glass, causing such limited visibility that he could not complete his run. Lt. Poole missed his initial point at St. Valary and entered the coast to a point approximately five miles west of Dieppe and flew up the coast to a point about three miles west of Boulogne. Through an error in navigation, Lt. Poole again entered the coast at Boulogue, drew intense flak, realized his error and broke away. However he turned his cameras on at Boulogne and got a short strip of the coast in this area. Lts. Holbury and Smith both completed photo runs over their respective areas without incident. With the completion of this last series of "dicing" missions enough of these detailed closeup photos had been accumulated to give Allied commanders planning the invasion a good idea of what their troops would face.

With the successful completion of these important "dicing" missions the 10th Photo Reconnaissance Group had proved to itself and all others that after only three months of combat flying they were second to none. So important were these photos to General Eisenhower and his staff that Ike and many of the commanders involved in the invasion planning sent glowing Letters of Commendation to the Group, each pilot participating in the "dicing" missions was awarded the Distinguished Flying Cross, and the Group was later awarded the Distinguished Unit Citation.* Another significant benefit derived from these missions by the pilots was the satisfaction that comes from close teamwork with the ground forces, the type that pays off in lives saved.

For the remainder of the month of May the Group went back to flying its conventional missions of high altitude bomb damage assessment, airfield surveillance and mapping, however they continued their training and experimentation programs which would prove most beneficial in days to come. On May 23, Major McCurdy took off in his F-5 and flew the 33rd Photo Squadron's first combat mission and successfully photographed the airfields at Morlaix and Ploujean. Of major importance during the closing

---

*Appendix 2—Text of Distinguished Unit Citation

days of May was the test mission which was successfully flown by pilots from Flight "D" of the 33rd and the 423rd Night Fighter Squadron.* In this test an Edgerton Lamp was mounted in one of the Squadron's F-3 (A-20) and good clear photos were made of the "target." With this successful test, the night photo boys now had the capability of taking 186 photos instead of eight as they were limited to when using the flash bombs.

Thus ended May 1944, a month of monumental accomplishment for the group. With the continued success of their high level surveillance missions, the introduction of "dicing," and the final development of improving night photography, the 10th was well rounded and a tactical unit in the fullest sense of the word. It would also be the last full month that the Group would operate as a strictly photo reconnaissance unit as the coming invastion would place entirely new demands upon recce units.

---

*The 423rd NFS was later redesignated as the 155th Night Photo Squadron.

Lt. Joe Conklin, 15th TAC R Squadron, who scored the first aerial victory by U.S. Forces on D-Day when he hit a FW-190 west of Paris. (R. Dawson)

CHAPTER III

D-Day and Aftermath

June 6–July 31, 1944 - Battlefield Coverage of the
Invasion Front and Group Reorganization

While May was a month of outstanding accomplishment for the Group, June was to be a month of accomplishment and change. These changes would be major and encompass both the command and organizational structure of the 10th Photo Reconnaissance Group.

From an operational standpoint, there was an air of great anticipation as everyone knew the invasion could not be far off. This had to be obvious to the pilots who had covered the beach areas of Normandy last month and were now spending the first few days of June mapping the Cherbourg Peninsula and carefully checking bridges, road junctions and known supply routes throughout Normandy and Brittany.

The Invasion of France

Finally in the late hours of June 5, 1944 the word came down to the Group that D-Day would be on June 6th, and that the honor of flying the first mission of the day would go to the 423rd (155th)* Night Fighter Squadron, whose mission would be the spotting of German movements by rail or road up the Cherbourg Peninsula. Shortly before midnight on the night of June 5/6, 1944, four F-3s (A-20Js) lifted off the runway at Chalgrove, climbed to 3,000 feet altitude and crossed the English coastline on their way to France. After passing the Channel Islands the aircraft climbed to 8,000 feet which would be the target altitude. Three of the F-3s, piloted by Lts. Starmont, Anderson, and Mackie carried flash bombs, and the fourth piloted by Lt. Lentscher carried the Edgerton

---

*The 155th Night Photo Squadron

Lamp. As they approached their target area the pilots encountered a heavy undercast and due to a lack of real experience with the Gee system experienced navigational problems which resulted in failure of three of the missions, but Lt. Lentscher's Edgerton Lamp ship brought back some very clear photos of Villedieu and Coutances. The photos showed no evidence of any enemy movement and indicated that the Germans did not expect landings in Normandy.

Later in the day when the landings were taking place the 10th dispatched its aircraft beyond the invasion area in order to keep a close watch on bridges and roads which the Germans might use to bring up reinforcements. Along with the visual missions many of the pilots were on mapping missions and were able to cover a large portion of the Cherbourg Peninsula. By nightfall the Group had flown 63 missions in support of the D-Day landings, but more importantly they had developed a real sense of pride from the realization of the role their preinvasion work had played in making the landings a success.

With a foothold established, the Allies continued to pour troops and supplies onto the beaches. To lend assistance to the battle on the ground, the 10th's pilots were keeping up with the German's activities day and night. The importance of their work was spelled out in the June 8 mission orders sent to the 31st Photo Squadron by Ninth Air Force, which said, "Get those photos regardless of weather." Three pilots, Captain Merritt Garner, Lt. Al Lanker, and Lt. Wendell Jackson took off to fly the mission, but they learned as they reached the English coast that the clouds covered the Channel area from the ground up to 29,000 feet. At this point Captain Garner was forced to turn back to base because of engine trouble, but because of their orders to get the pictures regardless of weather or other conditions, Lts. Lanker and Jackson proceeded on and attempted to get under the cloud cover. The two pilots were flying at 1500 feet when Lanker realized that the clouds went right down to the deck and pulled up and headed for home. Lanker made it back through the dense clouds okay, but Jackson crashed into a hilltop near Brighton, England while attempting to come out under the weather. This tragedy marked the low point in a most frustrating day of operations. The 10th had launched a massive effort of forty missions in support of Eisenhower's attempt to link up the two American beachheads, and had 19 missions aborted due to the weather.

The bad weather continued throughout June 9 and 10 and virtually shut down the 10th, however on the ground Bradley's First Army began its moves to effect a linkup of the two American beachheads and making contact with the British. In quick order the 29th Division took Isigny on June 9, and by June 12 the 101st Airborne had captured Carentan. With this type of movement Headquarters, VII Corps had already started looking toward Cherbourg, and on the night of June 10/11 the 423rd sent out four F-3s to photograph road junctions along the west side of the Cherbourg Peninsula. Again weather conditions plagued the pilots and resulted in an unsuccessful and tragic mission. An F-3 equipped with an Edgerton Lamp unit and piloted by Flight Officer Kulak was to photograph the road strip between St. Lo and Vire and was last seen heading for the Channel, but it and its three man crew vanished and were not seen or heard from again. In addition to the weather, flak had also been quite prevalent, but the fate of Kulak's crew can only be speculated. The other three F-3s returned to base with no pictures to complete the total failure of this mission.

Reorganization and Change of Command

The weather finally broke on June 12, and the 10th put up nearly 60 missions which covered vast areas of France. While the pilots of the Group continued flying their assigned missions, their commanding officer was learning that a major reorganization of reconnaissance groups within the 9th Air Force was being planned. Since the invasion was now well under way, the 10th would now be assuming the responsibility of providing aerial reconnaissance for the Third Army and would now come under the command of XIXth Tactical Air Command. As a result of these changes the Group's functions and organizational composition would be changed radically. What was now needed to support Third Army was an organization which was capable of providing not only day and night photography, but also extensive tactical reconnaissance in close support of fighter-bombers, artillery, and armored and infantry units. As a result of the new mission assigned to it, the 10th gave up the 30th and 33rd Photo Squadrons to the 67th Tactical Reconnaissance Group and in return received the 12th and 15th Tactical Reconnaissance Squadrons. The official date of these transfers was June 13th, 1944, although they did not actually begin until the latter part of June.

Coming right on the heels of the 10th's reorganization was a change of command. The change which took place on June 20, saw Colonel Reed turning over the reins of leadership to Lt. Colonel Russell A. Berg who had been Executive Officer of the 67th. Colonel Reed was reassigned to the 9th Air Force Headquarters where he served during the remainder of the war.

The first signs of the reorganization began to take place at Chalgrove on June 27 and 28 when the 15th Tactical Reconnaissance Squadron began moving in. The Mustang flying 15th, commanded by Lt. Colonel George T. Walker, was an aggressive unit which had been flying combat missions since March 26th. The Squadron had claimed the first aerial victory on D-Day when Lt. Joe Conklin clobbered a FW-190 near Dreux. Later in the day Lt. Clyde B. East and Lt. Ernest "Bud" Schonard returned to base from a visual recce with additional claims. Each of them had destroyed a FW-190 and Schonard had a probable FW-190 to add to his kill. At the time they joined the 10th Photo Reconnaissance Group, the Squadron had already destroyed seven enemy planes and probably destroyed two others. Captain John H. Hoefker was their top scorer with two Me-109s to his credit.

There had been much talk around the 15th TAC R that they would be one of the first units to go to France, and when word came down on June 26 that they would be transferred to Chalgrove there were mixed emotions. Lt. Fred Trenner recorded in his diary, "Just found out we're not going to France but to another field near Oxford. This move puts us further away from France and in a newly formed unit. The 67th has begun to move to the beachhead and will work in closer cooperation with the armies while we shall run deeper strategical reconnaissance." Again on June 28 Lt. Trenner states, "Our new field has a pretty nice set-up with good runways and Nissen Huts for all of us. Still don't like the idea of being so far from the coast. Stretching gasoline is a risky business."

Tactical Recon Missions Begin

The first officially recorded missions flown by the 15th TAC R as a member of the 10th Photo Reconnaissance Group were on June 29. Five missions were flown by its pilots that day, only two of which were successful due to weather. Lt. Trenner flew one of the unsuccessful missions of the day, and recorded in his diary a vivid description of flying recce missions in some of the bad weather encountered over Europe. "Went to the Brest Peninsula with Bud (Schonard) this morning. Ran into some foul weather and worked myself ragged flying cloud formation. One gets the damndest feeling inside thick clouds. Vertigo it's called and it makes one think he's doing everything but flying straight and level. In this type of flying the leader concentrates on his instrument while his wingman formates off his airplane. That way a section can keep together whereas if both flew individually through a thick overcast they might come out of it miles apart. We eventually turned around and came back to base after flying out our ETA and finding no break in the weather."

In direct contrast to Lt. Trenner's mission, Captain John Hoefker and

The crews on this and the following page flew the first mission of D-Day. This page, above l. to r.: Lt. Edward Lentscher, Lt. Cohn (MIA June 12, 1944), Sgt. James Willis. (J. Williams) Below, l. to r.: Lt. Vernon Red, Lt. Cliff Mackie, Lt. William McKeon. (C. Mackie) Following page, above, l. to r.: Lt. Douglas Hardy, Lt. Thomas Starmont, T/Sgt. J. Tackis. (J. Williams) Below, l. to r.: Lt. Nelson Huggins, Lt. Conoly Anderson, T/Sgt. John Palko. (J. Williams)

his wingman Lt. Joe Waits did not encounter bad weather on their visual recce over Bernay, Laigle, Belleme, and Alencon at all. Captain Hoefker was able to record the movement of several horse-drawn wagons, and several railroad cars sitting engineless, perfect targets for the fighter-bombers. However, while Captain Hoefker was watching and recording the enemy's movements below, he and Lt. Waits were also being watched and then quickly attacked by four Me-109s who came in from above. What followed is vividly described in Hoefker's encounter report, "We were 16 miles southwest of Bernay flying at 4000 feet when we observed four Me-109s approaching us from the southwest at 4500 feet. As we climbed for the clouds the 109s turned and dove at us from behind and I was attacked from below and to my rear by an enemy aircraft that opened fire at 500 yards. I broke left and we went into a Lufbury. I broke from the Lufbury while looking for Waits and was again attacked from my left rear. I pulled up into an Immelman and dove onto another 109, and fired three short bursts of one-half second each. After the third burst, I saw brownish-white smoke pour from the aircraft's engine, and then he rolled over and went down in a 60 degree dive, exploding as he hit the ground. The pilot did not get out." After the crash of the 109, the other three Germans hightailed it out of there and Hoefker and Waits headed back to Chalgrove. With his third kill Captain Hoefker extended his lead as the top recce pilot in downing enemy planes.

On June 30 the 15th TAC R was the only squadron from the 10th in the air, and they sent out 12 visual recce sorties. Again weather was a factor and five sorties were unsuccessful due to it. One of the sections up that day was Lt. Schonard and Lt. Trenner who recalled their mission in his diary. "Led my first mission today and got quite a kick out of it. After going over the route with our ALO*, Jim Clark, and checking on the flak defended areas I would have to pass, I received a few words of advice from Bud and we took off. I was slightly nervous about getting lost over there and bringing back an empty report. Concentrated on navigation down to Beachy Head on the south coast and once over the Channel dropped down to wave top level and flew on a compass heading. On reaching the coast of France and checking Le Havre on my left I crossed over and headed down the railroad track. The route I had to follow was of a circular nature and on reaching the start of it I had an easy time pinpointing myself. On a mission of this sort we mark down on our map and kneepad anything of interest that can be spotted on the ground. The contents of railyards, the

---

*Army Liaison Officer. See Appendix 1, TAC R area search.

highway and rail movement, possible supply dumps and anything else of a suspicious nature. Then too we can supplement our visual observations with photos. I relied completely on Bud to watch for aircraft and found that time really traveled and that I was enjoying myself immensely. Didn't see anything momentous and on heading north for the coast I passed over Liseaux—God was that town flattened. The only building left unscathed was a very beautiful church. Had some flak from Bernay but it was behind me. I wonder if Jerry is going to smarten up and put that stuff in front of us? Got back to the base and after being interrogated by Jim Clark and Buzz (Hadden, the 15th TAC R S-2), ate my combat ration and sat around comparing notes with the boys. Hanson and Khare returned, both excited having been jumped by two Me-109s and knocking down one each."

Lts. Henry Hansen and Frank Khare were flying a visual recce in the vicinity of Evereux and were charting some meaty targets, 50 railcars in the marshalling yards, a train in a tunnel, and a train of eight goods wagons sitting stationary, when they were jumped by the 109s. The Germans hit them from two o'clock, but inflicted no damage and soon found themselves the hunted instead of the hunters. Khare and Hansen each picked out their target and after a determined effort sent both 109s down in vertical dives trailing heavy smoke. The enemy aircraft were last seen entering heavy clouds at 1500 feet, so Hansen and Khare could not follow them down and had to settle for probables.

For the 10th Photo Reconnaissance Group June 1944 had been a very productive month. It had successfully inaugurated night photography and now could hinder the German by day and night, plus picking up excellent TAC R capabilities with the arrival of the 15th Tactical Reconnaissance Squadron. The 15th TAC R had given them the credit for destroying the first enemy aircraft on D-Day, and the 423rd Nightfighter Squadron (155th Night Photo Squadron) flew the first mission of D-Day. The unit's pride in their invasion support is neatly summed up in the final entry for June in the 15th TAC R's monthly historical report. "So ended the month. The squadron had made the decidedly unusual record for a recce unit of eight kills, three probables, and one damaged. *More important it had accomplished the primary mission of bringing back valuable information of enemy activity thereby making a significant contribution to the success of the Allied operations in France.*"*

Weather continued to be a factor during the early days of July 1944 and

---

*Emphasis the author's

during the first three days only six sorties, all by the 15th TAC R, were flown. Operations resumed on July 4 with the 155th Night Photo Squadron flying their F-3s on four sorties over the Cherbourg Peninsula, but due to weather conditions and Gee system troubles, only Lt. Verket was able to successfully photograph his targets. When daylight broke the 33rd Photo Squadron sent up four of its F-5s on TAC R type missions of front line coverage and checking the road on the Cherbourg Peninsula, and the 15th TAC R followed with eleven more sorties. With the need most urgent but ceilings dangerously low, TAC R received the task of running visual and photo reconnaissance regularly to determine the serviceability and repair status of railroad and highway bridges over the Seine and the Loire Rivers. So great was the importance of continuous isolation of the battle area by preventing German supplies and reinforcements from crossing these rivers that TAC R flew a number of low-level recce missions in almost prohibitive weather.

Again we find a good running commentary of weather conditions and how they affected the missions from Lt. Trenner's diary. "July 4, Went to Cherbourg with Bud today. We were after some guns that were holding up our troops but upon arriving there found the weather packed in tight. Cruised down along the beachhead for a while looking it all over and hoping we'd see some Jerries below us. Went back to the peninsula later and tried to get in, but no dice. July 6: First light mission this morning and it was really beautiful over England. Took off and went up through the low grey overcast and headed south. Over the Channel with the sun just starting to rise in the east was a sight I'll never forget. The sky above was shot with color and the clouds below were of a deep purple hue. It was really gorgeous. On hitting the coast though I forgot the scenery. Received a warm welcome with lots of flak. Flew down to Abbeville airdrome and kept a close watch for Herman's Yellow Noses. I guess all the Krauts were still in the sack as it was just 6:15 then. On further to Amiens and the railyards there have been pulverized. The 8th does a wonderful job, by God! Had a fair trip around and came out at Ostend, Belgium. After landing and interrogation I hit the sack for the rest of the day. Still have yet to see a Jerry in the air. July 10: Took off and headed for the beachhead this morning, there were six of us and we went over in formation. All three sections had photos to take of the Loire River. We landed on a strip there and had our ships refueled. This was my first trip to France so I picked up a small flower to send Nancy. Hung around for a while but the weatherman gave us a "duff" report so we went back to England. Would have loved to see some Krauts over the Channel right then. This business of flying in pairs isn't healthy with Jerry travelling in packs when he does come up. This afternoon we did the same thing with the same results. Pretty tired tonight so I'll hit the sack early."

By July 11, the need for information and photos of the Loire River bridges was critical and again the 15th TAC R dispatched its pilots into the "pea soup" to attempt to get the mission accomplished. Two pilots who went up that day, Lt. Fred Trenner and Lt. John Miefert provide a good picture through their reports of the day's events. First Lt. Trenner: "Finally got the job done on those bridge photos. Bud really got some beautiful pictures and its been an exciting day. We got over to the beachhead in the morning with orders from Operations to get the pictures regardless of weather. Gassed up and took off in a few minutes and were soon on top of a low overcast just skimming the tops of the clouds. It's like coming into a new world when you break through an overcast and find everything on top white, blue and sunny. We had a long way to go so Bud settled down flying a heading while I weaved, watching into the sun for bandits. After an hour's flying we dropped down through the overcast and ' jinked ' around trying to locate ourselves. The ceiling was down to 2000 feet and we were nervous as hell. Picked up the river and Bud headed for his first target. It was a highway bridge along side of Samur. We circled away from the town and Bud told me he was going to come in on the deck. At least we could have the element of surprise. I told him I'd go down with him and shoving the throttle forward we dove to the ground. Had my gun switches on and as I approached the river bank lined up on what I thought was a flak tower. Let go a long burst and watched my tracers bounce off the concrete structure— (then I) went over the top. Looked out on my left and Bud was about 50 feet higher than me just as we hit the river. I could see the bridge was caved in and a bunch of people were working on it. On the other side of the river was a train standing still so I gave it a squirt for luck.

"Just about then all hell broke loose with one shell exploding right in front of my ship. It was bright orange in color and I thought sure I had had it then and there. Jammed the throttle through the gate and swerved right and then up. Gunners followed me on up to the clouds and I've never seen so much of that stuff before. Broke out on top and I could feel the perspiration running down my neck. Called Bud on the RT, located him and joined up. We had two more bridges to photograph and I was hoping we'd get a better break on the next two. Went down to Tours and it was a piece of cake as was the third one. Up through the clouds again and headed back. On getting near the beachhead and not wanting to let down

Right: Maj. Robert Simpson and his F-6C "Heaven Can Wait" which was coded 5M-H. Lt Sal Mecca was killed in this Mustang on July 11, 1944. (J. Miefert)

Left: Lt. Col. Russell A. Berg, who assumed command of the 10th Group in June 1944. (R. Dawson) Below: Lt. E.M. Schonard and his F-6C "Peachy's Delight" at Chalgrove, England, July 1944. It was coded 5M-T. (C. Ochs)

Above: "Mary" of the 34th Photo Squadron over the English Channel during June 1944. (B. Rosen) Right: Lt. John Miefert of the 15th TAC R Squadron. (J. Miefert) Below: German officers captured at Normandy and flown to Chalgrove, England, shortly after D-Day. (W. Conard)

through the overcast with the possibility of running into the many barrage balloons there Bud decided to drop down a bit ahead of his ETA. We hit the deck again and ran into a hell of a lot more of light flak and small arms fire. It developed that we were slightly south of Caen where Jerry was still holding out fiercely. Landed at a Canadian Typhoon base and looked over our ships for holes. Didn't find any which seemed miraculous and ate a light lunch of 'Bully' beef and some hard biscuits. I was all in and it was a real treat to lay on the warm grass and smoke. Smoked about three cigarettes while our ships were refueled and then back off to England."

Lt. Miefert's account of the Loire missions begins with his afternoon mission of July 10 and continues through the mission of July 11. "Our squadron was assigned to do some behind the German lines reconnaissance to determine troop and tank strength. Sal (Mecca) drew the mission and I had been assigned as his wingman. It was late afternoon. The weather was bad so it was over the clouds we went with a let down near the Loire River so Sal could orient himself and then to fly north to the battle lines observing all he could see. The ceiling over the Loire where we let down was under 5000 feet. As we worked our way north, the ceiling got lower and lower. Normally we were not to go under 3000 feet. Sal got us down to 2500 and when the ceiling ahead appeared to be steadily lowering, he aborted the mission and we flew home, having observed nothing. Army was not satisfied and we were sent out the next morning with orders to go as low as necessary. Weather conditions were the same, but Sal kept on flying and looking. We came on some encampments (I guess as I was busy flying wing and saw little or nothing of the ground), and picked up some flak which I reported to Sal. He kept on going and the flak increased till I thought the whole Germany army was shooting at us. It was the worst flak I ever received. Sal finally gave the order to climb into and through the cloud cover. I was very excited and jammed the throttle as I 'jinked,' trying to throw the flak off aim and gain the clouds. There were two very loud noises and I thought I was hit and called Sal and told him so. I finally made the clouds and the flak quit. It seemed we were flying in and out of the clouds, but it seemed to take forever to get into them once we decided to do it. When I got on top of the thin cloud layer, Sal and I got together and he looked me over and could see no damage. We later decided that in my excitement, I added throttle but not RPM and the engine had detonated twice. We returned to base with my gas very, very low. It was decided the information Sal had gathered was not enough and he must go back again to try and complete this must mission."

By that afternoon when Lt. Sal Mecca was to make another attempt at his mission the weather had worsened to the point it was decided that wingmen wouldn't be necessary. The 15th TAC R then dispatched Lts. Mecca, Stelle, Reger, and Warenskjold, each flying without escort to try and bring back the needed information about the bridges and troop movements. All made it back with successful missions to report except Lt. Mecca. His target this time was a bridge near Paris, and he took off in a P-51 named ironically enough "HEAVEN CAN WAIT!" and never returned.

The reason behind these dangerous, tiring, and in the case of Lt. Mecca, tragic missions was that despite the Allies success in getting ashore in Normandy, the territory secured by the beginning of July was much less than had been planned. The British Twenty-First Army Group was stalled on a front stretching from the coast to the fields south of Caen and on to Caumont. Meanwhile General Bradley's First Army was engaged in a tough fight in the waterlogged, hedgerow fields of Normandy, and suffering horrible casualties because the weather was limiting both his tactical air support and use of armor. As a result of this situation there was a tremendous need for information and to try and get it the TAC R pilots continued to fly these risky missions.

TAC R Covers Operation Cobra

Because the need for tactical reconnaissance was so great the 9th Air Force sent its 67th Tactical Reconnaissance Group to France on July 2. It was to support Bradley's front and to provide up to the minute reports of German movements and positions. It was this need for TAC R that sent the 10th's other squadron the 12th TAC R to France along with the 67th Group rather than to Chalgrove. For the 12th TAC R their arrival at LeMolay ended a 25 year absence from France.

In the hedgerows the hard pressed infantry was still slugging it out with the determined German defenders hiding in emplacements concealed by the insidious hedges, and suffering terrible losses. The losses however did not restrict themselves to the fighting on the ground, and on July 14th, only two days after their arrival in France the 12th TAC R lost a pilot. Lt. Steve Canner and Captain Rusten were on their way back from a route reconnaissance of the Mortagne area when they were jumped from above by over 50 FW-190s. The section immediately took evasive action and broke for the deck in an attempt to lose the 190s, but Canner's P-51 was hit repeatedly by 20mm cannon fire and went down with Canner being listed as missing in action.

By July 18th, Bradley had captured St. Lo and on July 25th set

OPERATION COBRA in motion. This attack which called for a limited exploitation toward the town of Coutances was supported by a huge aerial armada of 8th and 9th Air Force Bombers. After an abortive and tragic attempt in which US bombers hit our own troops on July 24, another massive air attack was dispatched on July 25th and it destroyed much of the enemy's communications, shook his morale, and opened up the front in many places. As the infantry and armored columns exploited the opportunity to break through the lines of the dazed Germans, a second and vital phase of the aerial-ground cooperation was to begin, that of armed recce in support of the armor. These fighter-bombers would seek out and destroy enemy armor that might be attempting to block the route of advance of our troops and also in many instances came to the aid of our Tankers that were in trouble. Along with these fighter-bombers, the 12th TAC R also combined the area in search of enemy troop, and by their reports sealed the doom of many of the enemy. It was during one of these missions that the 12th TAC R suffered its third loss of the month (the second being Lt. Jacob Piatt who was killed while ferrying a P-51 from England to France on July 21). Lt. William Lacey was on a photo mission near Val D'Enhue on July 30th when he was hit by flak. He had just started his photo run over the target when his wingman called out "flak," but Lacy's attempt at evasive action came too late and his flak-riddled Mustang soon burst into flame, fell off into a steep dive and crashed.

As a result of hard fighting and excellent ground-air cooperation during the last week in July, a genuine breakthrough was accomplished. It was on the third day of the attack that a tremendous breach was made in the German line, and the Americans poured through. Seizing the initiative, General Bradley broadened the scope of the operation and sent all four Corps of his Army driving ahead. Within a week the VII and VIIIth Corps had advanced thirty miles, and American troops had captured Avranches and gained the base of the Cotentin Peninsula. The XIXth Corps had also played a big part in the victory when they blocked Kluge from sending two Panzer divisions into the Cobra area at Tessy-sur-Vire. Aggressive armored fighting along with the excellent tactical air support had trapped large numbers of German troops near Coutances and effectively crushed their left flank. With this the German defense was crushed and with his victory assured Bradley turned over command of his First Army to General Hodges on August 1st and assumed command of the 12th Army Group. On the same day the Third Army under General George Patton became operational, and the 12th TAC R now began its support of Third Army.

Meanwhile the 10th's squadrons operating from Chalgrove still continued their strategic coverage of areas surrounding the invasion front, ranging from St. Quentin, Lille, Cambrai, and Arras in eastern France to the bridges along the Loire River to Rennes and St. Malo on the Brittany Peninsula. One such mission was the one flown by Lt. Schonard and Lt. Trenner on July 17 and again recorded in Trenner's diary as follows, "Had a long haul over the water today, clear across the Brest Peninsula to Lorient. Had a good laugh as Bud got chased away from the town by some damn accurate heavy flak. Those boys were good and gave old Bud a good workout. This heavy flak, unlike the light stuff, the first indication of it is a black puff in the air whereas the other can be seen coming up from the ground. Back over the Channel we spotted several vessels with a large airplane cruising slowly above them. Thinking it might be an evacuation of Brest we peeled off and went down on them. It was a Coastal Command B-24, so we broke off and came home. Travelled 600 miles over water today."

The next day on July 18, Lt. Joe Waits and Lt. John Miefert were just completing a photo run on the Cherisy railroad bridge three miles east of Dreux when they were jumped by two Me-109s. The 109s made a pass and headed for the deck, and Waits quickly called Miefert on the RT to follow him, and they went diving after the 109s. Miefert recalls, "Joe made his turn quicker than I did and so I was well behind him, so I added throttle and RPM to catch up. He called again and said he had lost track of them but was sure they were following the railroad tracks and he was also following it. We were on the deck (50 feet) now and I could see the flak towers going by and cringed as we passed each one. I was gaining rapidly on Joe as the two 109s came into view. They were line abreast and Joe said, 'I'll take the one on the left and you take the right one,' and he opened fire at 200 yards. I could see hits all over the plane and it rolled over on its back and crashed. Meanwhile I have the throttle all the way back as I'm overrunning Joe and the other 109. I opened fire trying to keep the plane from an uncoordinated skid you get at high speed and no engine torque. I saw hits on the wing and the 109 turned left, right into Joe's area of fire. Joe fired a two second burst at 150 yards, and I saw strikes in the cockpit area, the canopy was blown off, the wings and engine were also hit hard, and this 109 rolled over and exploded into the ground." With the crash of the second 109 the two formed up and completed their mission, then returned to base and celebrated Joe Waits' victories.

On the afternoon of the 18th, the Luftwaffe was successful in attacking another section of the 15th. As Lt. Richard "Doc" Youll and Lt. Frank

Ristau were making their run in the vicinity of Avranches, they were bounced by a gaggle of at least thirty Me-109s. Ristau who was the leader of the section, radioed to Youll to run for it and to rendezvous at the beachhead landing strip. Doc made it to the clouds and safety, and then called Ristau on the RT but received no answer. By this time Ristau had gone down under the enemy guns, and soon afterwards became a prisoner of war.

July 20 also turned out to be a big day for the TAC R pilots of the 15th. Lt. Ted Trulson and Lt. Al Frick were checking the railroad sidings at Clastres when Trulson happened to see some twin-engine enemy aircraft on the ground at nearby Clastres airdrome. As they turned to check airdrome activity they saw two Me-109s at 1000 feet below climbing head on toward them. As Trulson and Frick started climbing the 109s started turning with them, so they did a wingover and dove on the 109s. The Germans immediately broke in the opposite direction and headed for the deck, but Trulson was gaining rapidly and opened up on one of them at 400 yards. His first burst enveloped the fuselage, and the second hit the cockpit and left wing root. As he broke upward, Lt. Trulson turned and saw a light colored object leave the plane which he believed to be a partially opened chute. While Lt. Trulson was firing, Lt. Frick had also pulled to within 300 yards of the 109 and opened fire and saw hits in the left wing root. As he broke away he saw the impact of Trulson's second burst, and also saw an object fly from the plane. The Messerschmitt then crashed into an open field, and his partner hastily left the area.

Later that day Lt. Raymond spotted a train moving southwest into Amiens loaded with armored vehicles and radioed in his report. Within twenty minutes he saw a flight of fighter-bombers beginning their bombing and strafing attack on the train and within minutes it was a smoking wreck; a classic example of good tactical reconnaissance work.

During the month of July 1944, the 155th Night Photo Squadron took a big step from its infancy and flew 64 sorties of which 60 per cent were successful, and as a result provided the night and day coverage desired by the 10th Photo Reconnaissance Group in order to keep the enemy reeling. Their excellent work along with the outstanding photo coverage provided by the 31st, 33rd (which had still not left the Group for its new assignment to the 67th TRG) and 34th Photo Squadrons gave the field commanders a decided tactical advantage during the breakout stage. The stage was now set for the entrance of the Third Army into the area and Patton's famous drive across France.

Above: A 155th Night Photo Squadron A-20. The port for the Edgerton Lamp is just forward of the bomb bay doors, toward the front of the fuselage. The round camera port is just to the rear of the bomb bay doors. (G. Pape) Below: L. to r., Lt. James Williams, 155th Night Photo Squadron, being briefed for a mission on September 4, 1944 by Lt. J.C. Thirwall and Lt. H.C. Crawford. (J. Williams)

CHAPTER IV

The Breakout

August – Early September 1944 - Move to France to Cover Third Army's Drive Across Europe

---

By the first of August it became very apparent that the 3rd Army and XIXth Tactical Air Command would need the 10th Photo Reconnaissance Group in France, but the campaign in Normandy was still behind schedule and as yet no airfield was available for them. Because of this it was necessary during the first few days of the Third Army's campaign for the 12th TAC R Squadron to handle its reconnaissance. During this period the speed of the drive into Brittany was so great that planned tactical reconnaissance had to be changed daily. Much of their work for VIII Corps, for example, was checking particular bridges, roads, and/or towns and woods for possible ambushes. In the first five days of the campaign the 12th TAC R flew 26 missions, all of which were successful.

The advance of Patton's Third Army was so fast that most of the emphasis was being placed on TAC R visual recce missions because photos were out of date virtually as quickly as they were made. With most of Brittany already in Allied hands after the first five days of Patton's assault, Third Army began to strike eastward. As it did planned reconnaissance had to be altered from routes to areas in order to give more complete coverage and to keep up with the enemy's movement on secondary roads. With the Third Army's spearheads continually outstripping their communications with its higher commands, TAC R pilots had also the task of reporting the movements and location of US armored columns and keeping ground commanders apprised of the situation. As a result of the great demand for tactical reconnaissance the pilots of the 12th and 15th TAC R Squadrons were operating from dawn to dusk protecting Third Army's flank and locating targets. The cost in maintaining this surveillance was high and resulted in casualties, the 12th losing two pilots killed, and a third shot down and injured. The first loss was on August 8 when a section was making a visual recce of the LeMans area and were attacked by 12 Me-109s. Both pilots broke and took evasive action trying to lose the German fighters. Lt. Dieckman was able to evade and returned to base okay, but Lt. Thomas J. Wood's Mustang was shot up by the 109s and he himself was seriously wounded. Woods was able to fly his crippled ship to A-13 (Tour-en-Bessin) for a crash landing, but died a few hours later in the station hospital).

At the time of Lt. Woods loss, the 12th TAC R which had been augmented in strength by the arrival of "C" Flight of the 15th TAC R was supporting the encirclement of the German 7th Army in the Argentan-Falaise Gap by combined British and American armies. Between the 8th and 20th of August of 1944 Allied forces trapped 50,000 German troops in this area, and sent the remnants of the German Fifth Panzer and 7th Armies back across the Seine in headlong retreat. The excellent battlefield coverage provided by TAC R helped immensely in guiding ground commanders, and more importantly directing fighter-bomber attacks on the retreating German convoys; attacks which killed 10,000 German troops and destroyed countless numbers of motor vehicles.

Move to the Continent

Rennes had fallen on August 6, almost without a struggle, and the airfield sites nearby were soon made available for US aircraft. On August 11, the 12th TAC R Squadron became the first squadron of the 10th Photo Reconnaissance Group to set up operations at their new base near Rennes, which seems appropriate since the 12th TAC R had been operating from English bases since September 1942, much longer than any other element of the 10th Photo Reconnaissance Group. The squadron was commanded at this time by Major Gordon L. Woodrow, the fourth of its overseas commanders.

When the 12th TAC R arrived in England as a part of the 67th Observation Group (later redesignated the 67th Tactical Reconnaissance Group) it was originally assigned to the 8th Air Force. At this time the 12th was commanded by Major James Haun, and although it was not on an operational status, many of the pilots flew their first combat missions while serving on temporary assignments with various Royal Air Force squadrons. In November 1943 the 67th Group was assigned to the 9th Air Force and Major Russell A. Berg assumed command. On December 6th 1943 Major Berg was promoted to Executive Officer of the 67th Group and command of the 12th was handed over to Captain D.R. French. In

January 1944 the 12th, now under the command of Gordon Woodrow, became operational and its first mission was flown on January 2 by Captain James L. Rose. In February and March the twelfth participated in the Merton Oblique* photographic missions of the invasion coast for which the 67th Group was awarded the Presidential Unit Citation. Much like its brother squadron, the 15th TAC R, the 12th TAC R began to claim aerial victories shortly after D-Day. It was on June 7, 1944 that Lt. William Lacey and Lt. Jacob Piatt were flying a visual recce of the Laval area when they saw three FW-190s circling their airfield in preparation for a landing. Attacking out of the sun Lacey and Piatt each shot down a 190, and sent the third German fleeing the area as fast as his FW-190 would carry him.

The 12th TAC R wasn't an orphan at Rennes for long however as the 155th Night Photo Squadron also reported in on the eleventh and the 15th TAC R came in on August 12. By August 15 all of the Group's squadrons had arrived, and the Group was now composed of the 12th and 15th TAC R, the 31st and 34th Photo Squadrons and the 155th Night Photo Squadron. Its other photo squadron, the 33rd, left for its new assignment with the 67th Tactical Reconnaissance Group. Also at this time there was a change of command in the 31st, with Captain Merritt G. Garner replacing Lt. Colonel Rudolph Walters, who was moved up to 10th Group Headquarters as Executive Officer.

With the Group now operating from Rennes, its reconnaissance capabilities were greatly increased; for example, during the first 13 days of the month its maximum number of successful tactical recce (visual) missions flown in one day had been 14, but with the addition of the 15th TAC R they were able to complete 36 missions on August 14. With the situation at the front still so fluid the month of August was to become a high point in the operational life of the TAC R squadrons and during the month they were to fly 432 tactical recce missions in support of the Army as compared to 81 photo reconnaissance missions. As was mentioned previously the pace was so great that photos were out of date as quickly as they were taken, so the burden fell on the TAC R pilots to search out targets, alert the ground forces of possible danger areas and protect Third Army's flank along the Loire River.

All of the activity was not taking place in the air either as the rapid movement of the ground forces had left pockets of German soldiers in and around the Rennes area. The airfield itself had a triangular runway setup

---

*Merton Oblique. See Appendix 1, TAC R Missions and Tactics

with some woods in the middle. Retired Colonel Edward L. Bishop, who at the time was Lt. Bishop of the 12th TAC R, recalled the German infiltration into these woods and attack made on 12th TAC R aircraft. "We got there before all the Krauts were gone and on about the second or third day they got into the woods and opened up on our aircraft with automatic weapons. It was a real shock for us and with no automatic weapons of our own we weren't sure what to do. Some of the crew chiefs wanted to jack up the P-51s and fire back with the 50s, but before that became necessary the Army came in and cleaned up."

This situation was also referred to in the history of the 31st Photo Squadron. "The situation at the front was very fluid and the advancing armor had left pockets of resistance all around Rennes with a big pocket at Falaise. This situation kept all members of the squadron on their toes and extra guards were detailed to insure security. Some men in the squadron were instrumental in capturing German soldiers at the base, but most sections were far too busy attempting to figure out what part photo reconnaissance was going to play in this fast moving war to come into personal contact with it."

The 15th TAC R swung back into action on August 13th and launched its first six sorties from Rennes, one of which was an excellent set of vertical and oblique photos of the fortress at St. Malo taken by Lt. Bud Schonard. By now Patton's drive had carried his armor and infantry into the area of Dreux and Orleans while his spearhead patrols were within 10 miles of Paris. With an assault on Paris itself seeming imminent, the Luftwaffe was becoming a little more active, and the number of encounters increased. On August 15 Lt. Colonel George Walker and his wingman Lt. Manuel Geiger were on a visual recce in the vicinity of Paris when Colonel Walker spotted a FW-190 climbing from behind towards them. He immediately turned into the German fighter to meet the attack, and after a hard fought dogfight with a skilled adversary, Walker shot the Focke-Wulf from the sky. His was not the only victory for the 15th TAC R that day as Lt. James McCormick also flying in the vicinity of Paris blasted a Me-109 from the sky.

Photo Missions August 15–25, 1944

Meanwhile the 10th Group's photo and night photo squadrons were now ready to begin operations from Rennes and play their part in the scheme of things. Even though the emphasis was being placed on tactical reconnaissance missions, there were some important photo missions for them. Several of them were to be flown over the Brest Peninsula where

Above: Ground crew checking out the tail-warning device on Lt. James Williams's A-20. (J.E. Williams) Right: A crated Bf109E found at Rennes, August 1944. (J.E. Williams) Below: Dr. Harold Edgerton and Col. Elliott Roosevelt with the commanders and staff of the 10th in an open air conference at Rennes, August 1944. (L. Davis)

Above: Members of the 155th Night Photo Squadron with a dummy tank left by retreating Germans near Chateaudun, France. (J.E. Williams) *Below:* The ground crew of this 155th Night Photo Squadron A-20J removing Invasion markings from the wings. Chateaudun, September 4, 1944. (W. Campbell)

Ninth Army was pushing the Wehrmacht back to the sea. In order to make this campaign a success, and to keep casualties to a minimum, detailed photo information was needed. At the same time they were covering Third Army requests to check for possible river crossing sites along the Seine, Marne and Meuse Rivers. Secondly, the Third Army was still running into strong points of resistance and was calling for photographic coverage of these areas.

The 155th Night Photo Squadron began its operations from Rennes during the early hours of August 15, and with the enemy moving by night as much as possible found their work becoming increasingly important. On this mission which was to check for movement in the Argentan-Falaise pocket area, two F-3s, piloted by Major Joe Gillespie, Squadron CO, and Lt. Barnes were sent out. They found little to report except for forest fires burning near Argentan and Le Loupe, but the mission nearly ended in tragedy when Major Gillespie's ship was fired on and hit by "friendly" anti-aircraft fire which damaged the plane and wounded the navigator.

The 155th was able to play a most successful part in covering the German retreat from the Argentan-Falaise pocket and provided the ground commanders with timely photos, but once the Army started advancing rapidly eastward the unit was not able to operate effectively.

August 17 found both the TAC R and photo ships in the air. The 15th TAC R dispatched 16 missions that day, one of them sending Lt. Colonel Walker back to the Paris area again. He and Lt. Bill Boyle were flying in the vicinity of Villeroche airfield when they were bounced by enemy fighters. The two immediately dived for the deck and as they outran the pursuing German aircraft they sighted two enemy planes directly in front of them, a Ju-88 and a Ju-52. Lt. Boyle caught the Ju-52 just as it entered the base leg of its landing pattern and sent it down in flames. Meanwhile Lt. Colonel Walker was firing on the Ju-88 and set the left engine on fire. As he finished his firing run, Lt. Boyle fired on the Junkers and set the other engine on fire, and moments later after its cockpit burst into flame the Ju-88 hit a tree and crashed.

While Lt. Colonel Walker and Lt. Boyle were engaged in an exciting mission, Lt. Trenner was lamenting his mission to Vienzon and Tours as a dull trip, one in which, "We didn't draw a bit of flak or see any movement." And a third section from the 15th, Lt. Zondlo and Posey travelled to St. Malo and got some excellent photos of the Citadel which had just surrendered that day.

The 31st wasn't as fortunate that day as it suffered the loss of Lt. Thomas L. Wood, their third loss to enemy action, when his plane burst into flames as he was returning to base. According to the 31st history, Lt. Wood was a soldier who took a very personal interest in the war as he was at Pearl Harbor on December 7, 1941, and wanted very much to end the war in Europe so he could get a crack at the Japanese.

One incident of incredibly good luck for the 31st Photo Squadron did occur during this period when Lt. James Matthews was on a mission over a strip of river southeast of Paris. After taking off in extremely bad weather, Lt. Matthews got off course and broke out over Chalons which is a hundred miles north and east of Paris. When he saw a river and other checkpoints that identified with his target area, he turned on his cameras, made a pass over the river and returned with some excellent photos. However, when he returned the plotting section could not plot the photos with the map, and reported that Lt. Matthews had missed his target. Afterwards, additional missions to his target area were cancelled because Third Army had already passed it. However in the meantime urgent requests had come down for photographs of some railroad guns in the Chalons marshalling yards. The unit made two attempts to fly the mission, but heavy cloud cover prevented any photography. By now Twelfth Corps was demanding the pictures and ordered that the mission be completed regardless of weather, and while Operations was trying to get volunteers to fly it, the plotting section called to report that they had discovered that Lt. Matthews had photographed Chalons. His photos were delivered to Army headquarters and the guns were quickly knocked out. The mission which had originally been declared a failure turned out to be of tremendous value and resulted in the 10th Photo Reconnaissance Group receiving a Letter of Commendation from General Patton in which he praised the Group for its "prompt attention."

By August 20, Patton's columns were driving toward the Seine below Paris and were about to cross the Loing River (a southern tributary of the Seine), but to do so the Third Army needed complete reports on the condition of the bridges along it. This mission was assigned to Lt. Robert Raymond and Lt. Eugene F. Balachowski of the 15th TAC R.

With Balachowski flying top cover for him, Lt. Raymond flew the course of the Loing twice at an altitude of 2500 feet, a distance of sixty miles, and took obliques from each bank so that shadows would not obscure the same portion of each bridge and also so that the bridge approaches might be studied. In addition, Raymond photographed the bridges over the canal and made visual observations which were forwarded to Army.

As in the case of Lt. Matthews mission, this mission drew high praise, and in a letter sent to the 10th Photo Reconnaissance Group by General O.P. Weyland they were told, "The spectacular successes achieved by the Third U.S. Army in recent weeks would not have been possible without the prompt and accurate observation and reporting of the enemy's dispositions and movements, which has so efficiently provided by the 10th Photo Group, Reconnaissance."

TAC R Support August 23–September 7, 1944

The Third Army had elements across the Seine above and below Paris by August 23. With XV Corps advancing northwest along the Seine toward Louviers and with the First U.S. Army, British and Canadian troops attacking north and eastward, elements of the German 7th Army which had been virtually destroyed at Falaise again found itself becoming encircled. With air to ground communications improving, tactical reconnaissance pilots were frequently able to report the location and movement of German troops directly to armored columns pursuing them.

In spite of poor visibility, clouds and showers on the 23rd, aircraft, both TAC R and XIXth TAC fighter-bombers, were pursuing the enemy. Fighter-bombers aided by recce information destroyed 114 motor vehicles, and damaged 38 others, destroyed or damaged 63 horsedrawn vehicles, and four tanks were knocked out. Additionally they destroyed four gun positions, two ammunition dumps, and a marshalling yard.

With all the activity on the ground Lt. Trenner decided to join the strafing. "Doc Youll and I went out today and ran into some excitement for a change. Spotted three trucks going down a highway. Told Doc to keep an eye out for flak and went down after them. Right near an airfield so I took a good look around and then hit for the deck. Lined up on the rear truck and then just moved my tracers right up the line. The Krauts had all hit for the ditch and I don't think I got any of them. Passed back over the spot about 15 minutes later and the trucks were still there. Some white smoke curling up, so I guess Jerry will have to walk. Spotted a lone engine puffing up a railroad track later on and really splattered the boiler. Gave the driver plenty of time to get out so I'm not worried about clobbering some Frenchman."

Next day the weather again limited missions, but the fighter-bombers again hit the retreating Germans hard. Aircraft of the 406th FB Group destroyed gun positions near Nantes, and 40 carts of an ammo convoy near Paris. The 371st did a "little working on the railroad" between Orleans and Tours, which is probably the action observed and reported in Lt. Trenner's diary. "Doc led today and we went down south of the Loire

River again. Quite a bit of activity mostly ambulances. Our troops are fighting in Orleans and Jerry must be holding on the other side of the river. The T-Bolts must have hit there just before us because the road is littered with burning vehicles. Several buildings are burning. Caught two hospital trains heading south but didn't strafe them. We're quite certain that Jerry is marking some ammo trucks with a Red Cross but have no real proof. I wouldn't want to strafe any wounded men although I wouldn't put it past the Germans."

On the ground, Third Army's XII and XX Corps, southeast of Allied occupied Paris, continued their rapid thrust towards the east, while XV Corps, now operating under First Army, moved eastward to aid in entrapping German troops remaining south of the lower Seine.

August 25 was a big day for the XIXth Tactical Air Force, both on the ground and in the air. On the ground the Seventh US Army was driving up through the Rhone Valley to meet up with the Third Army, when tactical reconnaissance reported large-scale movement of enemy rail and motor transport north and east below the Loire. The German trains were loaded with troops and equipment attempting to escape into Germany through the Dijon-Besancon Gap. A rail-cutting plan was begun immediately by XIXth TAC to try and cut off the escape attempt. This attack later had to be interrupted when XIXth TAC received orders to divert their fighter-bombers to support the attack on Brest, but by then they had inflicted some heavy damage on the enemy: 266 motor vehicles, 4 tanks, 44 locomotives, and 164 cars destroyed or damaged; five marshalling yards attacked and five lines cut; three gun positions, four troop concentrations, an ammunition dump and eight military buildings destroyed; five airfields attacked and five hangars destroyed. In anti-shipping missions off Brest, two naval vessels were claimed as destroyed and three naval and merchant vessels damaged. Four Mustangs of the 10th helped direct the artillery fire for Corps artillery at Brest and observed many hits on enemy gun positions and shipping.

In the air on August 25, the P-51s and P-47s of IX and XIXth Tactical Air Commands had a field day. In aerial combat and by strafing enemy airfields they destroyed 127 planes (77 air—50 ground) plus eleven probables and 33 damaged, and in doing so broke the back of the Luftwaffe in France. Pilots of the 15th TAC R were not going to let the fighter jocks claim all of the credit during the day and downed two of the 127 destroyed. The first was a Ju-52 which Lt. John Murtha knocked down while the Ju-52 pilot was trying to evacuate troops from Paris. After the clumsy transport was set afire its pilot tried crashlanding it in an open

Luftwaffe bombs line the road to the base at Chateaudun. (B. Rosen)

An F-5 of the 34th Photo Squadron in front of bomb-damaged Luftwaffe hangar at Chateaudun, September 1944. (H. Vaughn)

Above: "Sleepy Time Gal," the F-3 in which Lt. Fluhr, Lt. Joseph Rau, and S/Sgt. Charles Barren (below) were lost. (W. Campbell)

field, however Murtha strafed it and caught the escaping soldiers with a hail of 50 caliber fire. Meanwhile Bud Schonard and Lt. H.H. Hughes were halfway through their visual recce mission when Schonard saw a Me-109 at 12 o'clock. Almost simultaneously the 109 pilot saw the two Mustangs and immediately broke into them. Upon completing a 180 degree turn, the German dove for the deck and was followed by Schonard and Hughes. Bud opened fire at 100 yards, fired two bursts and saw hits on the wings, fuselage and engine, and then smoke and flame trailed back from the stricken 109. As Schonard broke away, Hughes followed the German into a steep climb and peppered both wings of the Messerschmitt with his fifties, then watched as the pilot jettisoned his canopy and jumped.

In his diary entry for August 25, Fred Trenner made note of the two aerial victories, and ended the passage with a significant note, "Everyone is now calling us the 15th FIGHTER SQUADRON."

August 26 found the personnel of the 10th's squadrons saddling up and preparing to move to their new base in Chateaudun. Headquarters had already made the move on August 24, and was ready to resume operations as soon as the aircraft arrived.

The new base did enable the TAC R aircraft to roam over eastern France and even into Germany itself, but it did not solve all problems of operations or communications for the 10th. For example, it was necessary for the Mustangs flying artillery missions to land at Rennes to refuel either before or after the mission. The distances involved were long and inefficiency was the result. Many times the planes would have to fly for an hour before reaching their target and then only be able to stay there for twenty to thirty minutes.

For the pilots covering Patton's drive eastward communications were a real problem. Many miles often separated HQ, Third Army, XIXth TAC and 10th PRG headquarters, and more times than not land telephone communications were inadequate, which resulted sometimes in delaying photo and tactical recce results to the users. Many times the pilots would fly over the airfield and radio the information directly to Corps level so it would still be timely, and then liaison planes were used to fly the information to higher headquarters.

Still the missions went on and August 27 was a day of triumph and tragedy for the Group. For the 12th TAC R, it was an extremely bad day which cost them a pilot killed and three planes. Over Brest Lt. Arthur Chinn and Lt. Garr were adjusting artillery fire when Chinn's Mustang was hit by flak. Lt. Garr reported the P-51 caught fire immediately and went straight down and crashed, Chinn being unable to get out. Meanwhile Lt. Karl Brandt and Lt. Smiley were flying a route reconnaissance and while in the vicinity of Bar-le-Duc Brandt's plane was hit by flak. Lt. Smiley saw Brandt throw back his canopy, but the plane was out of control and crashed and exploded. Smiley circled and flew back over the wreckage to see if there was any movement and seeing none headed back to base, only to run out of gas and have to crashland his aircraft short of the field. Brandt did survive the mission though. Even though Smiley had missed seeing it and reported that Brandt crashed, Brandt was able to jump just as the plane burst into flames and he lived with the French, posing as a farmer, until he was liberated several weeks later.

Flying in the same general area as Brandt and Smiley, Lts. Trulson and Goodermote of the 15th TAC R met up with a superior force of Me-109s and came out on top. They were over the St. Menehold marshalling yards at 4000 feet when 12 Messerschmidts bounced them from 9 o'clock. The section broke quickly to the left and ended up on the tails of the enemy aircraft. The Germans quickly dove for the deck with Trulson and Goodermote following in hot pursuit. Trulson opened up on one of them at 400 yards and got hits on the engine and canopy. As he passed the 109 Lt. Trulson was skidding to the left and opened up on a second German. The second 109 was hit in the cockpit and engine which began smoking, then rolled over on its back and went down. Trulson then turned his attention to a third 109, and had damaged it when his guns suddenly stopped firing. With this they headed for the deck and hurried back to Chateaudun. Claim 1 probable destroyed, 2 damaged.

Back at the base the 31st Photo Squadron photo lab was having problems of its own. After arriving at Chateaudun they learned that the nearest source of water for their lab was four miles away. This was a problem, but the section prided itself on the fact that no mission had ever been unsuccessful due to faulty processing, so they jumped right in and solved it by cleaning out a fire reservoir, and by using a captured German gasoline truck, carried water from Chateaudun to this reservoir.

On August 28 the First and Third Armies had crossed the Marne on a 90 mile front between Paris and Chalons and were pushing on toward the Aisne. Pilots operating over Chateau-Thierry that morning had seen the streets filled with American soldiers. Low cloud cover had again restricted the fighter-bombers but XIXth TAC aircraft still managed to seek out and destroy 34 locomotives, 148 freight cars, 158 motor vehicles, six tanks and several ground installations. In the air three German aircraft had been clobbered, one of them a Do-217 by Lt. Thomas Milner of the 15th TAC R. Milner was on a visual recce mission and was checking a train when he spotted the enemy bomber flying at 2500 feet above the tracks. He dived on it and opened fire at 50 yards, shattered the canopy and set both engines on fire before seeing the Do-217 crash and skid along the tracks in a ball of flame.

Continued bad flying weather on August 29 and 30 virtually shut down aerial operations, but on the ground US forces had secured the line of the Marne as far east as Vitry-le-Francois, only about one hundred miles from Germany. The famous battlefields of World War I, Chateau-Thierry and Aisne-Marne, were captured in hours rather than the months of hard fighting endured by the Doughboys of 1918.

As August closed four Allied armies were advancing north and northeastward on a front extending from the mouth of the Seine to the Meuse at Verdun, 60 miles from Germany. On the eastern end of the front, Patton's troops crossed the Meuse and were heading on past Verdun and into the Argonne Forest-St. Mihiel area, having already taken more than 70,000 prisoners. The battle for France was now ending and the battle for Germany was beginning.

It was during the latter days of August and the early days of September that Patton was slashing across France and pushing the Germans toward their own border when he was questioned about his exposed right flank. Patton's reply, "XIXth TAC would protect his flank," was military history. Never before in military history had an air force played such a part in vital military operations. To do this TAC R squadrons were keeping a constant watch on all of the roads and railways for enemy movement and the photo squadrons were constantly photographing strips of the Loire to determine if any bridging or construction was in progress.

The 10th Photo Reconnaissance Group's move to Chateaudun had helped in that it had brought the TAC R aircraft to a point where they could cover the extreme eastern areas of France and into parts of Germany, but even so Patton's continued advance in the early days of September made it plain another move would soon be required. In order to fly tactical recce to areas east of the Rhine River it was necessary to use F-5 photo reconnaissance aircraft with belly tanks. Even the 155th NPS was reverted to flying daylight TAC R missions since they were not able to fly night missions during this period.

Among the observations reported the first day of September was one of great importance: a report that the airfield at St. Dizier was operational and could be utilized by the Group in the near future. On the second and part of the third of September the weather closed in and no missions were flown on the second and only limited missions were made on the third. On one of the successful missions flown that day Colonel Berg went up with Lt. Colonel Walker on a visual recce of the Chateau-Villaine area and reported a huge fire in a German fuel dump and some railroad targets for the fighter-bombers to visit. Pilots of the 34th were not so lucky as Lt. Charles Hoy was shot down by flak while he and Lt. Robert Von Tempsky were over Etampes.

Meanwhile the 155th was trying to do its share of the work by flying its daylight missions, but they were finding out that although the F-3 was a good night photography aircraft it was a sitting duck in daytime work. On September 5, Lt. Fluhr flying "Sleepy Time Gal" on a mission south of the Loire River was shot down by a heavy flak concentration and he and his entire crew were killed. In addition to the loss of Lt. Fluhr and his crew, several other aircraft were damaged during the first few days of September.

It was on September 7 that the use of these F-3s was to pay a big dividend. Lt. Lloyd Verket was on a patrol south of the Loire in the Chateauroux-Issodun-Fourages area when he spotted a column of enemy vehicles that extended for miles. The Germans were heading for the Belfort Gap in the hope of getting back into Germany before their escape route could be cut by the junction of the Third and Seventh US Armies. In their rush they were travelling by daylight—hoping our reconnaissance planes would miss them. Their hopes were in vain as Lt. Verket not only spotted them, but he summoned the fighter-bombers of the 406th Group in on them. Even though the flak was intense over the convoy, and his F-3 was hit repeatedly, Verket continued flying over the column taking photos and reporting his observations back to XIXth TAC. When the P-47s arrived and went to work, he flew his riddled plane back to base, mission completed.

The P-47s of the 406th attacked the column until their ammunition was gone, went home and reloaded, and came back to hit the dazed Germans again. For the loss of one P-47, they destroyed 132 motor vehicles and 310 horse-drawn vehicles. When the news of the attack reached XIXth TAC they sent an immediate request back to the 10th for photos of the damage. What they wanted was low-level obliques of the destruction, and Lt. James Poole of the 31st flew a dicing type mission at treetop level to produce excellent photos of the target.

This was not the only dicing mission they were to fly from Chateaudun. Eisenhower's headquarters, anticipating long supply lines as a possible problem area which would hinder Third Army's advance, wanted to use rail cars to help ease the situation. To determine how much material and manpower would be needed to repair the railroads still in enemy hands, extremely detailed and accurate photos would be needed. The task was handed to the 31st Photo Squadron which sent its F-5s down the tracks deep into enemy country flying at treetop level to get the pictures. During these missions the foremost enemy was the terrain since the tracks wound through valleys and ravines, but by skillful flying the pilots returned with photos that enabled the Engineers to determine what tracks needed the most work. The result of the operation was that supplies would begin rolling to the front on these rails weeks ahead of what had been anticipated. However the use of these rails was still in the future and could in no way help with the logistical problems the Third Army was now facing.

During the first few days of September the supply of gasoline for Third Army had been reduced to a mere trickle and brought their splendid drive to a halt at the Meuse. What had happened was Third Army's drive had been so explosive and rapid they had completely outrun their supply lines. D-Day planning called for our armies to halt and regroup at the Seine, and at the same time set up new supply bases there before pursuing the Germans deeper and deeper into their own territory. No one could have really foreseen the devastating breakthrough Patton was to make, and prearranged plans had to go by the wayside in order to keep the enemy off balance and prevent him from regrouping.

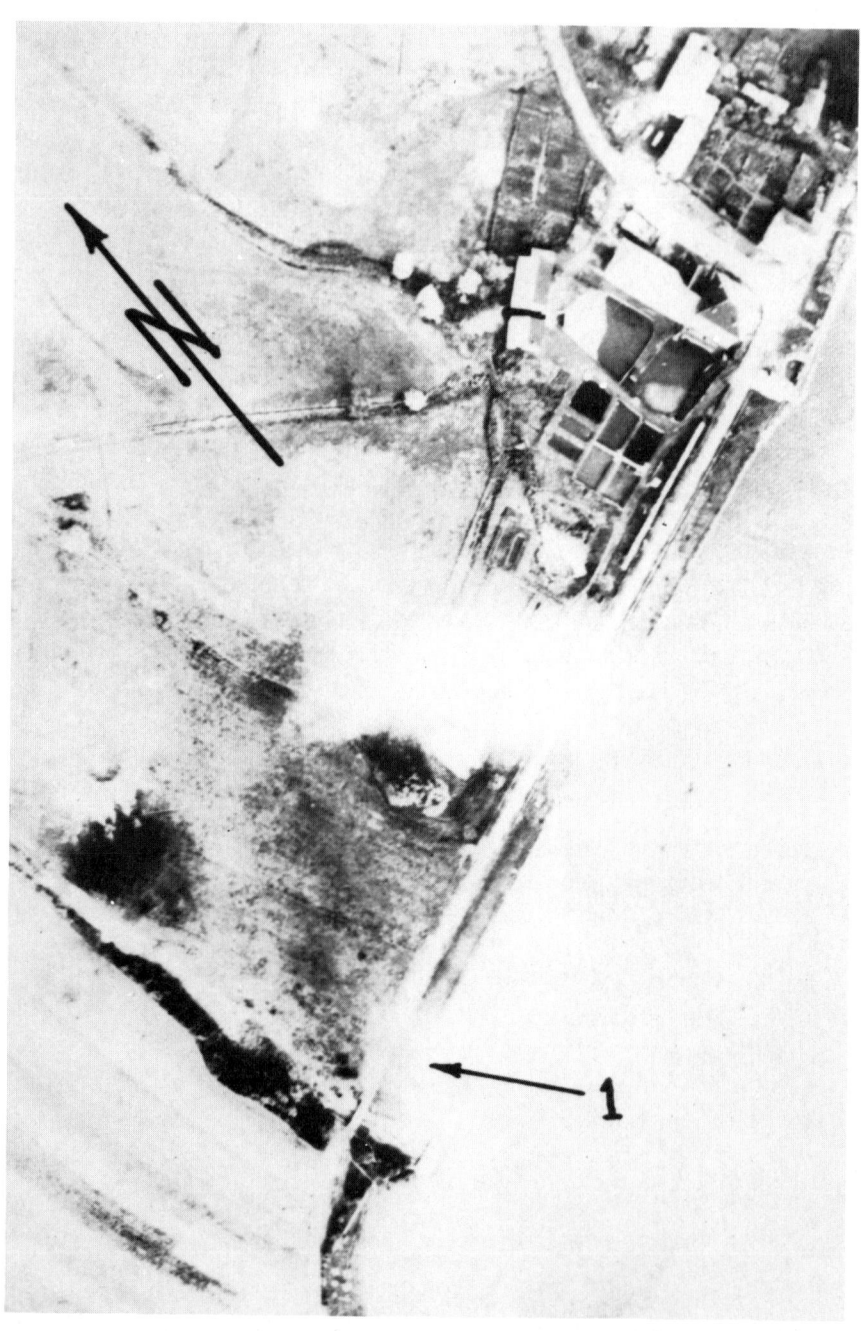

Lt. Fred J. Trenner's photo of the early stage of the attack on Dieuze dam on October 20, 1944. (L. Davis)

CHAPTER V

Stalemate

September–November 8, 1944 - Patton's Drive Stops,
Photo Recon and TAC R Missions Increase

The fuel crisis reached a peak during the first five days of September when Patton's armored legions, their fuel tanks dry, ground to a halt. General Eisenhower's decision to direct the limited stocks to First Army infuriated Patton even more, however the question became academic a few days later when First Army and some of the British units also began shutting down due to a lack of fuel. In spite of these formidable supply problems, Eisenhower was still determined to proceed into Germany on a broad front, an idea which sparked another argument between his two outspoken field commanders, Montgomery and Patton. Field Marshall Montgomery insisted that all Allied resources be concentrated under his control and then he would make a sustained drive all the way to Berlin. Patton heatedly argued that this was rubbish and stated that if he was given the proper support, his Army could reach the Rhine in a matter of days. As it turned out Eisenhower rejected both arguments, and then decided on another proposal submitted by Montgomery: an airborne invasion into Holland at Arnhem and Nijmegan.

While all this controversy was going on the 10th Photo Reconnaissance was trying to continue business as usual. On September 8 they were alerted for the move to their new base at St. Dizier, and the 15th TAC R flight section was attached to the 12th TAC R so the ground elements could prepare for the move. The 34th was completely shut down for the move and the 31st had to assume responsibility for the heavy photo workload during the move. During the period from September 10-13, they photographed approximately 10,000 miles of territory, and in the following week the 10th Photo Reconnaissance Group delivered more than 200,000 prints to the Third Army Photo Center. On September 12 the Seventh and Third US Armies junctioned, and many of the photos taken south of the Mirecourt-Strasbourg line for Third Army were turned over to Seventh Army.

While the photo squadrons were involved with their massive photo projects which began with obliques and verticals of Moselle River crossing points and continued into the mapping of the Siegfried Line, the other squadrons were maintaining their tactical recce missions.

On September 10, the brilliant work performed by Lt. Verket on September 7 began to pay further dividends. With his transport destroyed, and many of his troops dead, General Botho Elster announced he was ready to surrender his remaining 20,000 men and their equipment if TAC would stop its attacks on his positions. Since the combination of tactical reconnaissance and tactical fighter support had been the prime reason for Elster's surrender, General O.P. Weyland, the Commanding General of XIXth TAC, was there with the American delegation to accept his formal surrender.

Pilots of the 12th TAC R were also ranging throughout the area in search of the enemy, and Lt. Edward Bishop found some tempting targets for the fighter-bombers in the area between Metz and Nancy. He was over Luneville when he spotted a German train moving eastward, called for fighter-bombers, and watched them turn the train as well as a roundhouse into burning wreckage.

Fortress Metz and the Siegfried Line

September 12 found the planes of the Group up again and involved in various TAC R and photo missions over France and Germany. The 155th was still flying daylight tactical reconnaissance missions in spite of its losses and damage to its aircraft. Today would be no exception, important information would be obtained but again the squadron suffered. Lt. Bielinski and his crew were to make a visual recce of area Y, the vicinity of Nancy, and were able to photograph some German encampments on the west bank of the Moselle and some heavily camouflaged flakgun positions. Then they began to check for road and canal traffic and observed considerable activity. During this portion of the mission they were subjected to intense and accurate anti-aircraft fire and then attacked by two enemy aircraft which severely damaged the tail assembly and shot out the hydraulics in their F-3. Bielinski made it back to base, but in the crashlanding he and the navigator were badly hurt. Lt. Anderson flying in the same general area was much luckier. He was able to spot 50 goods wagons in the Nancy marshalling yards and 10 large barges in the Rhine near Breisach. He also noted that the railroad bridge across the Rhine had been repaired and a pontoon bridge had been built; all excellent targets for the fighter-bombers. Meanwhile over Metz, Lt. Verket was encountering the same hot reception that Bielinski had received earlier. Shortly after noting vehicular movement and a number of goods wagons in the marshalling yards, he too met intense and accurate flak which hit and heavily damaged his F-3.

While the 155th was busy on these missions along the Moselle, pilots of the 31st and 34th Photo Squadrons were mapping the Pirmasons, Germany area. Fifteen pilots were dispatched and successfully photographed the region, but they too were to suffer from the enemy flak guns and Lt. Becker of the 31st did not return.

The TAC R pilots were also to meet with mixed success during the day. The 15th TAC R was successful in getting some excellent oblique photos of the Siegfried Line, but had to abort its artillery direction missions due to their inability to contact Corps by radio. Lt. John Tillett and Lt. Dale Shimon of the 12th TAC R had an eventful day though, as they were able to note much motor vehicle, rail, and barge movement, as well as shooting up and damaging an Me-109.

The missions flown on the thirteenth turned out to be the last for nearly a week as bad weather crept in again, but the Group's pilots were able to note considerable activity behind the German lines. Lt. Donald Lynch and Lt. Charles Kinyon were operating between Sarrebrucken and Nancy and observed many vehicles moving east in an apparent withdrawal, plus thirty ambulances and clusters of German soldiers assembled in fields possibly awaiting orders for deployment. Lts. Ted Reger and Earl Ray of the 15th TAC R were kept very busy recording all the traffic in the area between Mainz and Frankfurt-am-Main. They recorded over 100 barges heading toward Weisbaden, nine engines with steam up between Bingen and Mainz, and on the highway between Frankfurt and Weisbaden a large number of trucks.

Meanwhile the photo pilots were continuing their massive coverage of the area. Captain Merritt Garner of the 31st was ordered up to photograph a strip 10,000 yards wide from Remick to Charmes while Lt. Rufus Woody was taking photos of an area covering Echternach, Trier, Beckingen, Sarrebrucken, and the Siegfried Line. Photo missions like the two just mentioned were invaluable to Army planners, and were delivered in such volume during the first two weeks in September that very detailed reports and information could be based upon them.

For example one photo interpretation report issued on September 14 consisted of 18 pages, and was later supplemented with 13 additional pages. This tremendous mass of information concerning the enemy and his defenses was incorporated into defense traces and collated maps, the first edition of which was distributed by Third Army on September 24.

Like its counterpart's drive on the ground, which had come to a halt due to a lack of supplies, weather virtually stopped all aerial operations from September 14 through September 20, and prompted the following entry in the 15th TAC R's monthly historical report. "The weather seems to be pro-Nazi, and activity between the 14th and 20th was limited to a few flights that returned with little more than weather reports."

During this lull Third Army was developing plans for taking the fortress city of Metz, plans which called for oblique and vertical photos of the fortifications west of the city. The weather began to clear a bit on September 20, but over the target area clouds and haze were encountered and the missions had to be rescheduled for the next day.

This period of forced inactivity had reached the crisis stage for the historian of the 15th TAC R, and with a definite lack of battlefield information to record for posterity, he had to take a look at human interest stories to fill the gap and came up with this jewel. "Six missions got off the ground on the 10th and met with some success. The importance of even this little information is undeniable, but the event that really marked the day happened that evening. Lt. Jones* answering a call from nature hastened to the latrine. Finding it unoccupied, he unbuckled his gun belt and laid it near him. After a moment or two of pleasant relief, Captain Silver* entered and began stripping for action. Lt. Jones, an obliging fellow, moved his gun to make room for the good captain, and heard a loud wet slap. Icy fingers of fear clutched his heart, he looked at Captain Silver, but the captain was not yet in firing position. With trembling fingers, he felt for his gun—but no gun. The last sound he had heard was a .45 caliber, Model 1911, Colt, semi-automatic (falling). You may search all the field manuals and all other publications of this army and every other army in the world, but nowhere will you find a directive on the tactics and techniques of recovering a pistol and gunbelt from a latrine pit. Lt. Jones proved equal to the occasion. He obtained a rake and deftly fished the fragrant weapon and belt from its bed. He spent the next day cleaning the elusive weapon with soap and a sheepish grin."

The weather lifted on September 21 and 22, and pilots were able to obtain the needed photos of the Metz fortifications. On September 22, Lt. Colonel Walker and Major Robert T. Simpson flew a very successful ar-

---

*The name has been changed to protect the embarrassed.

tillery direction mission near Metz, and direct hits were observed on two flak positions and a fort.

Again the weather turned bad and virtually grounded the Group until September 27. That afternoon the aircraft of both TAC R squadrons were in the air, but suffered losses of both life and aircraft. The 15th sent out seven missions, one of which was flown by Lts. James Warenskjold and Robert Culbertson. They were out on a visual recce during which Culbertson's instruments went haywire as they encountered 10/10s cloud cover and he was forced to turn back. Warenskjold went on alone and crashed into a hillside, apparently a victim of vertigo. Meanwhile Lts. Lonnie Grisham and William Winberry of the 12th TAC R were checking on railroads between Rastatt and Freudstadt when Grisham received a request to check the Dieuze area. As he attempted to make the requested recce intense flak was encountered and Grisham told Winberry to wait for him over friendly territory. Just as Winberry started back, he was hit by flak. Seeing his wingman in trouble, Grisham quickly aborted the Dieuze flight to escort Winberry back to base. Luck held and they were back over our lines when Winberry's engine seized and he was forced to jump. Within 2 hours Lt. Winberry had been picked up and returned to St. Dizier by an L-4.

During these closing days of September several fighter-bomber attacks were made, at the request of Third Army, on Fort Driant and other fortifications that composed the outer defenses of Metz. On some of these missions TAC R Mustangs were sent out with the P-47s to make strike photos. Lts. Fred Trenner and Chuck Rowland accompanied 358th FG Thunderbolts on one such mission September 28th and photographed the attacks on three small forts. These photos, which showed strikes on two of the three forts, pointed out as other photos had also shown that the fighter-bomber attacks had little effect on these heavy forts, and that it would fall back to the ground forces to dig them out.

While this attack was going on, pilots of the TAC R and photo squadrons were also out roaming over Germany and France and were able to report considerable movement of German equipment on the ground and that the Luftwaffe was again in evidence. Lts. Walters and Hooke of the 34th Photo Squadron both reported jet aircraft operating in the Koblenz area, and Lts. Byrd and Hooke reported seeing a rocket, possibly a V-2, in flight in the same area. These were not the only Luftwaffe jets operating that day as Lts. E. W. Dieckman and Mowery of the 12th TAC R encountered others in the Schweinfurt area. Their mission was especially successful as they were able to record much movement in the area, to in-

Lt. Fred Trenner and his Mustang "Nanki-Poo." (F. Trenner)

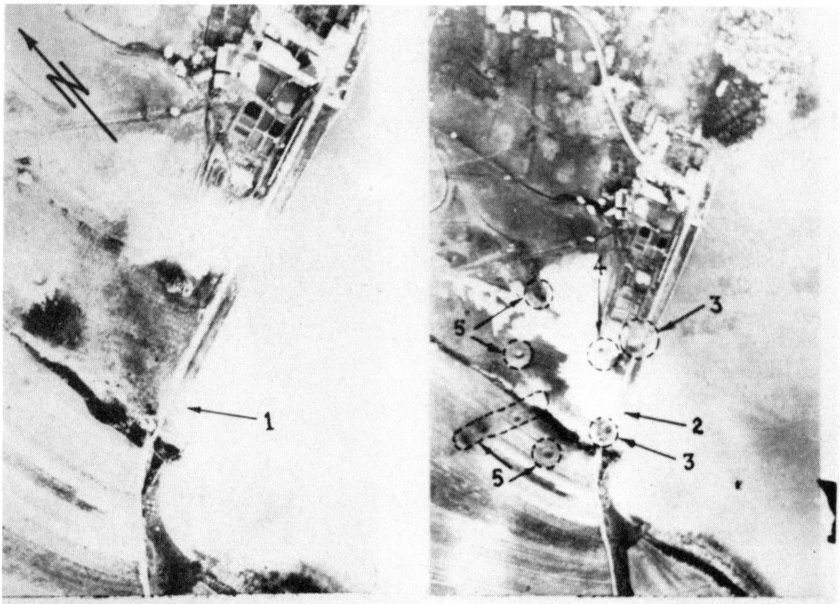

EARLY STAGE OF ATTACK   FINAL STAGE OF ATTACK
                                                             CONFIDENTIAL
                                                             20 Oct 1944

NINTH AF 2ND PHASE INTERPRETATION REPORT US10/D 468
(a) LOCALITY: DAM NEAR DIEUZE (GSGS 4416/V1-274225)
(b) SORTIE: US 15/3274   SCALE: 5,000   F.L. 6"
(c) DATE: 20 Oct 44   HOUR: 1300A
(d) PERIOD UNDER REVIEW: This report covers the attack by the 362 Fighter Bomber Group at the time of photography.
(e) COVER: The dam is covered on excellent quality photographs.
(f) STATEMENT:
    1. Direct hit on dam near the SW spillway has destroyed the granite facing and two-thirds of the earth backing.
    2. Water pouring through break at point of first direct hit and several near misses.
    3. Direct hits on road, damaging earth backing of dam.
    4. Smoke from burst.
    5. Craters of misses.
(g) ACTIVITY: No activity is noted.
ANNOTATED PRINT: 5004 & 5031   Sortie: US 15/3274 - 5002-04, 5011-14
                                                                                  5029-34.
CONFIDENTIAL   Hour: 1300A   Date: 20 Oct 44
20th P.I.D. at Hq. 10th P.G.

Photo interpretation photos of Lt. Trenner's picture of the Dieuze dam attack. (L. Davis)

"Puff," the personal mount of the 12th TAC R Squadron's commanding officer, Maj. Gordon H. Woodrow, at St. Dizier, France, September 22, 1944. (W. Swisher)

F-5E #974, 31st Photo Squadron, over France during October 1944. (R. Hibbert)

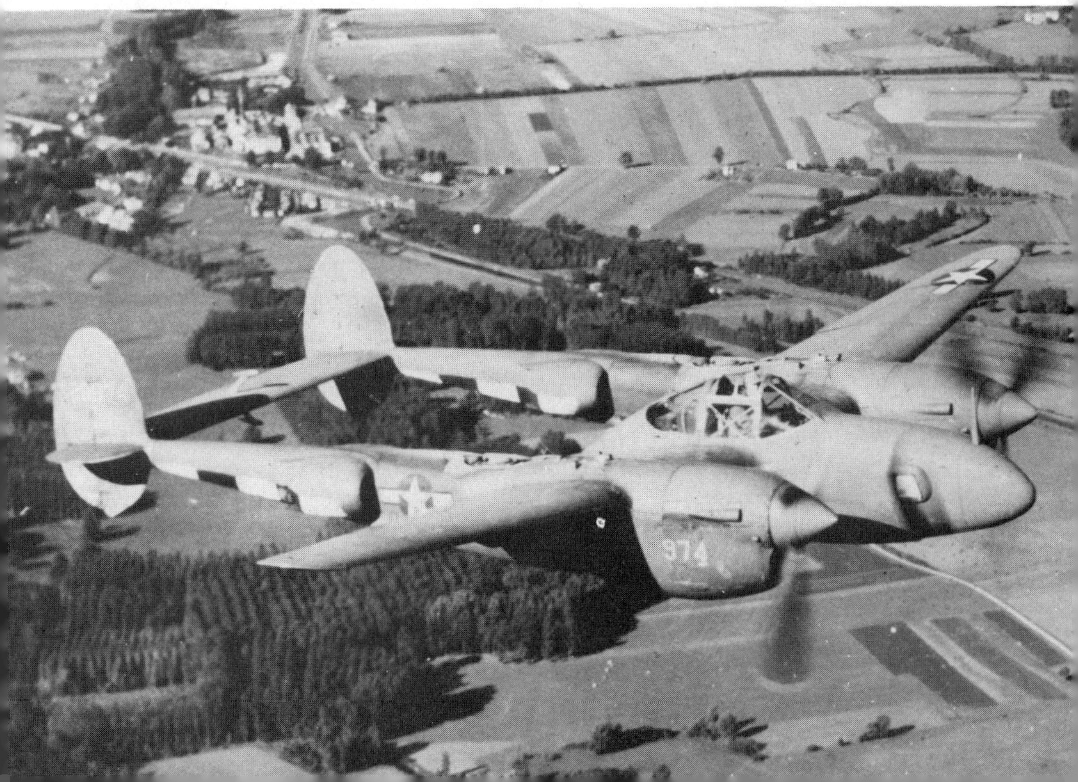

clude numerous trains, road traffic, and 15 plus Me-262s and 8 large transport aircraft at the Halle airdrome. However, the high point of the mission to Lt. Dieckman was catching an Ar-96 loafing along above the field and promptly shooting it down.

September 29 turned out to be the last operational day of the month for the Group as fog again settled in on September 30, and as on September 27 it proved to be a rough and costly day for the Group. Lt. Lively of the 34th Photo Squadron was flying bomb damage assessment missions over Bingen and Bad Kreuznach and encountered flak along the route. While he was over Ruschberg flak flipped his twin-engined Lightning completely over, and in his dive from 11,000 feet down to the deck his plane was hit 20 times but the dependable F-5 got him home. Flak was not the only problem that day, and pilots ran into trouble from several sources. For Lt. Claude Franklin who was involved in a visual recce with Lt. Ed Bishop in the Rastatt-Freudstadt area, it was a possible fuel leak. While over Zell he noted he was down to 15 gallons of gas, and as he and Bishop tried to make it to Toul for an emergency landing, his engine faltered and Franklin was forced to take to his chute. For Lts. Al Frick and Charles Johnson of the 15th TAC R it was the Luftwaffe that tried to interfere, but in this case the Luftwaffe pilots had to duck and run after Johnson peppered one of them with his fifties. Meanwhile Lts. H. H. Hughes and Ed Goval of the 15th were also bracketed by flak and both Mustangs were hit, but the most tragic event of the day was the mission flown by Lt. Colonel Walker and Lt. George Shaeffer. While they were on a visual recce mission in the Kaiserslautern Pirmasons area their section was bounced by 12 P-47s and separated. Colonel Walker made it back okay, but Lt. Shaeffer fell victim to guns of American pilots, a sad end to a productive month.

During September the photo missions had regained their importance and 299 were flown in support of Third Army—more than three times as many as they flew in August. Of the 299 missions, 223 were successful, 61 failing because of weather and 15 due to mechanical reasons. With the return of the photo missions and with the tactical missions still going strong, the Group entered October as a balanced, productive unit providing the type of support it was designed to do.

Weather continued to be a big factor at the beginning of October and affected ground operations as well as aerial operations. The 15th historian recorded that "The month got off to a dismal start with rain and fog keeping all planes on the ground. Sack time was the order of the day." For the 31st Photo Squadron which had spent the last couple of weeks getting their housing and operational sections set up in somewhat of a permanent and winterized basis, the rains had a more serious effect and their historian wrote the following account. "The first week of October the Marne River threatened to wipe out the Thirty-first in one stroke. One morning the men of the squadron found the river on a rampage with water coming up around the floors of the tents. Personal articles were floating around from tent to tent. Operations were forgotten. With everyone cooperating to the fullest, the squadron was able to move all sections and living quarters, as well as equipment and planes to high ground which although not as picturesque an area, was far safer and healthier. The entire squadron was moved that day and the following morning the old area was under nine feet of the Marne River."

This miserable weather experienced during the first week did not end there but plagued the 10th during the entire month, limiting the number of missions that could be flown and again flooding the 31st Photo Squadron's area three weeks after the first flood.

Group Operations Intensify

The ground warfare was still relatively static in October. It was a month marked by limited objective attacks to get favorable positions for a major offensive and by relieving and resting of troops which had been attacking steadily since August. As a result of these conditions on the ground, photo reconnaissance would continue to play an extremely important part in carrying out operations. Strangely enough, just when it seemed the number of photo requests would increase, the Group lost, on October 6, the services of the 34th Photo Squadron which was transferred to the 363rd Reconnaissance Group. This left the 31st Photo Squadron with a big job on its hands, especially in view of the number of requests which had piled up during the period of bad weather. These requests were pouring in from all agencies. The Third Army, in addition to its front line coverage requests, was asking for large scale photos of forts, obstacles, roads, and individual artillery concentrations. The Ninth Air Force, with its tactical bombing was anxious to have bomb damage assessment photos of all targets and placed a high priority on all requests. These requests called for photography at any altitude, of bridges, railroad yards, and fuel dumps, to determine the damage done to targets and to take advantage of it. Secondly with the anticipation of moving into bases in Germany itself, Ninth Air Force Engineers needed photos of suitable air field sites as well as photos of bases the Luftwaffe was using. Additionally, the strategic planners of the war were very interested in the Luftwaffe's strength and disposition, and therefore requested photo coverage of all German airfields within the 10th's operating area. Most of this crucial work was assigned to the 31st Photo Squadron and its pilots, in spite of miserable flying weather and increased flak, proved themselves equal to the task. Their historian summed up the 31st operations by saying, "Constantly trying to accomplish all requests, it was necessary for the squadron to do its utmost, whenever the weather would permit, in order to cut down the vast amount of targets. One day in October, when the weather broke, the unit flew thirty-six missions totaling eighty targets and 4000 square miles of mapping. This was accomplished in only five hours of photo light allotted by the short fall days. October saw the 31st change from a green combat unit to a compact efficient organization that was capable of handling all tasks assigned to it. The many lessons learned in England and while crossing France were paying dividends now. The trial and error methods were out, for teamwork prevailed throughout the squadron in intersectional relations."

In the early days of October the Lightnings of the 31st were ranging deep into Germany to photograph the Luftwaffe bases and found to their dismay that the Luftwaffe was not gone. On October 6, eleven sorties were dispatched to photomap the Kaiserslautern area and in the course of this mission, Lts. Wassom and Ward had to take evasive action to rid themselves of nosy Me-109s. Next day while photographing over Mannheim Lt. Mykyten encountered heavy, intense flak and was chased all over the sky by two 109s, but it was Captain Robert Holbury who had the dubious honor of being the 31st's first pilot to be stalked by the Me-262. He was on a photo mission covering the Munich-Stuttgart-Metz area and was flying in the vicinity of Heilbron at 33,000 feet when he encountered the jet. His report of the mission reads as follows: "I was intercepted by a jet aircraft (Me-262) southeast of Heilbron. The interception was at 33,000 feet from 6000 feet below. I estimate the jet was indicating 350 miles an hour in a 45 degree climb, coming into position within 15 seconds after I sighted him. I pulled my plane into a 270 degree turn to the left as the jet closed in, and turned inside of him as the jet mushed on by. I then went into a 450 mph dive with the jet following me. I went into the turning maneuver three more times, and escaped by continually turning inside of him. After losing him I dove to the deck and came home." Captain Holbury's escape tactics were quickly put into a report and made the standard evasive tactics for reconnaissance pilots encountering the jets.

While the photo reconnaissance planes were ranging into Germany the TAC R plans for October called for a visual coverage to a depth of 120 miles all along a front approximately 100 miles wide. Like the photo reconnaissance pilots, TAC R pilots were also hampered by bad weather which grounded them 15 days out of the month, more intense flak, and a more aggressive Luftwaffe. The 15th TAC R sent out ten flights on October 2 and in spite of many encounters with the Luftwaffe the results were quite satisfactory. Captain Henry Hanson and Lt. Steve Zondlo were jumped by six Me-109s, while Lts. Dale Goodermote and Ed Goval were jumped by a mixed bag of German aircraft but both sections escaped without loss. Missions of the third also met with success. The 15th TAC R brought back some interesting information on German rail activity and an aerial victory, while pilots of the 12th TAC R directed a devastating fighter-bomber attack. Lts. Frank Khare and Norborne A. Thomas of the 15th were flying a long route reconnaissance when they were attacked by an aggressive but undoubtedly stupid German pilot flying a twin-engined Me-110. The intended victims easily outmaneuvered the 110, and then got on his tail and took turns blasting the helpless German fighter out of the sky. Meanwhile over Sarrebrucken, Lts. Lawrence Leonard and R. R. Ricci of the 12th TAC R were bounced and pursued by two suspicious P-51s, neither of which was marked with the normal US code markings, but evaded them without any shots being fired. While this was going on two of their squadron-mates, Lts. Robert Walker and Mingo Logothetis were on a visual and photo reconnaissance mission in the vicinity of Metz. Their mission was to photograph an attack on one of the forts. Weather prevented attacking the primary target, and while they were covering the attack on the secondary target they spied a German assembly area east of Chateau Salines. Lt. Logothetis quickly climbed 500 feet above Lt. Walker and watched for enemy aircraft while Lt. Walker circled the area and gave coordinates to a fighter-bomber group whose P-47s quickly arrived at the scene and wreaked havoc on the target below.

Bad weather again set in and virtually grounded the Group on the 4th and 5th, but the time was put to good use. It was football season and also the time of a presidential election back in the States and the 15th TAC R's activities were recorded as follows: "The men of the Squadron cast their votes in the national election under the direction of Lt. Frazier Adams. Allegiance was divided and there were many lively discussions highlighted by the bombastic eloquence of Pvt. Frank O'Dowd who took the stump for Dewey. On the fifth the Squadron football team got into action and played its first game. However in spite of an array of talent, to include former Little All-American fullback Martin Pitts, the team suffered a setback at the hands of the 155th Night Photo Squadron."

Success on the football field was the only bright spot for the long suffering 155th though. After it had been virtually limited to the dangerous and costly daylight missions in September, hopes had been raised by the MEW (Microwave Early Warning) navigational system they had received in late September. It was on the sixth of October that the unit attempted to put the system into use and to get back into operations, but that mission and four others between the 6th and the 13th ended in failure due to equipment problems.

Weather did improve on the 6th and for three consecutive days the TAC R pilots enjoyed good flying weather. During this period they were able to pick up considerable information concerning enemy canal traffic and guide some good artillery shoots. On the 7th Lt. Lonnie Grisham and Captain William Winberry of the 12th TAC R observed P-47 strikes on trains in the Saarbrucken marshalling yards, then turned their attention to directing artillery fire on suspected armor and gun positions the Germans had camouflaged inside of a forest. While they were enjoying a productive mission, Captain Henry Hanson of the 15th TAC R was having his problems with active and accurate anti-aircraft fire which protected a suspected rocket launching site he was attempting to photograph. In the course of the barrage Hanson's Mustang took eleven hits, but he was able to limp back to base in it. With weather still excellent on the 8th, the 15th TAC R launched 15 sorties, during which Lt. Ted Trulson was able to get some excellent photos of rocket launching sites, and Bud Schonard directed Third Army artillery fire on a railroad tunnel. Schonard's expertise in providing artillery adjustment was certainly demonstrated on this mission as the artillerymen scored twenty-three hits on the tunnel entrance and completely shut it down.

After rain and ground fog prevented operations on the 9th and 10th the Group resumed flying on October 11. For the 15th TAC R's top gun, Captain John Hoefker who had just returned from a Stateside rest and recuperation leave, the Luftwaffe's show of strength was quite a surprise. While flying his first mission since returning to the unit, he and his wingman, F/O Henry Lewis, ran right into a huge gaggle of 40 Me-109s over Worms, and although he had no trouble in disposing of them before, this time Hoefker figured discretion was the better part of valor. He radioed Lewis with instructions to head for the deck and get out of there, kept an eye on the 109s while Lewis got away and then headed for the deck himself. While this took place over Germany, Lt. Charles Kinyon and Lt. William Burdick of the 12th TAC R were directing more artillery attacks on railroad tunnels in the Metz area, scoring several direct hits on the

Above: F-3 (A20-J) "Starize" of the 155th Night Photo Squadron, St. Dizier, September 22, 1944. (W. Swisher) Middle: F-5 of the 31st Photo Squadron taxis past a partially deflated rubber dummy of a P-51, St. Dizier. (M. Renner) Right: B-24s unload fuel at St. Dizier for Patton's Third Army. (J. Williams)

Above: 10th Group Headquarters staff pose by the access panel to the vertical camera of a 15th TAC R Mustang, St. Dizier, October 9, 1944. L. to r.: Lt. Col. Rudolph Walters, Group Executive Officer; Col. Russell Berg, Commanding Officer; Major Simpson, Group Operations Officer; Captain Eisman, Supply; Major Williams, S-1 (Admin.); Lt. Col. Richard Hibbert, S-2 (Intelligence). Photo taken at St. Dizier, Oct. 9, 1944. (J. Conroy) Below: Dr. Harold Edgerton, inventor of the Edgerton Lamp. (J.E. Williams)

mouths. The 31st Photo Squadron also got to resume their photo runs during this respite in the foul weather and launched five missions covering parts of Germany between Saarbrucken and Strasbourg.

A change of command in the 15th TAC R also took place on the 11th with Captain Lyon L. Davis replacing Lt. Colonel George T. Walker. Lt. Colonel Walker, who would now assume command of the 12th Reconnaissance Group at Dijon, had joined the 15th TAC R in 1943 as a First Lieutenant and had served as its Operations Officer prior to assuming command in April 1944.

Friday, October 13, 1944 is a day Lt. William Brackett of the 15th TAC R will probably never forget, for he and Bud Schonard are lucky to have made it back in one piece. They were reconnoitering over the Sarreburg area in search of a break in the clouds so they could get under it. Finally they spotted a big hole in the clouds but when the two Mustangs entered it, all hell broke loose. Apparently the German flak gunners had zeroed in on it and opened up with the planes and flak reaching the spot in a dead heat. Schonard's Mustang was almost blown completely over on its back by the force of the explosion but somehow he escaped being hit. Brackett on the other hand was not so fortunate, as his ship was hit 96 times, and he was wounded in the leg. After collecting their wits, they headed back to St. Dizier with Schonard keeping a constant watch on Brackett's crippled P-51 in case of trouble. When Brackett rolled old 3215 into the revetment, his crew chief stared in disbelief at the bedraggled P-51, wondering how in the world it got back.

A special project in October was the breaching of the Etang De Lindre Dam, three miles southeast of Dieuze. The dam was to be bombed in an attempt to inundate the area and cut off a portion of the German Army. In order to study possible weak spots in the dam, large scale photos were requested. To the 31st Photo Squadron fell the responsibility of obtaining these photos. Flying through intense and accurate flak the pilots of the 31st were able to get the needed photos, but at the cost of Lt. Harry Butler's life. He had volunteered for a mission over the dam during the early afternoon of the 20th, even after hearing reports of the dangerous flak from the pilots who flew the morning missions. Apparently his plane took a direct hit from flak because he or his plane were never found. Later in the day the hard earned photos paid off though, as the fighter-bombers of the 362nd Fighter Group successfully breached the dam, and that attack was recorded for us by Fred Trenner in his diary.

"Quite a big day today, and I feel quite satisfied with everything. A teletype came in this morning calling for two ships to go out with a P-47 group. Chuck (Rowland) wasn't around so Louie (Henry Lewis) was chosen as my wingman and we took off at 11:30 to go over to this 47 base. On landing there we met the Group C.O. Colonel (Joseph) Laughlin who briefed us on the mission. The target was a dam south of Dieuze and the 'gens' wanted it breached before our troops reached that sector. Jerry would do it himself when the time was ripe and they hope to scratch now what might prove to be an ace in the hole for him later on.

"The Colonel was a rugged looking man and looked like the type you'd like to have on your side. He gave me all the 'gen' I would need and wished us luck. Walked out to the ships with Louie and plopped under the wing of my kite. We both lit up a cigarette and I told Louie just how I'd like him to fly. Louie had gotten a small stick of wood caught in his airscoop and we messed around trying to get it out, but had to give up as we couldn't reach it. I was going to make several photo runs over the dam and wasn't too keen about it as Dieuze has been a hot flak spot for a long while. One run is okay, but when you repeat the same one Jerry gets a chance to correct his mistakes.

"At 1300 the Thunderbolts started their engines so we climbed into the ships and cranked up. A narrow runway, so Louie followed me off instead of taking off in formation. We had gone off after the second squadron and circled the aerodrome while they got into formation. All the ships were carrying bombs and I would have liked to have had two myself just for the hell of it.

"Finally got all squared away and on arriving at Pont a Mousson one squadron stayed there while the Colonel led the others to Dieuze. In ten minutes we were over the dam and the flak started up. Louie and I went up to 10,000 feet so we'd keep out of the way and waited for the show to start. I told Louie to stay up high and keep his eyes open for Jerry. Didn't believe he'd care to stick his nose around those Thunderbolts. The flak was very spotty and not too accurate. When they toss it up like that it's simply a matter of luck if they hit you.

"Watched the first ship go in and he came down and across the lake going from south to north. The town was off the north west end of the dam and after dropping his bomb he broke to the right—away from town and started climbing. The bombs were delayed action type, which permit dropping them at a low altitude without getting the ship caught in the explosion. His bomb went off a few seconds later causing damage to the spillway. The rest of the squadron then went down singly, dropping one bomb at a time.

"The sky seemed a mess of planes and flak which left black puff balls all over the area. After everyone had made their first run, I drove down to 3000 feet and made my run over the dam. Watched my camera indicator and when I had a stage of 4 pictures, I broke up and climbed back again to 8000 feet. I noticed three direct hits on the dam.

"No tracer received and I felt pretty good. When the first squadron finished with its bombs, the second squadron came in and duplicated the performance of the first. I'd made three runs and when they finished and had left, I made a fourth one. This time I really caught it. The light flak machine-guns opened up on me, but I had too much speed for them and came out untouched but nervous.

"Called Louie on the RT and we headed home. As we left you could see the water spilling over the dam and heading for Dieuze. All the Thunderbolts got back and they had accomplished what they set out to do. On checking on the time I was surprised to find that I'd been over the target for an hour.

"My photos came out beautifully and I'm very pleased. I know Colonel Laughlin will like these pictures of his squadrons' work. Went up to the club that night and bored Frankie (Khare) stiff telling him about the show. Louie got a big kick out of it too. Going to bed early as I'm quite tired."

October 20 was also a big day for the 12th TAC R, as it climaxed the search for the "Phantom Gun." The Germans had taken advantage of the bad flying weather during October and had employed harrassing fire from 280mm railroad guns against various headquarters behind the lines of Third Army including XX Corps at Conflans and and XIXth TAC at Nancy. Tactical and photo reconnaissance did not locate the guns, but did discover numerous railroad spurs not shown on existing maps. Third Army sound and flash devices and ground intelligence located several possible lairs of the guns, and fighter-bomber attacks on tunnel entrances and bridges, in an effort to destroy or bottle up the guns, obtained good results in some cases.

Finally on the twentieth, Third Army received information that a railroad gun was hidden in a shed at Metz and submitted a request for an artillery adjustment. By 4:35 that afternoon Lt. Donald Lynch and his wingman Lt. Max Burkhalter were over the target. When they arrived on the scene, Lt. Lynch tried to make contact with the artillery commander, but found communications so poor that contact could only be maintained if he remained over the radio car. Lynch had no intentions of letting the elusive gun get away though, and quickly checked the radio contact between his aircraft and Burkhalter's. Finding it perfect, he directed

Burkhalter to remain over the artillery commander's car and relay the necessary information. With these arrangements made Lt. Lynch called for the first round and at the same time started a very shallow dive toward the target. In this way he could follow the path of the shell and reach the target at approximately the same time. The first round was observed and corrections were relayed to the artillery commander through Burkhalter, while both pilots were dodging flak being fired at them from Metz. With Lynch's corrections our batteries bracketed the target perfectly, and then with the third round right on target, Lynch radioed, "Fire for effect." He saw 70 rounds fall into the target area starting fires and causing explosions. Gathering darkness forced them to return to base while the artillerymen were still firing, but later that night word came of the destruction of the "Phantom Gun" along with twenty-two of its crew. For his part in the destruction of the gun Lt. Lynch was awarded the Silver Star.

Between the 21st and the 29th weather again was a problem and the Group's missions were limited for TAC R and photo pilots, but the 155th Night Photo Squadron was able to launch successful night missions on the 25th and 28th. On the latter date Lts. Mackie, Montgomery, Williams and Major Gillespie flew quite successful night missions, with Major Gillespie obtaining excellent photos of twenty German gun positions near Dillengen.

The weather cleared on the 29th of October and it became a productive day for all of the Group's squadrons. This was the day the 31st Photo Squadron launched 36 missions and successfully photographed 80 targets and accomplished photomapping of 4000 square miles. The 15th TAC R launched 13 missions with excellent results. At 9:25 that morning Lt. Eugene Balachowski found eight engines with steam up and quite a number of boxcars in the Zweibrucken marshalling yards. He immediately radioed his find to the fighter-bomber controller and by 11:00 P-47s of the 406th Group began bombing and strafing the yard, claiming seven engines and twenty-five boxcars destroyed. After witnessing the attack, Lt. Balachowski feeling quite pleased with himself, headed back to the base.

The 155th Night Photo Squadron also went back into action on the 29th photographing targets in France, but again the squadron suffered a tragic loss. As Lt. Hulse was crossing back over the American lines near Commercy his F-3 was hit repeatedly by flak thrown up by American gunners. His navigator, Lt. W.C. Leavenworth was killed outright during the attack, and the mortally wounded pilot ordered gunner S/Sgt. C.H.

Whiteman to jump. Lt. Hulse was able to get his flak-riddled Havoc back to St. Dizier for a crash landing but died shortly afterward.

To the crews of the 155th these frustrations of weather, problems with the MEW systems and now losses due to our own people were certainly demoralizing, but as the only Night Photo Squadron in the Ninth Air Force, it was developing under the stress of operational missions procedures which would normally take years of careful experimentation. To the Third Army, the night missions to check road and rail junctions were of paramount importance as they prepared for the next offensive. It was imperative that they keep up with German troop movements, which because of our air superiority were taking place more and more by night. Progress was slowly being made, and the squadron was aided by the return of Dr. Harold Edgerton, but there was still room for improvement. The successful missions flown at the end of the month was an indication that the unit was about to begin playing a bigger role in the 10th Group's operations.

A wet takeoff for 12th TAC R Squadron on December 7, 1944. (R. Dawson)

Lts. Dale Goodermote and Charles Johnson walking toward their Mustangs for their November 17, 1944 mission. (R. Dawson.)

CHAPTER VI

The Fall Offensive

November 8–December 17, 1944 - Third Army Offensive
Resumes While Aerial Combat Intensifies

Recce Points the Way

During the waning days of October General Eisenhower became encouraged by the steady although unspectacular improvement in movement of supplies to his troops which had been dormant since September and ordered that a new offensive be begun in early November. The main effort was to be made by the First Army around Aachen with Ninth Army making a supporting attack on the left, while Patton's Third Army launched a thrust from the vicinity of Metz. Air support was vital, and for the first time Patton's Third Army was to have a large scale aerial preparation for a jump-off and nothing would be left to chance. Before his attack, photos had been made of each fort in the Metz system and photo cover of the entire terrain in and around Metz was complete. Also verticals and obliques had been made of the Moselle River crossings, defense traces prepared by Third Army's Photo Center, and collated maps were placed in the hands of XX Corps, which had the task of crossing the river. Information about the critical area between the Moselle and the Rhine was totally inadequate, so the 31st was asked to photomap the area. With these photos the Third Army Engineer was able to produce an updated map on which the latest information about enemy dispositions and movement could be overprinted.

Meanwhile the A-2 of XIXth TAC had assembled detailed target material for the widespread air attacks which were to accompany the offensive. Photographs taken by 10th PRG pilots of all enemy installations suitable for aerial bombardment were obtained along with information from ground forces, and target photographs were produced by the 10th Group's 20th Photo Interpretation Detachment. Preparations for the offensive were now complete and all that was needed was the word "go" from the weatherman. Threatening weather on the morning of November 5th postponed the start of the offensive, although that afternoon bombers hammered the Metz fortifications with high explosives and napalm bombs. The weather worsened and it rained on November 6 and 7, but a decision was made to go on November 8 no matter what the weather.

When the offensive began in the early hours of November 8, German forces were caught totally by surprise by the combined ground and aerial assault. The accurate and devastating artillery fire combined with the destructive fighter-bomber attacks made by XIXth TAC pay tribute to the thorough reconnaissance work provided by the 10th Photo Reconnaissance Group during the weeks of the stalemate. XII Corps began its attack with a tremendous artillery barrage pinpointed on targets which included 221 artillery positions, 40 command posts, 14 assembly areas, and 12 defiles. Because planning by Photo Intelligence was so complete and accurate in regard to this attack, not one round of enemy artillery was received while the pinpointed enemy positions were being obliterated.

From the air XIXth TAC fighter-bombers hit five troop concentrations, four enemy command posts, nine motor transports, 22 locomotives and 12 cars, along with 34 buildings and a bridge. One of their attacks that proved quite effective was the destruction of the Headquarters of the 17th SS Panzer Grenadier Division which served as the mobile reserve to the Metz sector; an attack which left the Division disorganized and ineffective for quite a while.

On November 9, the day after the offensive was launched, a new tactical reconnaissance plan was placed in operation—a combination of areas and routes. Eight areas were laid out, four on the immediate front of Third Army which were 20 by 60 miles in dimension and were covered twice daily, weather permitting. The four areas beyond them, each measuring 20 by 30 miles were flown once daily when operations were possible. Five routes were selected and these were more strategic in nature, since they dealt primarily with rail and road movement and extended out 250 miles beyond the Third Army front.

The day began badly for the 15th TAC R which launched 10 missions. On the first of the day, a weather recce, Captain Glen Staup of 10th HQ and formerly assigned to the 15th, was killed in a mid-air collision with a P-47 over Pont-A-Mousson, and the next two were aborted due to cloud cover. Later in the day the weather did improve enough that other pilots were able to bring back some important information.

Between the 10th and 16th of November bad weather again virtually eliminated effective operations, but the time was used by Headquarters for making operational changes. Daily front-line coverage was cancelled on November 15 and a new photo cover plan combining routes and areas was adopted. Priority was given first to the designated areas, then to the main roads and good secondary roads leading to Corps objectives. Pinpoint photography also gave way to strip photography, with Corps requesting many oblique photos for planning river crossings and for artillery firing data. On November 17 areas covered were increased 20 miles to the northeast and the five route recce zones were reduced to four. These plans really paid off on November 17 and 18 in terms of enemy movement being observed and aerial victories. On November 17 more than 300 trains or engines were reported east and west of the Rhine River with the principal movement being to the southwest and west into the zone of Third Army. One of the more successful missions flown that day was the visual recce of the Metz-Merzig-Sarrelautern area made by Lt. Mingo Logothetis and Lt. Max Burkhalter of the 12th TAC R. During their mission they reported, "Merzig marshalling yards ½ full, 7 engines with steam. Haze and smoke made observation difficult over Merzig. Photos taken at Q-1391 small marshalling yard—5 trains, no engines with steam up. Several oil tank cars in trains. L-3101 one train headed east with 5 plus boxcars. Scattered vehicular traffic east and west along highways. Q-3799 one train stationary, headed west with steam up. 5 oil tank cars and several boxcars. Q-2495 entrenchments and tank traps running north and south. L-5012 train headed northwest, makeup undetermined. Q-5996 steam coming from underpass, probably train at marshalling yard St. Wendell—1/3 full three engines with steam up. Q-0875 Photos taken of town. Q-3789 enemy vehicles along side of road—stationary, headed north. Q-3369 train moving north with 10 plus boxcars. Q-9669 appears to be railroad siding or spur. U-9974 Convoy of 12 plus trucks, some with trailers in village between Worms and Mainz. 5 plus trains, unable to pinpoint due to weather. No flak or enemy aircraft encountered."

The 15th TAC R also launched 13 missions that day and brought back detailed accounts of rail and barge movement along the Rhine River, in addition to some aerial victories. Lt. Dale Goodermote and Lt. Charles Johnson were over an enemy airfield near Kirch-Kons when they caught four Me-109s in their landing approach and immediately dove to attack them. They teamed up and blasted the first 109 out of the sky and then Goodermote attacked a second 109, scoring hits all over it and claimed it as a probable. While attacking the second Messerschmitt, Goodermote ran into a barrage of ground fire. An armor piercing shell exploded right on his gunsight, part of it lodging in the sight and part of it wounding him in the hand and chest. At this point Goodermote reported, "I decided it was time for us to get out of there." Almost at the same time, Lt. Jackson Marshall and Lt. Bill Brackett were raising hell with a flight of Ju-87 Stukas. Flying in 8/10s weather with a ceiling of 1900 feet near Worms, they sighted one Stuka. Marshall opened fire and numerous hits were noted by Brackett as the Ju-87 rolled over on its back and went into a vertical dive through the overcast. Almost immediately after the first encounter Marshall began firing on a second Stuka which also went into an uncontrolled dive after taking numerous hits. Like ducks in a shooting gallery, another Ju-87 appeared and Marshall again attacked and fired until he ran out of ammunition and then Brackett took over, blasting the Stuka with his fifties. With smoke pouring from it, the riddled Stuka went into a shallow dive into the overcast. They spotted two more of the lumbering bombers, but with Marshall out of ammunition and Brackett low, decided it was time to head back to St. Dizier.

Again on the 18th TAC R pilots noted heavy enemy traffic, to include 226 trains many of which were made up of heavy flat cars of the type used to carry tanks and other equipment. Lt. John Kimler of the 12th TAC R noted 29 trains, 15 of which were pulling a combined total of over 200 of these flat cars. Also in the air was Colonel Russell Berg flying as wingman for Lt. Ward Kieffer of the 12th TAC R and they noted the following in the area of Thionville, Luxembourg, and Trier. A half-track with five support vehicles deployed in a field along with numerous dug-in troops, plus numerous engineless trains dispersed throughout the Trier area. Unusually heavy flak was encountered throughout their mission, a good indication that the enemy was up to something big and wasn't welcoming any visitors.

Meanwhile pilots of the 15th TAC R were also roaming throughout the area and noted many observations. Captain Bob Raymond photographed 18 targets of opportunity for the fighter-bombers to attend to while Captain Hoefker turned in a long report and photos concerning airfields at Kirch-Kons, Giessen, and Frankfurt-Am-Main. Later in the day Lt. Clyde East witnessed fighter-bombers destroying many of the twin-engined aircraft which Captain Hoefker had noted at Frankfurt.

Armed with the photos and information brought in during these two days, Intelligence was able to determine that the Germans were rushing at least one Panzer Division in to help shore up their defenses which faced the Third Army, and for its efforts the 10th received numerous Letters of Commendation. Probably the one that gave them the greatest sense of satisfaction was the report rendered by Captain C.C. Chambliss, the 12th Army Group Ground Liaison Officer, who stated in part. "TAC R reports received on November 17 concerning German rail movements gave evidence that at least one Panzer Division was moving into Third Army area. It added that the 10th Photo Group, more than any other group had been reporting trains and flats by type and that this had favorably impressed the 12th Army Group. Three days later, Third Army G-2 report verified arrival of the armor through prisoner of war interrogation."

Although TAC R missions grabbed the limelight for their work on the 17th and 18th, the 31st Photo Squadron and the 155th Night Photo Squadron were in action too. On the 18th, pilots of the 31st flew 20 missions and successfully photographed the areas of Metz, Saarbrucken, Homburg, Sarrebourg, Frankfurt, Weisbaden, Muelheim, Thionville, Trier, Wurzburg and Limburg. Virtually all of the pilots experienced heavy concentrations of flak and Lt. James Poole had to play hide and seek in the clouds over Darmstadt to evade two Me-262s which were attempting to intercept him.

Night Missions Increase

With the onset of winter, night photography became increasingly important due to Europe's short amount of daylight hours during this period and accordingly the 155th was assigned more targets than ever before. In addition to the missions flown in support of Third Army, they would also be flying missions to the Aachen-Cologne area for 12th Army Group.

During the evening of November 18, the 155th launched nine sorties, seven of which aborted due to navigational failure, but the two others were quite successful and seemed to begin a new and important life for the unit. One of these missions was flown by Lt. C.G. Anderson. He and his crew, Lt. N.B. Huggins, navigator, Lt. W.C. McClendon, observor, and Pvt. T.G. Nelson, encountered heavy flak enroute but located their target and their photographs revealed a train consisting of 170 goods wagons in the marshalling yards at Julich and several light flak positions which guarded the area.

All squadrons were airborne again on the 19th to take advantage of available flying time before the bad weather which was approaching set in. The 15th TAC R dispatched a number of missions of which the results were satisfactory, and in the case of Captain Howard Nichols and Lt. Phillip Hunt a little humorous. While they engaged in a visual recce over Germany, they observed some activity at Lachen-Speyerdorf airfield. As they steered across the field they noted 8 to 10 twin-engined aircraft north

Left: Members of the 34th Photo Squadron photo section (l. to r.): Cpl. Ben Rosen, T/Sgt. Jack Quinn, Pfc. Roy Tiefield. (B. Rosen) Below: Flight line of the 15th TAC R at Giraumont. (M. Renner)

*Capt. John H. Hoefker's F-6D (code 5M * A) St. Dizier, (J.H. Hoefker)*

An F-6C of the 12th TAC R, St. Dizier, September 1944. (F. Pfeiffer)

*Above: "A" Flight of the 12th TAC R Squadron. (On wing, l. to r.) Captain Winberry, Lts. Ricci, Davenport, McCotter, (standing) F/O Williams, Lts. Logothetis, Oswald, and Worrell, (kneeling) Lts. Franklin, Ellis, Rhodes. (W. Davenport) Below: Mission Ahead—The ground crew readys the 15th TAC R Squadron's 5M * B for an oblique photo mission. (H.S. Edwards)*

of the airfield in revetments, and that on the runway a single engined fighter was scrambling to intercept them. Apparently the Messerschmitt pilot must have looked up and upon sighting his opposition thought, "Mine Gott in Himmel, zwei Indianer," because he promptly did an about face and hurriedly taxied his 109 back into the safety of his hangar. Meanwhile Captain Hoefker and his wingman Doc Youll were checking on the Giessen airfield when they were jumped by a not so timid FW-190 pilot. The 190 lined up on Hoefker's Mustang, and before Doc could finish calling out a warning in his slow western drawl, the German was firing. Unfortunately for the German he missed and within an instant Captain Hoefker was on his tail and firing. With his Focke-Wulf mushing all over due to the pasting it took from Hoefker's guns, the pilot jettisoned his canopy and jumped, but was killed when his chute failed to open. With this victory, his fourth, Captain Hoefker increased his lead as the Group's top scorer. Other pilots in the squadron were again checking the rail traffic and Captain Raymond and Lt. Rowland both brought photos and information of more trains with numerous heavy laden flat cars.

The success enjoyed by the TAC R pilots did not completely carry over to the 31st pilots though as about 50% of their missions were unsuccessful due to heavy cloud cover. One of their pilots, Lt. Renton, was a little thankful for the dense clouds though when he encountered thirty FW-190s over Kaiserslautern and used them to good advantage in staging his getaway.

That night the 155th was again up in force and five of nine missions were successful. Their photos indicated much German movement by road and rail. Lt. Neal Barnes' crew spotted vehicle movement heading northwest and through the town of Delem, and a locomotive with steam-up in the Forbach marshalling yards while Lt. Anderson noted two four-gun flak emplacements and vehicular traffic headed southwest through Machern.

Of course the big news of the day was that Patton had completed his pincer movement around Metz. Using information about German troops provided by pilots of the 10th Photo Reconnaissance Group, the 10th Regiment of the Fifth Infantry Division launched a surprise attack at night on November 18 and cut off the last escape route from the city. In doing so, it cut off a large enemy column trying to escape and with the help of a tank company from the 6th Armored destroyed 100 vehicles and killed over 200 German troops. On November 19th, 1944 U.S. troops entered Metz and for the first time since 451 AD Fortress Metz had fallen to assault troops.

With the exception of November 21st, weather again curtailed operations between the 20th and 25th. Twelve TAC R, three photo, and two night missions were flown on November 21 but met with limited success due to cloud cover. The high point of the day was Lt. John Tillett's destruction of a FW-190. He and Lt. Bill Enneis of the 12th TAC R were on a weather recce northwest of Frankfurt when they spotted six Focke-Wulfs preparing to bounce them. Tillett yanked his Mustang into a steep climb to 14,000 feet and then hurled himself at them in a diving attack, opening fire at 450 yards and pulling away at 75 yards after blasting big chunks of metal from the 190 and seeing the smoking wreck go over on its back and plummet straight down.

Even with aerial operations curtailed, Patton continued to advance and capture one after another of the forts and fortifications surrounding the city of Metz, and it came as no surprise to the 10th Photo Reconnaissance Group when they received alert orders on the 24th to prepare to move to a new base. While the air echelons of each squadron remained at St. Dizier and resumed flying on the 25th, advance and ground elements were on the way to prepare the new base at Giraumont. The most successful squadron of the day was the 155th which flew strip coverage between seven and ten PM and noted much road and rail movement. Some of their aircraft were sent to photograph movement in the First Army area, and just as they were beginning their photo runs the controller warned of bogies operating in the area. The crews strained their eyes looking for enemy night fighters, but when none could be seen decided someone was feeding them bad information. However when the photos Lt. J.E. Williams and his crew took in the Aachen area were developed they showed a Me-109 flying directly under his plane. Fortunately for them German crews were having night vision problems too.

On another mission the next night a 155th F-3 had just finished its run and started back over First Army lines when a V-1 appeared below and US gunners opened up on it with everything they had. The buzz bomb's course intersected that of the F-3 almost at right angles, and nearly resulted in another of the F-3s being downed by American anti-aircraft fire. Prompt firing of the colors of the day stopped the firing long enough for them to get out of there, then the gunners blazed away again.

Operational flying for the Group was closed out with the missions of the 27th, and it turned out to be a big day for Fred Trenner who had so often lamented his lack of an opportunity to take on an enemy plane. He and Frank Khare were out on a weather recce, and while flying in the vicinity of Weisbaden Trenner dropped down to investigate the extent of a cloud bank and found himself right on the tail of a He-111, the first enemy plane he had seen in seventy-six missions. Almost simultaneously Lt. Khare saw the bomber and called out, "Kraut bomber right in front of you Fred, clobber him." Not wanting to blow his opportunity, Trenner took careful aim and fired, but observed no hits. He then pulled his Mustang up into a chantelle to the right while the Heinkel turned left into the clouds, and as he was still climbing Lt. Trenner felt and saw a tremendous explosion; his Heinkel had crashed into the side of a hill.

The last few days of November were spent in completing the move from St. Dizier to the new base. Unlike Chateaudun and St. Dizier which were actual airfields, A-94 was merely a steel mat runway laid out near a cluster of mining villages. Headquarters 10th Photo Reconnaissance Group set up in Giraumont, and the squadrons selected other sites, with the exception of the 155th Night Photo Squadron which remained at St. Dizier. The 31st Photo Squadron set up base in the town of Jarny in buildings belonging to an iron mine. The Germans had operated the mine and used it as a prisoner of war camp for Russian troops, and many of the prison barracks were put into use as supply buildings, day rooms etc. While the 31st was making itself a comfortable new home in Jarney, the 15th TAC R was preparing to make its new home in a 14th century chateau at Tichemont, and the 12th TAC R was setting up in Giraumont. The weather was horrible and the rain and ankle deep mud were playing hell with the engineers' attempts to finish laying the runway, not to mention the morale of the men of the 15th TAC R, since they had to remain in cold, wet tents on the chateau grounds until the Engineers who were currently occupying it finished their job and moved out. Another new element for many of the 10th's ground personnel was the close proximity to the shooting war. Security had to be tight as their new base was on the edge of Lorraine province and many of its inhabitants were pro-German, and secondly the formidable Fort Jean D'Arc which lay about four miles east of them had been bypassed by Patton and was still occupied by some aggressive German troops. Each squadron diary mentions its "combat patrols," or more accurately its daily coal and supply details ducking potshots taken at them by German snipers. The 31st Squadron can even lay claim to the capture of German soldiers by one of these details which came upon two wounded Germans lying on a backroad near the base.

While the unit was settling into its new home the war was still going on, and as XX Corps fought its way into the Siegfried Line defenses it was on the receiving end of some of the most intense artillery fire it had ever experienced. It was apparent that the Germans were prepared to defend the area, as evidenced by this artillery fire and the reinforcements whose moves into the area had been traced by the 10th pilots and now identified as the 130th Panzer Lehr Division, the 245th Infantry Division and the 256th Infantry Division. To assist Third Army in its campaign, TAC R pilots were checking the extent of flooding along the rivers, serviceability of roads and bridges as well as locations of troop and tank concentrations. The Germans had also come up with a new sound and flash suppressor which was making location of their artillery positions more difficult, so locating them from the air became an urgent project.

Tactical reconnaissance plans were revised on December 2 to provide coverage from Trier to Koblenz to Mannheim to Zweibrucken, and the areas near the battle zones were to be covered three times daily. In addition four reconnaissance routes were to be flown twice daily covering the main rail lines and highways as far northeast as Kassel.

On December 2 TAC R pilots were up in spite of continued foul weather, and even though cloud cover was thick in many of their target areas many of them were able to bring back long reports of rail and highway movement. The weather did cause the 15th TAC R to abort an urgent check of the Saar River bridges and delayed another attempt until December 5.

With the weather breaking again on December 5, TAC R was up in force to try and honor requests that had backlogged during the last two days. Lts. Logothetis and Burkhalter of the 12th TAC R, took off in their Mustangs for an early morning visual recce into Germany and were in the vicinity of Limburg when a quartet of Me-109s tried to interfere with their business. The enemy leader cut into Burkhalter but Logothetis drove him off, and then continued on to attack the other three 109s. He fired at and damaged two of the 109s, but had to break off because he had become separated from Lt. Burkhalter and his guns were jamming. While Logothetis was busy evading his 109s, Lts. Ray and Goval of the 15th TAC R were running into the same problem with FW-190s near Worms, but they too were able to sidestep the enemy fighters. The big news for Third Army was that Lt. Howard Nichols of the 15th TAC R was able to check the Saar River bridges and brought back a full report.

On December 8 Lt. Clyde East of the 15th TAC R checked 13 of the Saar bridges again as plans for a drive into the Rhineland proceeded. In conjunction with these plans the 31st was directed to provide frontline photo coverage to a depth of 15,000 yards, but weather prevented this until December 11. Lt. Mykyten flew a successful mission of this type over Saarbrucken on December 12 and met some flak, but when Major Garner and Captain Rufus Woody returned to the area three days later both of them got a very hot welcome from flak and FW-190s which successfully disrupted the mission. Other pilots from the 31st and the TAC R squadrons were also meeting up with increased aerial activity on the part of the Luftwaffe, as well as the continued heavy rail and road movement on the ground, indicators that should have spelled out to Army Intelligence that something big was about to happen. Nevertheless, the significance of all this activity was missed and while Allied commanders continued to plan for their next push, Von Runstedt launched his massive Ardennes offensive.

Capt. Robert Holbury of the 31st Photo Squadron. (R. Woody)

CHAPTER VII

The Battle of the Bulge

December 17, 1944–January 1945 - The 10th Helps Turn Germany's Last Offensive

The German Offensive

It was under the cover of some of the worst flying weather of the winter that three German armies totaling 25 Divisions struck on a 70 mile front defended by only six Divisions. The surprise and force of the attack had its effect and German columns broke through in a number of places. The most notable breakthrough occured south of St. Vith and by nightfall of December 17, elements of the 5th Panzer had entered Luxembourg and headed toward the Meuse River by way of Bastogne. With Army commanders unsure as to the disposition of their own troops it became the task of TAC R to pinpoint our troop positions as well as the enemy's.

December 17 began with a flurry of activity on both sides. Both TAC R squadrons put up a maximum effort, and the Luftwaffe was also out in force to support the German offensive. The aggressiveness of the Luftwaffe was first felt during the morning missions, some of which had to be aborted. The 12th TAC R had sent Captain Winberry and Lt. Karl Brandt out to check the area of Lamstein, Cochan, Bingen, Algesheim and Sobernheim, but the section was lucky to escape with their lives when they were suddenly attacked and chased fifty miles by twenty Fockewulfs and Messerschmitts. The same thing occurred to Lts. Goodermote and Merlin Reed of the 15th TAC R who were also able to evade the attack, but unable to complete the recce. The morning was not a complete loss for the 15th though, as Lts. Eugene Balachowski and Donald Dowell were able to fly successful artillery shoots.

During the course of the afternoon the enemy continued to fill the skies with aircraft, but for those who found themselves in the Frankfurt-

Giessen-Wiesbaden area it spelled disaster. In three separate encounters all which took place at about 2:45 p.m., seven German planes were blasted from the sky by pilots of the 12th and 15th TAC R. At 2:35 Lt. Clyde East and Lt. Henry Lacey of the 15th saw a Me-109 with gaudy white and orange paint flying down the autobahn east of Giessen at 200 feet altitude. East immediately jumped this sitting duck and blasted it with two short bursts from his fifties, after which the 109 went up on one wing and fell to the ground and exploded. While Lt. East's attack was taking place, Lt. Ronald Ricci and Lt. Lawrence Leonard of the 12th TAC R came upon two He-111s near Weisbaden. Ricci immediately attacked one of the bombers and scored hits on his first pass. On his second pass his guns blasted a huge chunk out of the left wing and the Heinkel crashed into the trees with all aboard. As the first bomber was going in, Lt. Leonard began firing at the second and set its right engine on fire. He then attacked from the other side shattering the left engine and scoring many hits on the fuselage, sending the bomber to its doom. As the second He-111 was crashing, two Me-109s approached the area but after witnessing the fate of the bomber crews, turned tail and ran.

The top scorer of the day was Captain John H. Hoefker who blasted three German fighters from the sky and shared a bomber with his wingman, Lt. Charles White. They were engaged in a route recce covering highways and railways in the Frankfurt, Giessen and Hanau area when two 109s passed under them near Giessen. Captain Hoefker hauled his Mustang into a turn and locked onto one of the Me-109s. As he fired a burst at the 109 from a range of 150 yards down to 75 feet, he observed hits all over the enemy plane and then the German pilot jettisoned his canopy but could not jump as his plane went into an uncontrolled wingover at 100 feet and crashed. As the first 109 crashed, the second attacked Captain Hoefker who quickly turned into the 109, circled and got off a 1½ second burst from 100 yards hitting the Messerschmitt's right wing root and fuselage. The 109 pilot then climbed to 1500 feet, did a wingover and leveled out just above the trees but found to his horror the persistent blue-nosed Mustang was still there and its guns were firing. On this pass Captain Hoefker closed to 100 feet and tore the already damaged Messerschmitt apart with a two second burst and sent it crashing to the ground.

After photographing the wreckage of the 109, Captain Hoefker headed south along the autobahn toward Kirch and within a few minutes met a FW-190 flying north and under him. He quickly turned, dived and began firing from about 50 yards and got hits on the wings and fuselage, and the

Focke-Wulf's engine began smoking. The German turned right and Hoefker broke left and turned right onto the tail of the German again. He hit the 190 with three more bursts and its pilot suddenly threw back his canopy and jumped just as Lt. White arrived at the scene to confirm the victory.

With the three victories under his belt Captain Hoefker joined back up with Lt. White to continue his route during which he noted the movement of much rail, barge, and road traffic. At about 3:40 they had completed the recce and were heading back when a Ju-188 blundered into their path northeast of Wiesbaden. This time the German pilot was alert and started taking evasive action while his gunners began to blaze away at their tormentors. With the inaccurate return fire missing badly, Captain Hoefker slipped in behind the bomber and hosed the right wing and fuselage with his first two bursts and then set the right engine and wing root on fire with his second two bursts. Lt. White followed up by firing two more bursts into the already burning right engine causing it to explode into flame. The pilot of the 188 rolled his plane over on its back and into a dive, leveling out at 4000 feet in a desperate but hopeless attempt to escape. As it leveled out Hoefker raked it again and this time it was fatal, for the escape hatches flew open and the crew of four jumped and the burning bomber crashed into a house in the suburbs of Wiesbaden. With the destruction of this bomber Captain Hoefker and Lt. White returned to base after climaxing the biggest day in the 10th Photo Reconnaissance Group's history. With his 3½ victories Captain Hoefker raised his total to 7½ kills and became the European Theatre's first reconnaissance ace in World War II. Additionally this mission which was to earn him the Silver Star was only the beginning of an incredible two week period for the Captain, one that would also see him decorated for outstanding recce support given to the beleaguered troops at Bastogne.

It was not all TAC R on the 17th though, and the 31st sent out 19 missions over Germany, 18 of which were successful. One of their pilots, Lt. James Butler, received an extremely hot reception over his assigned area and had to dodge intense flak over Merhausen and Bad Nauheim airfields plus flak and enemy aircraft at Merhausen on his second pass. This time he was intercepted by four FW-190s, one of which chased his F-5 until Butler made it back to Allied lines. Upon landing and checking his Lightning Lt. Butler found out how close his escape had been for his stabilizer had a gaping hole in it and the fuselage under the cockpit looked like a sieve.

With the German offensive beginning not only in bad weather but at the time of year when the days are shortest, the night photography capabilities of the 155th became increasingly important. The need for photos showing the direction and size of enemy movements was urgent and beginning on the 17th the Squadron began flying missions to support this effort. Three successful sorties were flown that night with Lt. Bielinski's crew being particularly successful in photographing rail traffic consisting of moving trains pulling several hundred cars plus three other trains sitting motionless in marshalling yards.

Meanwhile, on the ground, reports relating the size and speed of the breakthrough were filtering back to the 10th Group and contingency plans had to be made for defense and/or possible evacuation of the base. Third Army too had to re-evaluate its plans to meet the new threat. Patton had already sent the 10th Armored to the VIIIth Corps on the 17th and realized Third Army was going to have to halt its offensive and help out in stopping the German offensive.

Captain E. L. Bishop of the 12th TAC R had been detailed to Third Army Headquarters as a reconnaissance officer early in December and became involved in planning Third Army's next strike. On December 17, General Patton asked Captain Bishop to fly over the Luxembourg sector and report what was happening. Bishop took his war-weary P-51B over the area and saw US forces in headlong retreat, an event which Bishop recalled, "scared me quite a bit and I turned my Mustang around and headed back to report the sad situation to General Patton." The next day he sat in on the meeting between Patton and Bradley in which they planned a counter attack that would involve Third Army. During the meeting the Generals talked with General Eisenhower by phone, and Captain Bishop recalled that during the call an argument between Patton and Eisenhower occurred. It was finally terminated by one of Patton's famous outbursts in which Patton said, "You stay out of it because you are a politician, not a tactician, and Bradley and I'll figure out what to do with these Germans." Shortly after this conference Captain Bishop asked for and was given permission to return to the 12th TAC R so he could help out with some of the important missions to come.

When General Eisenhower summoned Patton to his headquarters in Verdun on December 19, Patton had already prepared his plan of attack, a three Corps attack with VIII Corps in the west hitting the spearhead of the German attack, III Corps in the middle, and XII Corps in the east. After his presentation, Ike asked how soon he could attack the enemy's flank, and Patton's reply of "the day after tomorrow" left those officers in attendance speechless, for what he had proposed here and did accomplish was without parallel in military history. What it entailed was taking an entire Army poised for an attack in one direction, turning them around and racing 125 miles to launch an attack within 48 hours. By December 20, some of Patton's troops were already in the Bastogne area helping the 101st resist a breakthrough. Although the Germans did succeed in surrounding Bastogne on December 22, they now had to contend with three Corps under Patton which was totally unexpected, and which threw its weight into the attack that day.

Missions of the 19th found the 31st Photo Squadron meeting with mixed success due to heavy cloud cover over about 50% of their target areas, while TAC R pilots flying into Germany were able to spot more rail and highway movement. The 15th TAC R got seven missions off the ground which included a successful artillery shoot by Lt. Goodermote and a very long report of enemy movement by Captain Hoefker, but in doing so came close to losing one of its most aggressive pilots, Lt. Clyde East. Lt. East and his wingman Lt. Henry Lacey were also involved in a successful visual recce and East had already detected four concentrations of trucks, six motor convoys and photographed a V-2 launching site when a Me-109 slipped on to his tail. The sudden appearance of the Messerschmitt didn't escape the watchful eye of Lt. Lacey though. Lacey quickly bounced it and fired a burst catching the German pilot, intent upon his prey, completely by surprise. His first burst struck the 109's fuselage and the second destroyed its engine, and moments later the German jumped from his burning 109. After returning to base, a somewhat shaken Clyde East penned this terse remark in his log book, "Lt. Lacey shot down a Me-109 off my tail! TOO CLOSE!"

The day was closed out by the 155th Night Photo Squadron who again turned in an excellent night's work. Only four of its nine F-3s were able to complete their missions, but these four returned with useful photos of enemy movements.

Recce Over Bastogne

With Third Army on the move towards the Ardennes Forest, TAC R was receiving urgent requests to provide reports of enemy and friendly positions but terrible weather over the battle area was frustrating the effort. Captain E.B. "Blacky" Travis and Lt. Newman of the 12th TAC R had made an attempt on December 19 but weather had forced them back, and on the 20th it was so bad no attempts could be made. By December 21, the need was so critical some single plane volunteer missions went up to make another attempt in locating troop positions. Clyde East went out

*Left: Lt. Howard Nichols and his Mustang. (R. Dawson) Below: Lt. Arnold Meyer's F-6C (coded 5M * N) of the 15th TAC R over France, late 1944. Lt. Meyer was killed in this aircraft in February 1945. (R. Dawson)*

Tichemont Chateau, which housed the TAC R Squadron during its stay at Giraumont, France, winter 1945. (M. Renner)

Cleaning snow from the runway at Giraumont. (J.F. Miefert)

looking for US troops that had been cut off, but had to abort due to weather. However, his squadron-mate John Hoefker was able to observe some German troop movement, but the truly outstanding mission of the day was flown by "Blacky" Travis.

Captain Travis' mission was to make another attempt to locate the cut-off US troops he had searched for on the 19th. Knowing their situation was growing more serious by the hour, "Blacky" took off in his Mustang without an escort to try and get through at all costs. In weather which was as bad as it could possibly be, ceiling 50 feet and visibility 100 yards, he located the target area and made his first pass but the overcast was too low. He then pulled his Mustang, "Mazie, Me and Monk," above it and searched for a hole but to no avail. After checking his position with the controller Captain Travis went in again and on his fourth attempt struck paydirt. There were many enemy vehicles all over the area as he streaked across the treetops and he was receiving heavy fire from German positions, but Captain Travis successfully charted the dispositions of our men and returned to base with it. With this information a rescue effort was now possible, and because of his dogged determination to get the mission accomplished, Captain Travis received numerous Commendations in addition to the Silver Star.

To coincide with Third Army's arrival in force in the Bastogne area on December 22, all previously assigned TAC R routes and areas were cancelled and operations were shifted to cover the breakthrough area. On December 23 TAC R was reinforced by the arrival of the 160th and 161st TAC R Squadrons of the 363rd Reconnaissance Group led by Major E.A. Poe, former Assistant Operations Officer of the 10th Group.

December 23 also brought an answer to General Patton's famous prayer for good weather when a mass of dry, stable air from the east entered the area and cleared away the overcast, and for more than a week good flying weather prevailed. With his weather shield gone, the enemy's movement was laid open to aerial observation and attack. Consequently all roads and railroads leading to the breakthrough area were put under constant surveillance. During this period heavy movement of tanks and motor vehicles was observed and information was quickly forwarded to the fighter-bomber and Third Army units pushing into Belgium and Luxembourg. In many instances the TAC R ships were able to lead the fighter-bombers right to the target thus increasing the element of surprise and damage to the targets. A very critical area was the Trier-Merzig zone where the right flank of XII Corps was exposed, and as he had during the battle of France, Patton entrusted the TAC R to cover it for him.

Missions began on December 23 just as soon as the early morning ground fog began burning away, and the fighter-bombers were up in strength in the Bastogne area. The 15th TAC R dispatched six missions to help locate targets for the bombers and came close to losing Captain Hoefker. As he and Lt. Charles White covered their sector, seven red-tailed P-47s bounced them and it took some expert flying on the part of Captain Hoefker and Lt. White to convince the P-47 jockeys of their error, but in doing so they became separated and Captain Hoefker flew into intense light flak. The flak caught his Mustang, destroyed the glycol tank and within minutes its Merlin engine seized. John jettisoned his canopy and tried to jump. He tried twice to get out but each time the slip-stream pinned him to the aircraft. Just as he was beginning to think he would have to ride it down, he remembered a trick he had heard about while on temporary duty with the RAF. He raised the nose just slightly and then jammed the stick forward with his feet and was propelled out as if he had an ejector seat. The chute opened beautifully but this still was not the end of his ordeal as trigger happy members of the 4th Infantry Division started blazing away at him with their M-1s. The combination of constant rumors of German troops in US uniforms infiltrating the area and his plane nearly crashing into their mess hall made it very hard to convince the GIs that he hadn't attacked them, and John recalls, "what probably finally convinced them I was American was the blistering profanity I hurled at them. No German would have known some of those 'colloquialisms.'" Finally the shooting stopped and Captain Hoefker stepped out from behind his cover of rocks and introduced himself to his "liberators." The next day he was delivered back to base by his 4th Infantry hosts.

In conjunction with the TAC R coverage on the 23rd, the 31st Photo Squadron began photo coverage of the breakthrough area to aid in determining enemy positions. Their pilots found it necessary to fly two or three missions a day over heavily defended areas at suicidal altitudes in order to supply units in the Ardennes with current photo files, and in doing so kept the photo labs and photo interpretation sections working night and day cranking out this important information. The Luftwaffe was also in evidence that day and did succeed in forcing back some photo missions, but the Focke-Wulf pilots that tangled with Lt. James Poole were in for a surprise. He was on a mission to Euskirchen, Germany and was at 20,000 feet on his target run when he was attacked. He immediately threw his F-5 into a screaming dive to the deck. Three of his attackers soon gave up the chase but the fourth was more aggressive and began to close in on

Poole after he leveled out on the deck. As the distance between them grew closer Lt. Poole pulled up into a vertical climb and into an Immelman, but the enemy pilot lacked the skill to follow and spun in and crashed. Lt. Poole was exuberant when he reported his victory to his squadron S-2, Captain Bill Hohner, and Hohner equally proud sent the following message to Group, "We shall not be outdone. Chalk the 31st up with one FW-190 destroyed."

Because of the Luftwaffe interference on the 23rd, the bombers of the 8th Air Force and the Royal Air Force hit at Luftwaffe bases the next day while 9th Air Force bombers hit at bridges and communications centers; missions which also required the services of the 31st Photo Squadron and put a further strain on the crews. Nevertheless, the 31st reorganized its photo interpretation and kept up with this demanding schedule.

TAC R also took advantage of another day of good flying weather and dispatched many missions. The 15th TAC R sent out eight of which most were successful, but they suffered the loss of two aircraft and one pilot. Lts. Don Dowell and A.R. Tenny were flying a visual recce over the front when a wall of light flak and tracer caught both P-51s at the same time and Tenny immediately called out that he was going to have to jump. Lt. Dowell implored him to stay with his plane as long as possible, but Tenny turned west and jumped at 3000 feet and Dowell never saw a chute blossom. Dowell circled for five minutes looking for some sign of Lt. Tenny but could not see him in the air or on the ground, so he headed south and sounded a "May Day." Within seconds after sounding "May Day," his engine caught fire, causing him to jump and moments later Dowell came down virtually into the waiting arms of US troops who promptly returned him to base. Unfortunately Lt. Tenny was not located and had to be carried as MIA.

Two of the 363rd Reconnaissance Group pilots, Lts. Norman and Maher, operating with the 12th TAC R were a lot more fortunate during their visual recce in the Ansbach-Koblenz area. They were bounced by a very aggressive FW-190 who made two passes at them before Lt. Norman was able to turn inside and rake the Focke-Wulf with two bursts. Apparently the second burst killed the pilot because the 190 dropped off into a lazy spiral, crashed and exploded.

Christmas Day 1944 was celebrated as a working holiday because the skies were still clear and every attempt was made to fly as many missions as possible. The 101st Airborne which was surrounded at Bastogne needed photo cover of its area, and Captain Rufus Woody of the 31st Photo Squadron volunteered to make the drop. What his mission involved was loading the prints into an empty drop tank and flying in low and slow in order to accurately drop the photos within the 101st's limited perimeter, and Woody accomplished his mission even though he had to fly through heavy flak. The photos were helpful to the "Screaming Eagles," but they radioed back that they needed more up to date photos, and missions were laid on for the 26th.

The high point of the day for the 10th came Christmas night when a Ju-88 buzzed the airfield and paid for its folly. John Hoefker recalled that "he came over the runway low and slow on his first pass giving the impression that he was lost. The German continued on beyond the base, made a big lazy turn and started back over the base and this time our gunners were ready and lit up the December sky with their tracers. There was no way that 88 could have made it through that barrage, and after it received numerous hits, the burning bomber crashed on the base scattering wreckage and bodies everywhere. I recall I found one of the crew in the middle of the runway and picked up his wallet and identification papers, and kept some of his money as a souvenir."

Next morning the 31st Photo Squadron dispatched twenty missions to try and get those photos so badly needed by the 101st and other units, and in doing so covered areas around Bastogne, Luxembourg, Sedan, and Sarrebrucken. Captain Roger Wolcott flew the mission in support of the 101st, even though he had completed his tour of duty, and obtained excellent vertical photos. The films were rushed through the labs that day, and Lt. Al Lanker, who flew the first "Dicing" mission, volunteered to fly the drop mission. Apparently the deadly flak at Bastogne blasted his Lightning from the sky because he was not heard from again and the photos were not received at Bastogne. After a two hour wait for Lanker's return, Captain Wolcott took off with a duplicate set of the prints and suffered the same tragic fate as Lt. Lanker. Months later, the shattered wreckage of Wolcott's F-5 was found near Bastogne, but Lanker was never found.

Pilots of the 12th TAC R were up and keeping an eye on German movements throughout the area, and were still running into the irritating attacks by those red tailed P-47s. After detecting numerous trains composed of hundreds of flat cars and box cars in the Bingen-Algesheim area Lts. Logothetis and John Rhoads had to fend off repeated attacks by two of these P-47s and finally evading them, hustled back to Giraumont with their photos and reports of inviting targets for our bombers. In addition to this encounter, Lt. Ricci brought back reports of sighting a possible German flown P-47, noting it was painted green with a bright yellow nose and tail sections with black cross markings on the fuselage. The attacks on 10th Group Mustangs by the red tailed P-47s continued the next day and two of them damaged Lt. Don Lynch's P-51 as he and Lt. Leon Canady were flying in the Bastogne area. Meanwhile Lt. Burkhalter and Captain Winberry operating virtually unmolested in the same area were able to bring back a long report about motor transport movement and a possible bivouac area near Bastogne and numerous enemy aircraft over St. Vith.

A large portion of the battlefield coverage of Bastogne fell to the 15th TAC R during the period of December 23rd through December 31st and they performed the task so well that the Squadron received a Letter of Commendation from General Maxwell D. Taylor, the Commanding General of the 101st Airborne stating in part, "The success of this defense is attributable to the shoulder to shoulder cooperation of all units involved. This Division is proud to have shared the battlefield with your command." A great deal of this help came from missions flown by Captain Hoefker beginning with his mission of the 23rd. On December 26th he observed an enemy column of 15 plus Panther or Tiger tanks and five plus motor vehicles moving toward a column of US tanks. Realizing that time was short, he began circling over the enemy tanks in sight of the American column, then dived and fired his guns at the enemy from an altitude that could be seen by the US tankers. He then circled the US tanks and returned to the enemy position until the Americans could deploy into battle formation and go into action. Afterwards, he reported another eight sightings of enemy motor vehicles.

On the 27th, Captain Hoefker reported two enemy tanks, nineteen locations of enemy vehicles in groups of 3 to 100, and twelve gun emplacements. No missions were flown on the 28th, but he returned on the 29th and located six dug-in enemy tanks, three small convoys of enemy vehicles, and a large concentration of enemy vehicles concentrated in the woods. In his mission on December 30th he was able to locate eight tanks in two locations, thirteen groups of enemy vehicles, and rendered a follow-up report on the concentration of vehicles he had found the previous day.

When Captain Hoefker went back on December 31st, his luck ran out and he had to jump for the second time in eight days. He was over enemy lines looking for a hole in the 10/10s overcast when his aircraft was hit by light flak and burst into flames which quickly enveloped the cockpit area. Using the "ejector technique" he had used on the 23rd, he was propelled out with such force that he lost his flying boots and came down in German held territory near Bastogne. After taking refuge in some woods he wrapped his freezing feet in material torn from his chute and used the remainder for warmth and camouflage. During the next two days that he spent in the woods, German patrols were constantly searching for him and some came within 15 feet of his hiding place, but on the third day he was able to make his way to American lines under cover of a dense ground fog and was returned with frostbitten feet to his unit on January 2, 1945.

The constant need for current, round the clock intelligence information was helping make December the busiest month in the 155th Night Photo Squadron's history. During the month they flew 99 missions and drew high praise from General Hoyt Vandenburg and General Weyland for their work on December 24th and 25th. In his letter General Vandenburg stated:

"I would like to commend the efforts which the 155th Night Photo Reconnaissance Squadron has made since 14 December, especially since 22 December, and with particular reference to the very fine performance on Christmas Eve. The intelligence derived has been of exceptional value in this very critical phase of our operations. Their operations of 24-25 December without doubt comprise the outstanding performance of night photography done anywhere at any time. My congratulations and may we have more."

The pictures of the marshalling yards at St. Vith taken by Lts. Porter and Meltzer on December 23rd had shown a large concentration of railroad cars and locomotives, and three squadrons of heavy bombers were sent out to bomb the yards, followed up by RAF bombers at night. On Christmas Eve the 155th was up again and some crews met up with strong opposition from flak and night fighters, especially Lts. Camp and Kezziah whose F-3 was hit at least 45 times by night fighter guns, slightly wounding both of them. Nevertheless, Lt. Loomis and Reeves flying in the same area were able to bring back clear photos which showed the bombers shattered the roads and railroads leading into St. Vith. Christmas night the 155th crews completed 13 of 17 missions successfully in spite of harrassment by night fighters. Lt. Bielinski became the prey of two or more Me-410s who in turn were being chased by two P-61s, and at the insistence of his radar controller who kept shouting, "Can't you go any faster," shoved the throttles forward all the way and made a record shattering dash back to base. One of the German pilots was so enraged at letting Bielinski get away, he tried unsuccessfully to strafe a gasoline truck rolling along the perimeter of the base before departing.

The 155th's successful missions continued throughout the month in spite of strong night fighter opposition, flak, and our own guns. The run of

Left: Sgt. Anderson of the 15th TAC R Photo Section looks over one of his cameras, Giraumont, December 21, 1944. (R. Dawson) Bottom: Mobile photo lab of the 15th TAC R at Giraumont, Christmas Day, 1944. (R. Dawson)

Right: Film washing equipment in a mobile photo lab. (B. Rosen) Below: Capt. Robert Dawson, 15th TAC R Squadron, prepares for a mission over the Bulge area, December 1944. (R. Dawson)

good luck came close to being spoiled on December 29th when two of the F-3s were attacked by P-61s which shot up Lt. J.E. Williams plane before they realized their error, but fortunately Williams was able to fly his plane home safely. The following night Lt. Bielinski came over the field for a landing and was subjected from fire from just about every "friendly" battery on the field but through a miracle his aircraft was not hit. Obviously Major Joe Gillespie, the Commanding Officer of the 155th, was upset with this situation and demanded that better recognition systems be devised and reminded all of the problem by this caustic comment. "Day flyers are killed in combat it has been said. Night flyers kill themselves. There is certainly no reason for our friends to aid in the destruction."

As 1944 was ending, the situation on the ground was stabilizing as a result of the battering given to the German troops by the combined effort of US airpower and a determined defense by our ground forces. During the last four days of December fierce fighting took place along the entire Third Army front, and in spite of heavy losses, Patton's men blunted the assault. The last day of the year saw particularly heavy fighting with the Wehrmacht launching 17 attacks supported by 64 Luftwaffe raids against Third Army troops who suffered terrible losses but stood firm and not only repulsed the attack but made a few small advances. It was truly a victory. To celebrate it and welcome in the New Year Patton ordered a spectacular greeting to his adversaries, a twenty-minute rapid fire barrage by every battery under his command into their positions.

Tracking the German Retreat

The Germans tried to return the greeting with a massive air attack, called OPERATION HERMANN, against Allied air fields during the early morning hours of January 1, 1945. This attack did destroy numerous Allied aircraft, but at a cost the failing Luftwaffe could not afford. With this failure the Germans realized their offensive was doomed and went on the defensive in the Bulge area. With their strength concentrated in the Bastogne area, the Germans began an orderly withdrawal under cover of their old ally, the weather which had turned harsh again and severely hindered aerial operations during the first four days of January. Along with their holding action at Bastogne the Germans launched a diversionary offensive in the Strasbourg area in order to draw US air and ground units away from the Bulge and protect their withdrawal. This thrust into the Alsatian Plain was first indicated when aerial reconnaissance detected roadbed covering on barges along the Saar River between Merzig and the Moselle to the north, and that bridge ends were under construction at several points. Intelligence was convinced that the barges could be quickly moved into place at these bridge ends to provide an avenue of attack for Panzer units located nearby to launch an assault into our thinly held sector. With the weather getting worse, it was absolutely necessary to obtain photos of German movements, and with a ceiling of only 600 feet that day, a "dicing" mission was the only available method to accomplish the mission.

When the mission request came in at 10th Group on a day all other missions had been scrubbed due to the weather, Captain Robert Holbury, assistant Group Operations Officer, volunteered to fly the mission himself rather than assigning it to another pilot.

Taking off in F-5 #608 Captain Holbury headed toward the heavily defended twelve mile sector and began his camera run at Merzig north along the Saar to the Moselle, then made a left turn down the Moselle to complete the mission. The mission itself is best described in Captain Holbury's own account of it:

"It occupied my full attention to follow the river and at the same time avoid hitting obstacles. Hills were above me on either side most of the way and I concentrated on staying down as low as possible. Jerries were firing at me, but I was too busy to do anything but follow the river. Suddenly red balls, about three-quarters the size of billiard balls, were arching around me. I felt several sharp impacts as the wheel tried to jerk out of my hands and the right rudder pedal went forward. It took heavy pressure to neutralize the controls, but they responded normally.

"I flew as close to the ground as possible while I looked for the damage. My left coolant gauge began creeping past the red line. A glance in the rear view mirror showed a stream of white vapor behind me. I immediately feathered the prop. By this time I didn't know where I was—all my careful memorizing of the route was forgotten.

"I was plenty frightened, but it soon changed to anger. As my speed dropped off from 330 to 250, I saw several Jerries shooting at me and I would have given anything to have had guns to dish out some lead myself. I received fire in several places, but as they didn't hit me I didn't consider it necessary to break away from my camera run.

"After I rounded a sharp bend intense flak again arched up. I felt my rudders jar and knew I had been hit again. The right engine was hot; the coolant radiator on it had been hit three times. I stayed on the deck to the last minute and pulled up over the hills with plenty of speed to spare. I got a vector to base and soon was circling the field at 300 feet with visibility about one mile. I landed OK—climbed out and patted that good right engine."

The F-5 Captain Holbury landed was a virtual wreck. Its left vertical stabilizer was shot off, large holes were in the horizontal stabilizer and the left rudder was just hanging on, and there were numerous hits all over the plane, but he had brought back 212 very revealing photos. His photos indicated that there was no imminent threat from the Panzer units across the Saar and that redeployment of US forces to the area was not required. For his outstanding mission Captain Holbury was awarded the Nation's second highest award for bravery, the Distinguished Service Cross.

The weather got considerably worse during the next several days and for all practical purposes operations stopped until January 10. A slight improvement in the weather on the 10th allowed the 15th TAC R to dispatch nine missions and its pilots reported a general lack of activity in their areas. On a special mission to check the road network in the Sarrebrucken, Trier and Koblenz area Lt. Clyde East found only a few scattered vehicles but didn't leave the area without calling on them. In an instant Lt. East had his Mustang in a dive and began strafing the terrified Germans before they could even react, leaving one heavy truck burning and a motorcycle wrecked along the roadside. With continued reports of a German buildup in the Sarrebrucken-Neukirchen area, Lt. East returned to the area on January 12th and 13th and on the latter mission saw several hundred troops, scattered trucks and tanks. The sight was too much of a temptation for East to let pass and again he went down after them and as he later recorded in his log book, "Pranged four trucks and lots of Krauts."

January 14th was a day of considerable activity for the 10th Group and a big day for the 12th TAC R in particular. Captain Edward L. Bishop set the stage by directing one of the most outstanding artillery adjustment missions flown by the Group. He was over a small town in Belgium directing artillery fire when he saw a long column of enemy armor moving into Houffalize, and immediately contacted the fighter-bombers. When the fighter-bombers arrived Captain Bishop led them to the target but the flak was so intense they could not bomb, so he contacted the artillery and had them fire into the German flak positions. While the artillery fire kept German gunners in their shelters, the fighter-bombers attacked and destroyed the entire column. By the time the attack was finished, Bishop had located some gun positions and had our artillery lay smoke markers on them to point them out to the fighter-bombers, who once again went in and destroyed them.

Shortly after Captain Bishop performed his classic mission, Lts.

Logothetis and Franklin of the 12th TAC R were intercepted by a Me-262 during their visual recce in the Diekirch area. The jet made a firing pass at their section from 6 o'clock, missed and as it pulled up into a wingover Lt. Franklin fired at it. Lt. Logothetis then followed it into a series of diving turns and blasted pieces from its wings, canopy, and left engine, and then broke off the attack after he saw pieces fall away from the burning jet's tail section. Claim one Me-262 destroyed. (He had reported the jet as a He-280 but as far as the author can determine no He-280s were used operationally.)

Lts. Ed Goval and Leland Larson of the 15th TAC R also met up with aerial opposition and each damaged his respective FW-190 when both pilots suffered the frustration of having their guns jam right when they had 190s in their sights. Lt. Clyde East and N.W. Kirkpatrick found their targets on the ground in the form of two truck convoys and East clobbered six trucks and numerous German soldiers.

Lady Luck still seemed to smile on the 10th Group as F-3s of the 155th took to the air that night, and particularly so in the case of Lt. W.A. Wolfe's crew. When they arrived over their assigned target, Kaiserslautern, it was undergoing a particularly heavy RAF raid and the sky was filled with flak and searchlight beams, so Lt. Wolfe elected to head north and look for a more promising target. After a short while they noted some lights on the ground, so they dropped their flash bombs and began filming the area. When Lt. Wolfe's film was developed and plotted it turned out that they had taken a dramatic photo of marshalling yards just north of Stuttgart which contained over 1800 goods wagons, fifteen engines with steam up and several trains in motion. North of the yards they had photographed fifteen twin-engined and one single engine aircraft dispersed on a field thought to be vacant. The very next night 500 RAF bombers paid a visit and obliterated the marshalling yards and aircraft that Lt. Wolfe and his crew had found.

On January 16th, the 12th TAC R went back into the convoy destruction business when Lt. John Tillett found a convoy of forty vehicles during his recce of the area between St. Vith and Prum. He contacted the P-47s and within a few minutes they attacked and annihilated the column. Later on in his mission Lt. Tillett located another group of trucks parked in some woods and led the fighter-bombers to the attack. Lt. Howard Nichols of the 15th TAC R came back with a long and valuable report on seventeen bridges across the Moselle and evidence of considerable German highway traffic between Trier and Bitburg. Lt. East and Major John Florence checked the Saarbrucken, Forbach, and Neunkirchen area

Left: Capt. E. L. Bishop, 12th TAC R Squadron, who directed a classic artillery adjustment mission for the group on January 27, 1945. (R. Dawson) Below: Bridge at Merzig photographed by Capt. Robert Holbury. (N. Jarrard)

and reported the marshalling yard at Neunkirchen as quite active in addition to locating numerous small convoys in the area and clobbering a truck.

It was becoming obvious from the many reports of German road movement that their retreat was accelerating and Patton was keeping the pressure on them especially in the St. Vith area. A second factor which was aiding the US push was the Russian winter offensive which was making steady gains toward Berlin, and made it essential for the Germans to move many of their Panzer troops to that area. The German retreat was favored by a return of miserable weather between the 19th and the 21st of January, but on January 22nd, XIXth TAC planes were in the air and due to the sharp eyes of the 10th Group's TAC R pilots, began a wholesale slaughter of German motorized units which were jamming the roads.

The massacre began when Lt. Howard Nichols sighted a concentration of over four hundred vehicles lining the roads near Dasburn. He radioed for fighter-bombers and flight after flight of Thunderbolts bombed and strafed the enemy columns until over three hundred of the tanks, half-tracks, and trucks were burning wreckage. On the same day Lt. W.M. Brackett, also of the 15th TAC R, was enroute to his assigned artillery recce when he was informed his original target had been cancelled and he was directed to a new target. When he arrived at his new target area it was under 10/10ths cover, but he was able to spot a small concentration of vehicles and direct fire upon them. As he approached Dasburg he saw another convoy consisting of over 150 vehicles. Before he left he saw the fighter-bombers he had directed smashing it with bombs and machine gun bullets.

In order to get an idea of exactly how much damage was being done, the 31st Photo Squadron was requested to do a "Dicing" run over the area which was protected by at least ninety 88mm flak guns. Lt. Thair W. Best volunteered for the mission and took off at 3:28 p.m. to get the photos, and upon arriving at the scene, circled the area first and then began his run. His F-5 was less than half way through its run when it was hit repeatedly by a flak barrage, burst into flame and crashed. (Lt. Best was considered to have been killed, but shortly before VE Day the 31st learned that he had been a prisoner of war.) Later in the day the ceiling lifted enough to permit Lt. Ray Krone to photograph the area from 16,000 feet, and his photos confirmed the slaughter which had been reported.

The aerial assault on the retreating Germans continued the next day and Lt. Clyde East reported several concentrations of vehicles northeast of Vianden, including one consisting of over 2000 vehicles. He contacted two flights of P-47s and led them to the attack in a mission which he recorded in his log book as his "best mission yet." In the attack Lt. East destroyed four trucks himself and observed the P-47s clobber another fifty before he had to leave the scene. Before the day was out pilots of the 362nd, 368th, 354th, and 365th Fighter Groups claimed 317 motor transports destroyed, 168 damaged; 6 tanks destroyed; 3 armored vehicles destroyed; 11 horse drawn vehicles destroyed; 12 gun positions destroyed, 4 damaged, and many other miscellaneous targets at Vianden damaged.

To assist in the attacks on these convoys 9th Bomber Command dispatched some ot its twin-engined bombers on their first low-level mission since the disastrous May 10, 1943 mission in which the 322nd BG lost all ten of its attacking B-26 Marauders at Ijimuiden. For the 416th Bomb Group attacking at Dasburg, January 23rd was almost as bad.

Just before noon Lt. Howard Nichols rendezvoused with five A-26s of the 416th's 670th Squadron over Luxembourg and led them to their targets. After he pointed out the target, the A-26s began their pass at the enemy convoy but were repulsed by extremely intense and accurate light flak. The lead ship had its left engine shot out and it and another Invader crashlanded in Allied territory.

Lt. Nichols then returned to Luxembourg and met six more Invaders of the 671st Squadron which he led back to Dasburg for another try at the convoy. He guided them around flak positions on the way out and then damaged six trucks personally as he led the attack on a convoy of seventy-five truck. The A-26s followed and again the lead ship was sent down in flames by flak. Seconds later it was followed down by a second A-26. The third ship received heavy flak damage to its left wing and Lt. Nichols escorted it back to Luxembourg while the other three headed back undamaged.

The results of this A-26 attack were disastrous, but operations by 9th Air Force as a whole were extremely successful. They had reaped a harvest of German equipment that exceeded the destruction at the Falaise Gap!

On the ground US troops recaptured St. Vith on January 23rd and within the next few days Third Army troops had cleared the "Skyline Drive" which overlooked the Prum valley from St. Vith to Diekirch. On January 28th US forces had regained the original positions held by the First Army at the time of the breakthrough.

After a very productive month in the air, all the officers and enlisted men of the 10th Photo Reconnaissance Group were assembled on their air strip during the early hours of January 29th to take on another enemy, deep snow. From Colonel Berg on down they struggled in sub-zero weather to clear their runway in preparation for upcoming operations.

While the 10th was involved in its massive "snow-job," Patton was beginning his assault against the Eifel and the destruction of German Army Group G. From their positions in the St. Vith area, three of Patton's divisions jumped off across the flooding Our River toward Prum, a key communications center and key to the German northern Eifel defenses. By the end of the day our infantry had cleared five fortified villages and pushed two miles into Germany.

15th TAC R sortie over Bavaria, spring 1945. Ed Maxwell is in J and Ray Montes is in U. (S.A. Wilson)

CHAPTER VIII

The March to the Rhine

February–March 1945 - Third Army Supported by the 10th's Battlefield Coverage

---

February 1945 began with a big thaw that quickly melted the snow and ice, flooded the streams, brought back the mud but gave the promise of a busy month for the 10th Photo Reconnaissance Group. There was no flying on the first, but on the second all squadrons were up in force. The 31st Photo Squadron dispatched numerous front line photo missions to cover the area stretching from Sarrebrucken to Trier. The 15th TAC R sent out sixteen missions, one of which was a very successful Merton Oblique mission flown by Lt. Goval. Lt. Wayne S. Patrick had the most harrowing experience of the day when his engine failed just after completing a visual recce mission with Lt. East in the Hanau-Aschaffenburg area. His engine had given him some anxious moments in the area but cleared and he was able to complete the recce; however as they were heading back to base it cut out completely just west of Trier and Lt. Patrick jumped. His chute opened beautifully but as he floated down into US territory, about twenty trigger-happy infantrymen opened up on him. Fortunately for Patrick, their marksmanship left a lot to be desired and he landed scared but unhurt in an area of real estate controlled by a heavy weapons company of the 76th Division. A Regimental headquarters apologized in the form of a hearty steak dinner and then returned Lt. Patrick to Giraumont.

The weather turned sour again on the third and the Group was forced to stand down until the sixth, but on the ground Patton's troops had pushed halfway to Prum and the center of the Siegfried defenses. Even though Third Army was making steady advances at this time political infighting was taking place at Eisenhower's headquarters where SHEAF was forcing a change of operations. The offensive would be shifted to the north and placed under the command of Field Marshall Montgomery for OPERATION VERITABLE, and like the Ninth Army, the Third would have to transfer some of its Divisions to Montgomery to help carry out his plan to "dispose several Divisions on my flank and lie in wait for the Hun. Then at the proper moment, I shall leap on him like a savage rabbit." (The preceding is a direct quote from Monty during his briefing to Ike.)

Third Army's part in this plan was to continue its push into the Eifel as vigorously as possible in order to draw German troops away from Montgomery's sector and to do so Patton began a simultaneous assault on Prum and Bitburg on February 6th. Reconnaissance support on the 6th was limited primarily to TAC R as the 31st Photo Squadron only sent one mission up. The overcast hampered early TAC R flights but later in the day they were able to observe considerable barge and rail traffic especially in the Oppenheim and Aschaffenburg areas.

Operations resumed again on February 8th with the 31st flying photo reconnaissance and bomb damage assessment missions throughout Germany including one run to Cologne. From the 15th TAC R came some detailed reports of rail movements, one of which was a very long and detailed report by Lt. Goodermote covering the rail lines from Wiesbaden to Aschaffenburg. On another such mission Lt. Haylon R. Wood almost lost his argument with a German flak battery, and he recalls the mission as follows, "My wingman, Lt. C.D. White and I were covering the area generally south of Koblenz through which ran the river Rhine. We had been briefed of the danger of exposing ourselves to flak barges, however in my eagerness to stop a train of some 60 flatcars loaded with tanks, motor transports etc, I temporarily forgot all warnings. I had called Central Control and had a squadron of P-47s on the way, but the train was headed full steam for a tunnel paralleling the river. My wingman and I made one pass and realizing the boiler had not blown, I banked sharply to the left at an altitude of 300-500 feet—intent on stopping this fine target. Midway through the turn I was almost literally slapped in the face by flak which exploded some 1½ feet behind me. The explosion ripped a large hole in the fuselage, and the sensation was something like banging your head against a door or wall while groping your way through an unfamiliar room in the dark. I broke down and into the line of fire—the standard procedure—and leveled off at tree top level. I actually felt as if I had been blown apart but I quickly realized that my engine was OK, but my radio equipment had been knocked out. Unable to locate my wingman, I headed homeward. Arriving at the base, it was obvious that they were waiting for me to return in a beatup condition, for firetrucks and ambulances lined the runway. Lt. Colonel Simpson and Colonel Berg were standing at the turnoff, and Simpson with that gaping hole in the fuselage staring him in the face shook his fist at me, but with his characteristic smile. I was flying his plane that day."

The 12th TAC R also dispatched eight missions to check rail traffic and marshalling yards behind Third Army's front, one of which was flown by Lts. Elmer Olson and Edward Kenny who found the yards quite active at Giessen, Fulda, and Hanau.

The unpredictable European weather turned bad again on the ninth and limited operations by the Group for the next several days, but Patton was continuing to advance toward Prum and Bitburg. By February 10th, Patton had ringed Prum on the three sides and was closing on Bitburg, so many of the days TAC R missions were front line coverage and artillery adjustment missions. Captain Winberry and Lt. John Ellis of the 12th TAC R were checking for serviceable bridges along the Saar River when they observed enemy vehicles along the edge of some woods and called for the P-47s. They requested the artillery to fire some smoke markers to pinpoint their target and in doing so their shells hit the woods and revealed a much larger concentration of vehicles. The section watched the fighter-bombers attack for a while and recorded the destruction, then with gas running low returned to base. While this was going on Lt. Claude Franklin ran a very successful artillery adjustment and destroyed a gun position near Merzig, and Lt. Leon Canady adjusted fire on a suspected enemy command post in Bitburg, scoring a direct hit which completely destroyed it.

Covering Patton's "Creeping Offensive"

The 15th TAC R and 31st Photo Squadron covered targets beyond the front lines with the Mustang pilots bringing back more long reports on German rail and highway movement while the photo pilots covered the Trier area. That night the 155th Night Photo Squadron flew one of its last missions as a part of the 10th Group and in spite of "Gee" failure brought back some excellent photos. "Gee" jamming aborted four of ten missions, but Lt. Robert Davis and his navigator Lt. J. King returned with photos of the Andernach marshalling yards which showed 200 goods wagons and two other trains with steam up, 600 goods wagons at the Neweid marshalling yards, and 40-50 barges in the river, and made the evening's effort worthwhile.

The low point of February 10th had happened on the ground though, when General Bradley called Patton to inform him that Montgomery's

"Savage Rabbit" had fallen on its face and that the Third Army would have to go on the defensive. After a heated argument with Bradley over this, Patton got permission to continue probing attacks from his positions, but he had no real intentions of going on the defense, and continued right on toward Prum by use of a "creeping defensive." Prum fell on February 12th, but this gain was somewhat offset by the loss of III Corps to First Army, the first of a succession of moves to placate Montgomery and shift the headlines to him.

Even with the behind-the-scenes politics going on, Patton continued on toward Bitburg and Trier with the idea of breaking out through the Palintate region. During the remainder of February the 10th Group's TAC R aircraft directed most of their emphasis in covering his "creeping defensive" with artillery adjustment, front line coverage, and route recces checking the rail systems, while the photo ships were photographing strips along the front line area and doing bomb damage assessment work deeper into Germany. Unfortunately the 10th lost its 155th Night Photo Squadron about this time when it was transferred to the 67th Group.

On February 13th, Lt. Robert Bruce of the 12th TAC R noted a large number of bivouac areas, tanks and rail cars in the Bitburg-Trier area which set the scene for a concentrated effort in this area the next day. Lt. Bruce flew two of the 12th TAC R missions on the 14th and during his first had his wing tip blown off while checking rail traffic in Trier. On his second mission he noted numerous gun positions, tanks and zig-zag trenches near Remagen. The 15th TAC R launched 17 missions with Captain Nichols, Lts. East, Thomas, and Zondlo flying outstanding missions. Lt. Steve Zondlo flew a long and difficult bomb damage assessment mission along the Canadian front, while the others brought back long reports of rail movement. The squadron did pay a price for its successful day though when 15 Focke-Wulfs attacked Captain Robert Dawson and Lt. Arnold Meyer near Kaiserslautern. The 190s jumped them from out of the sun, and sent Lt. Meyer down before he could even react to the attack. Captain Dawson was able to evade the attackers, but was unable to get a fix on the spot where Meyer went down.

The 31st Photo Squadron also had a big day on the 14th and launched 36 missions which carried them over a number of targets, during one of which Lt. Daniel Davis had a bird's eye view of a heavy B-17 attack on Bonn, and like the bombers had to evade a heavy barrage of flak over the city.

Next day the pilots of the 15th TAC R returned to artillery adjustment and achieved excellent results. On one of them Captain Dawson, with Lt.

Stewart A. Wilson flying his wing, successfully put a serviceable bridge across the Saar River out of commission with three near misses that completely twisted the bridge out of shape.

As Patton continued to "probe" the enemy defenses, a fortunate situation was developing in the Eifel. In their attacks from the east and south from Prum, VIII Corps had driven nine miles into the German lines while XII Corps striking northeast had pushed halfway to Bitburg and formed a semi-encirclement of German troops between Prum and Echternach. During the next four days they reduced this pocket of resistance and by February 24th, Third Army troops were beginning to close in on Bitburg.

On the 21st of February the 15th TAC R flew several more artillery adjustment missions in support of this advance, including one very successful shoot flown by Captain Dawson with Lt. Colonel Jack Dingle of XIXth TAC and formerly of the 10th Group flying his wing. A second good shoot was flown by Lt. Don Dowell and Captain John Hoefker, who had recently been transferred from the 15th to 10th Group Operations.

The 23rd was a day of mixed success and found Lts. Gilbert Nicklas and Wallace Mitchell recording the presence of numerous trains in the Trier marshalling yards and pinpointing a prisoner of war camp on the outskirts of town. Lts. Eugene Balachowski and R.C. McFadden brought down heavy artillery fire on a concentration of enemy tanks and troops while Lt. Clyde East directed fire for an hour and a half into the targets in the Trier marshalling yards. Lt. Norbert Kirkpatrick found an excellent target for the fighter-bombers, but when he located a flight of twenty P-47s, they not only refused to follow him to the target but one of them tried to shoot him down.

The most severe mistake of the day occurred as Lt. Dowell and Lt. Floyd Lofland were covering a route recce in the Wurzburg area and encountered a flight of six P-51s. Three of the P-51s peeled off and attacked Lt. Dowell, whose plane was hit and caught fire. While Dowell was jumping, Lt. Lofland broke into the attacking Mustangs and pulled up in front of them waggling his wings but they attacked him too. Lofland again evaded the pass and formed up on the wing of one of the Mustangs just as a second P-51 started firing at him again. With that he just tucked his Mustang in tighter on the wing of the Mustang he was in formation with and stayed with him until they reached the Rhine, then gunned his Merlin and parted company with his overzealous "friends."

February 24th was just about a complete repeat of the day before. TAC R was having an excellent day directing artillery fire in support of advancing ground forces and Lt. Haylon R. Wood of the 15th TAC R was having

*Above: The 15th TAC R Squadron's 5M * A "Miss Minookie" over Germany, spring 1945. (S.A. Wilson) Middle: 5M * G over Germany, March 15, 1945, with Lt. Edmund Maxwell at the controls. (E. Maxwell) Below: Lt. R.J. Montes in his F-6C "Alma" over Germany, May 1945. (S.A. Wilson)*

Above: A Ninth Air Force A-26 crash-landed at Trier March 25, 1945. (R. Dawson) Right: A 15th TAC R Squadron F-6C at Trier, Germany, March 1945. (H.S. Edwards) Below: Clyde East's F-6D undergoing field maintenance at Trier, March 1945. (C.B. East)

*Above: "Kitten" was flown by Lt. A. O. Frick of the 15th TAC R Squadron and was coded 5M*X. (R. Gaudette) Below: Lt. Stanley Newman's "Azel" at Furth, May 1945, 162nd TAC R Squadron. (S. Newman)*

better luck with the fighter-bombers than Lt. Kirkpatrick did the day before. He found two separate targets for them and personally destroyed one enemy vehicle while leading the attacks. Wood's success carried over to Lt. William Brackett who found a train consisting of thirty boxcars and twenty flats in the Homburg marshalling yards and directed a destructive P-47 attack against it.

The chronic problem of aerial identification reared its head again and this time Lts. Gilbert Nicklas and Wallace Mitchell of the 12th TAC R were attacked by six or eight P-47s over our lines. The hail of bullets missed Nicklas' ship but clobbered Mitchell's Mustang, forcing him to immediately abandon ship. In this case Lt. Mitchell was a lot more fortunate than Lt. Dowell was the day before because US troops and jeeps were waiting for him when he landed.

The 15th TAC R suffered its third loss of the month on February 25 when Lt. F.B. Bunker was shot down by Focke-Wulfs near Worms. The section had just entered the vicinity which had been identified as a hotbed of Luftwaffe activity that day when fifty FW-190s swarmed over them. Both pilots quickly broke for the deck and became separated. Five FWs continued chasing Lt. Henry Lacey while the bulk of them went after Lt. Bunker, who radioed Lacey about five minutes into the chase that he had had it and was jumping.

Trier Falls

The aerial coverage and sacrifice was paying dividends to the GIs on the ground, especially the artillery adjustment, and by the 26th Bitburg was virtually surrounded. Before the month was out Bitburg was captured, and the Prum River was crossed in VIII Corps area. In the XII Corps area the high ground overlooking the river was taken, and US Infantry was on the outskirts of Trier.

The 376th Infantry Regiment stormed into Trier on March 1st and was met by savage and fanatical resistance by the German defenders, but by nightfall Patton was able to claim it as his prize. Along with the city the excellent airfield at Evren (Y-57) was captured and soon it would become the 10th's new home. Two days later the Third Army began a major attack to gain the Rhine north of Koblenz and link up with the First Army along the Ahr River south of Remagen; an event which would lead the 10th Photo Reconnaissance Group to its busiest month in its operational history to date. The 31st Photo Squadron aided by pilots of the 39th Photo Squadron roamed far and wide over the Third Army front performing photo recce and bomb damage missions. TAC R missions provided a thorough coverage of highway and rail movement and enemy activity in the zone of Third Army's smashing drive. A new high was reached in the coordination of TAC R and fighter-bombers as evidenced by the increased number of incidents in which recce units found and led fighter-bombers to profitable targets. In addition to directing the destruction of ground targets, pilots of the 15th TAC R had a field day at the expense of the Luftwaffe and shot down fourteen enemy planes during the month.

As usual the month began with bad weather and the 15th TAC R had 10 of its 13 missions on March 1st aborted by weather, but in one of the successful missions, Lt. Balachowski distinguished himself with an excellent mission flown at low altitude in 10/10s weather. His long report in support of XII Corps included tanks, motor transport, flak positions, trenchwork, rail activity and a check of six bridges. On the 2nd and 3rd Lts. Byrne Warren and Henry Lacey each found large concentrations of enemy motor vehicles and armor and led fighter-bombers in to attack their respective targets.

During the next several days continuous rain and low visibility virtually grounded the 10th's aircraft as well as the rest of XIXth TAC, but Patton's drive was off and running. They blasted out of the Trier-Koblenz corridor on March 6 and by March 7th had completed its 50 mile drive to the Rhine, smashed German resistance and captured thousands of prisoners and pieces of equipment. With this accomplished Third Army turned its attention to the Palatinate region where German Army Group G was manning the Siegfried Line defenses against Seventh Army in its western sector and Hunsruck Mountain positions against Third Army. The new attack began on March 13th and was reinforced by XIXth TAC fighter-bomber support on the 14th. Flying 643 sorties, the P-47s aided by the target finding TAC R hit 16 towns and seven marshalling yards, destroyed or damaged 58 tanks, 19 locomotives, 393 rail cars, 289 motor vehicles, and killed over 600 enemy troops.

15th TAC R Moves to Trier

In order to get closer to the action the 10th Group began making plans to move to its new Trier-Evren airbase, and the 15th TAC R, the first of its squadrons to make the move, began operations there on March 15. Nineteen missions were flown by the 15th TAC R during the course of the day, and excellent flying weather resulted in long reports, especially on rail traffic. The Luftwaffe was out in strength again and Lt. Dale Goodermote nearly fell victim to the same fate as Lt. Boyden had the day before when thirty Focke-Wulfs jumped him and his wingman Lt. Henry Lewis.

Goodermote's P-51 took a cannon hit in his left wing that knocked out his guns and wounded him, but managed to escape before any more damage was done. Ten miles east of Giessen Lts. Henry Lacey and T.P. Davis ran into the same problem but were able to evade 35 FW-190s with no damage. Over Aschaffenburg the odds ran in favor of Lt. Clyde East and his wingman Lt. E.A. Ray when they ran into a lone Me-109, and East shot it down for his third kill. With East's victory the 15th TAC R added another first to its record. It had been the first unit to score a kill on D-Day and now was the first to score while flying from a German base.

TAC R was up in force on March 16th and searched out numerous targets for the fighter-bombers along Third Army Sectors. The 362nd Fighter Group alone destroyed 3 tanks and 6 armored vehicles, 7 locomotives and 28 railcars, 40 horse drawn vehicles, 402 motor vehicles in addition to numerous gun positions, buildings and other targets. The 15th TAC R flew sixteen missions and provided a thorough coverage of highways, rail lines, and airfields, but lost another pilot in doing so, Lt. E.A. Ray, near Bingen. He and Lt. Bob Shively became separated in the clouds while they were maneuvering to meet a bandit coming in at them from the southwest. A short time later Lt. Ray contacted Shively on the radio and told him that he had been hit by flak near Mannheim, then called a second time and said he was okay and was bailing out near Bingen.

On March 17th, German Army Group G was caught between Seventh Army and Third Army and its annihilation began. The sledgehammer blows of the two pronged attack forced the Germans on to the roads in retreat and then XIXth TAC fighter-bombers went to work on them in a devastating attack. The crowded highways were turned into flaming ribbons of death, especially so on one fifteen mile stretch east of Kaiserslautern where the road was filled with burning vehicles, dead and dying animals and men. With the help of this excellent air support Third Army troops captured Bad Kreuznach and pushed within ten miles of the projected contact point between it and Seventh Army.

The new day brought no rest for the shattered Germans as the pressure on the ground was maintained, and the XIXth TAC recorded a record kill when it destroyed or damaged 1033 motor vehicles, 416 horse drawn vehicles, 176 tanks or armored vehicles, 69 locomotives, and 588 rail cars. TAC R stayed quite busy during the course of this aerial siege locating targets and directing the fighter-bombers to them. Captain John Hoefker joined Lt. William O. Davenport of the 12th TAC R for a mission to the Worms, Bad Kreuznach and Bingen area and located a small convoy of forty vehicles which they directed the P-47s to. At the same time two other sections of the 12th were checking the Frankfurt, Koblenz, St. Wendall area and Lt. Leon Canady reported German road blocks located on the roads leading to Kirchberg and numerous barges in the river, while Captain E.L. Bishop and Major John Florence, who had assumed command of the 12th TAC R in February, reported US troops entering Bad Kreuznach and a three mile zig-zag trench at Worms. Lt. Don Lynch and Lt. Melvin Strange helped discourage the German retreat by supplying a battery of artillery with an excellent target of opportunity after their primary fire mission was unsuccessful. They spotted a column of German infantry trying to struggle out of Immeldorf, and put the very first round into the head of the column causing considerable casualties and panic.

The 15th TAC R also had a busy day but at the cost of an excellent recce pilot and two of its aircraft. Lt. Robert Kirkpatrick had to belly his Mustang in about 20 miles south of Luxembourg when his engine failed, but the most serious loss occurred when one of the squadron's most skilled pilots, Captain Howard Nichols, hit high tension wires near Merl, Germany and was killed.

On the plus side of the ledger, the squadron added two more confirmed victories and two probables to its scoreboard. Lts. N.A. Thomas and Guy Cary were bounced over Hanau-Langenchibach airfield by eight Me-109s and two FW-190s and a dogfight ensued. Lt. Thomas turned into the attacking 109s, fired a long burst and the first 109 went into a snap roll and then dove straight into the ground and exploded. He then locked on to a second 109, scored hits all over its fuselage and tail section, and watched it head downward trailing heavy black smoke. Lt. Cary took on a third 109 and set its engine on fire with his first burst, then followed it down and saw the smoking 109 crash into a grove of trees and explode. As Cary climbed back up he fired on a FW-190 and sent white smoke trailing back from its engine with a well aimed burst but could only claim it as a probable because he did not observe it crash.

The 31st Photo Squadron flew sixteen missions on the 18th and covered the Frankfurt, Darmstadt, Koblenz, and Bingen areas and brought back excellent photos showing German defenses, and the heavily damaged conditions of their airfields throughout those areas.

The Third Army battering ram really broke out and exploited its mobility by overrunning 950 square miles on March 19, virtually eliminating organized German resistance in the Palatinate area. With so much real estate changing hands so quickly, Patton's aerial eyes remained over the area continually to keep commanders up to date on the highly fluid situation, and to locate tempting targets for fighter-bombers.

In his mission Major John Florence of the 12th TAC R noted eight bridges still intact along the Nahe River and the contrasting situations of US troops heading through Bad Kreuznach after white flag waving enemy soldiers positioned outside of the city, and German soldiers hastily constructing road blocks outside of Alzev. Lts. Henri Lefebure and Robert Marple flying in the same general area directed the attack of fighter-bombers on a fifty vehicle convoy, and then called in the P-47s to attack a huge convoy of over 500 assorted vehicles. As they left the area twenty-eight Thunderbolts were turning the stretch of road into a blazing junk pile, and Lts. Ronald Ricci and Bill Davenport, who had just arrived at the scene to take over, charted four more good sized convoys for the P-47s.

With speed and surprise being a big part of Patton's success during the breakout, the use of Germany's autobahn highway was incorporated into his plans for advancing through Germany. In order to take advantage of these autobahns, detailed photos of every mile along its plan advance were needed, and the 31st Photo Squadron was called on for some low-level runs down them. These would not be "on the deck" "dicing" runs as at Normandy, but the pilots would fly at the vulnerable altitude of 5000 feet photographing every foot of it with their nose cameras. The one safety factor in the "dicing" missions was that they were so low to the ground it was difficult for the defenders to bring their guns to bear, but at 5000 feet they were endangered by flak and enemy fighters alike.

The first of these missions was flown on March 19th by Lt. Russell Mykytan who volunteered to cover the stretch between Kaiserslautern to the Rhine River. He solved the problem of defense by diving from 12,000 feet to 5000 feet and streaking down the autobahn at more than 400 MPH, and returned with photos that helped the 10th Armored to shove all the way to the Rhine in record time. His success resulted in many requests for similar photos of nearly all the main highways in central Germany, and a Distinguished Flying Cross for himself. A second very successful mission of this type was flown by Captain Johnston between Frankfurt and Giessen which helped our armor keep its drive in high gear.

"Mazie Me & Monk" over Germany, late spring 1945. At this date its code had been changed from ZM * O to ZM * A. (F. Pfeiffer)

CHAPTER IX

Across the Rhine to Victory

March—May 8, 1945 - Aerial Recon Aids Patton,
TAC R Scores Its Final Victories

During March 20 and 21, the 10th Photo Reconnaissance Group covered the battlefield and assisted in Third Army's race to cut off the escape routes across the Rhine and close its Rhineland campaign. With the doors to escape closed to the enemy on the 21st, Third Army stormed and captured Mainz, Ludwigshafen, Worms, and barricaded the Rhine between Worms and Mannheim, thus ending a fantastic eleven day campaign with a magnificent victory.

For their part in the activities of the 21st Lt. Claude Franklin and Lt. "Dusty" Rhoads of the 12th TAC R checked out the bridges between Ludwigshafen and Mannheim and found them unserviceable. Then they called in P-47s to attack numerous rail cars located in the Mannheim marshalling yards, while Lts. Mingo Logothetis and Bill Davenport were calling in the Thunderbolts to attack a column consisting of 800 tanks, half-tracks and self-propelled artillery.

The Luftwaffe was up in force and tried unsuccessfully to intercept several of the 31st Photo Squadron's Lightnings, and one FW-190D made the fatal mistake of entering airspace occupied by Captain Clyde East and Lt. Leland Larson of the 15th TAC R. As the section passed over it, Captain East turned and made a diving pass at the long-nosed 190 but his bullets missed their mark. Lt. Larson then took over the attack and with two long bursts into the fuselage sent the Focke-Wulf to its doom. Apparently one of his bursts killed the pilot because it went into a slow roll and straight into the ground. As Larson started to climb back to altitude after his victory, Captain East spotted 10 more 190s coming in after them and radioed a warning to Larson to hit the deck and get out of there. The Mustang section then skimmed along the deck, easily outran the 190s, then pulled up and continued their recce.

While these aerial engagements were taking place on the 21st, plans for a Rhine crossing were being discussed by Generals Bradley, Patton and Courtney Hodges and the decision was made that the Third Army would cross first. Patton quickly put the plan into action and on the night of March 22/23 sent troops of the 5th Division across at Oppenheim, completely surprising the German defenders. By nightfall of March 24th he had crossed the Rhine at four points and by nightfall on the 26th had captured Darmstadt, Aschaffenburg, and had thrown a ring around Frankfurt.

With Third Army waging war in three different directions; mopping up in the Palatinate, one spearhead headed for Kassel, and another for Limburg to meet up with First Army, the 10th Photo Reconnaissance Group was kept well occupied.

The 15th TAC R had a big day both in the air and in finding fat targets for the fighter-bombers. Early in the morning of March 24, six Me-109s bounced Captain East and Lt. Larson in the vicinity of Eisnach. The 109s hit them from out of the sun, but the section made a 180 turn to the left and caught two stragglers as the Messerschmitts followed them into the turn. East and Larson chose their respective targets and opened fire almost simultaneously, with devastating results. East's 109 exploded in the air and pieces of it slightly damaged his plane, and Larson's Messerschmitt spun into the ground and exploded. After they climbed back to 7000 feet, Captain East spotted another Me-109 getting into firing position on Lt. Larson's tail and blasted it out of the sky for his fifth kill and became the second 10th Reconnaissance Group ace.

TAC R Pursues the Wehrmacht

Lt. Haylon R. Wood found a damaged train near Neustadt with engines at each end pulling fifteen flat cars loaded with heavy tanks and led a squadron of P-47s to the train and made the first pass at it. In doing so Wood received such intense flak that the fighter-bombers refused to follow and they flew off in search of a less hostile target. While that was going on Lt. Chuck Rowland led another squadron of P-47s against a convoy of over 300 mixed vehicles and watched the destructive attack mangle many of them. On his second mission of the day, Lt. Wood provided more targets for the Thunderbolts and led them in on two different attacks. The first was a concentration of 75 vehicles near Wiesbaden, and in the second, an airfield near Limburg, Wood himself flamed a Focke-Wulf on the ground.

These unrelenting aerial assaults led by the TAC R pilots did not end there, but continued throughout the remainder of March and resulted in enormous damage to the crumbling German war machine. On March 26, the 15th TAC R flew sixteen more of these successful missions with Lts. Leland Larson and Henry Lacey and A.O. Frick overseeing the destruction of three large columns of enemy vehicles, but Lt. Haylon Wood found the biggest target of all. He recalls the day's events as follows:

"My wingman was Lt. James Webb and our mission was to recce the Remagan bridgehead and areas around and beyond it. Visibility was unlimited on a beautiful day and as we approached the area I immediately realized things were happening. That our forces had broken out was obvious, that the breakout had occurred only a short time prior to our arrival was apparent; that this was a field day for our forces was quite soon to be a fact, a reality. A relatively small town [Limburg]—but a key communications center—was located only a few miles east of the bridgehead. From this point some half dozen roads radiated generally eastward. Our troops and armor were fanning out along each road, preceded by bedraggled groups composed of German soldiers and civilians. I was amazed that such an enormous operation was taking place in the absence of massive air assistance, no US or Allied aircraft were in the area. My amazement was confirmed when I contacted Central Control, for neither was that center aware of such an undertaking. With overcharged elation I apparently convinced Central that 'the war can be ended here today.' Please send every squadron of P-47s that you have available.

"Within moments my radio conversation with Central Control made it apparent that word was spreading, an onslaught was in progress. Central assured that P-47s were on their way from virtually every point of the compass, and nine squadrons were to arrive before my departure. As they began to come in I informed them, incorrectly, that there was no flak. I had strafed an enemy column prior to the arrival of the first P-47 squadron and had led the first squadron to arrive on their first pass and no flak was encountered. That my first assessment of 'no flak' was in error was soon to become evident. Upon the arrival of the third or fourth bomber squadron I led the strafing run and as I pulled up and banked sharply to the left, the sky was suddenly filled with 20mm and 40mm 'golf balls.' Scared and angered by the flak which had passed dangerously close, I turned and dived into the line of fire and began a strafing pass which I have regretted ever since. I rolled out at 50 feet and pressed the trigger, sending streams of 50-caliber fire into the mass of people in the road before I realized a white banner was being waved by civilians mixed in with the German soldiers. I quickly released the trigger, but it was too late to undo the damage."

Unfortunate as it was that the Germans did mix civilians in with their military column, Lt. Wood did lead a very successful attack against German troops and armor and before he had to leave the scene, fighter bombers had destroyed over 200 vehicles.

The next day the coordination of TAC R and fighter-bombers continued and Captain East led them to 45 motor transport at Idstein and saw 15 of them burning before he had to leave. Lts. James Webb and Haylon Wood found another big concentration of 400 vehicles parked bumper to bumper near Wetzler and led the P-47s in an attack which destroyed 200 of them and left the woods ablaze. Lt. Richard McFadden, also of the 15th TAC R, found another 1100 vehicles in his area and got another P-47 squadron to administer their hellish treatment to over 100 vehicles.

The Luftwaffe did not escape either. Lts. Wayne Patrick and Leland Larson of the 15th TAC R during a morning mission chased a Me-109 into German flak and saw it shot down, and Captain Clyde East and Lt. Henry Lacey turned an abortive recce mission into a very successful fighter attack. Here is their report of the mission.

"We ran into bad weather and were returning from our route when seven Ju-87s were observed dive bombing [our troops] in the town of Hammelburg. We were at 2000 feet when we attacked the Ju-87s which scattered as we approached. I [Captain East] got on the tail of one E/A who took violent evasive action. After several two second bursts, I observed several strikes on the left gas tank and radiator and the E/A began streaming coolant. The canopies suddenly flew open and its crew jumped and landed very near where their plane crashed. I then closed on a second Stuka and fired a three second burst and missed, and the E/A dove steeply for the deck and jettisioned his bombs. He then proceeded west on the deck and I followed firing several deflection bursts that hit him in the landing gear and engine. Shortly afterward the E/A started trailing smoke and coolant and its pilot took it in for a crashlanding. I took photos of both aircraft after they crashed.

"Lt. Lacey attacked a third Ju-87 and it dove vertically, jettisoned its bombs, and pulled out on the deck. A long chase ensued with the Stuka taking violent evasive action and Lt. Lacey firing several short bursts from various angles and observing hits on its tail section and tail. On his next to last burst Lt. Lacey saw coolant start streaming back when his shells hit the Stuka's engine and cockpit area, and then it went into a shallow dive and crashed into some woods. The rear gunner in the Stuka continued firing all the way in."

Wiesbaden was seized by the 80th Infantry Division on March 28, and First Army's crack 9th Armored Division raced twenty-five miles south of Limburg to meet up with them, thus joining and cutting off a large pocket of enemy troops and capturing over 8000 prisoners of war.

XIXth TAC also had a record day and its fighter-bombers damaged or destroyed 1527 motor vehicles, many of which they had been directed to by TAC R. The 15th TAC R flew nine missions and reported roads full of military and civilian equipment. Lt. Henry Lewis located 1000 vehicles in a column and called in fighter-bombers but they couldn't strafe because of the large numbers of civilians in the mob, however Lts. Alfred Reed and Henri Lefebure of the 12th TAC R located another large convoy in the Bad Homburg area and called in a squadron of P-47s which destroyed it. Lts. Don Lynch and Elmer Olson detected a small convoy of US troops heading through Hammelburg toward Diebach or the Prisoner of War camp at Hammelburg. (Possibly these were the troops General Patton had sent to try and liberate the camp.)

In the day's aerial action, four Me-109s attacked Lts. Leland Larson and Robert Landers of the 15th TAC R near Neustadt and paid dearly for their effort. The P-51 section broke right as the 109s attacked and then Lt. Larson got in some deflection shots on one of the Messerschmitts causing it to trail black smoke. The enemy plane pulled up into the lower edge of the clouds but did not escape from Lt. Landers who attacked and tore its cockpit apart and sent it crashing to the ground in an uncontrolled dive. Lts. Wayne Patrick and Henry Lacey had located two trains for the fighter-bombers and were now heading back to base when they encountered a lone Ju-87 Stuka. Lt. Lacey yanked his Mustang into a dive and went after it, opening fire when he could "see the whites of the gunner's eyes." After Lacey's initial bursts the enemy pilot crawled out on his wing and jumped at 300 feet but his chute did not open, and his rear gunner rode the plane down firing all the way.

Weather shut down Group operations for the next two days and gave the 12th TAC R and the 31st Photo Squadron the opportunity to make their move to Evren airfield and join up with the 15th TAC R. For the 12th TAC R the move was a case of history repeating itself, for the unit had operated from this same airfield in World War I and it was only the first step in a series of moves that were nearly identical to the path it followed in the last war.

Frankfurt fell on March 29th and Third Army's powerful armored and

"B" Flight, 15th TAC R Squadron, at Trier, Germany, March 1945. (On wing, l. to r.) Lts. Wayne Patrick, Charles Johnson, Phillip Hunt, (on ground, l. to r.) Lt. Henry Lacey, Lt. Leland Larson, Capt. Clyde East, Lts. Merlin Reed, Fairfield Goodale, Robert Ober. (L. Larson via W. Hess)

Maj. Leon L. Davis, commanding officer of the 15th Tactical Reconnaissance Squadron from October 11, 1944 to the end of the war. (R. Dawson)

*Above: Lt. Don Lynch of the 12th TAC R escorting in a surrendering FW-190 on May 8, 1945. (D. Lynch) Below: Comedians Jerry Cologna and Bob Hope pose in front of Lt. Ed Kenny's F-6C which was decorated in their honor. The plane was coded ZM * E.*

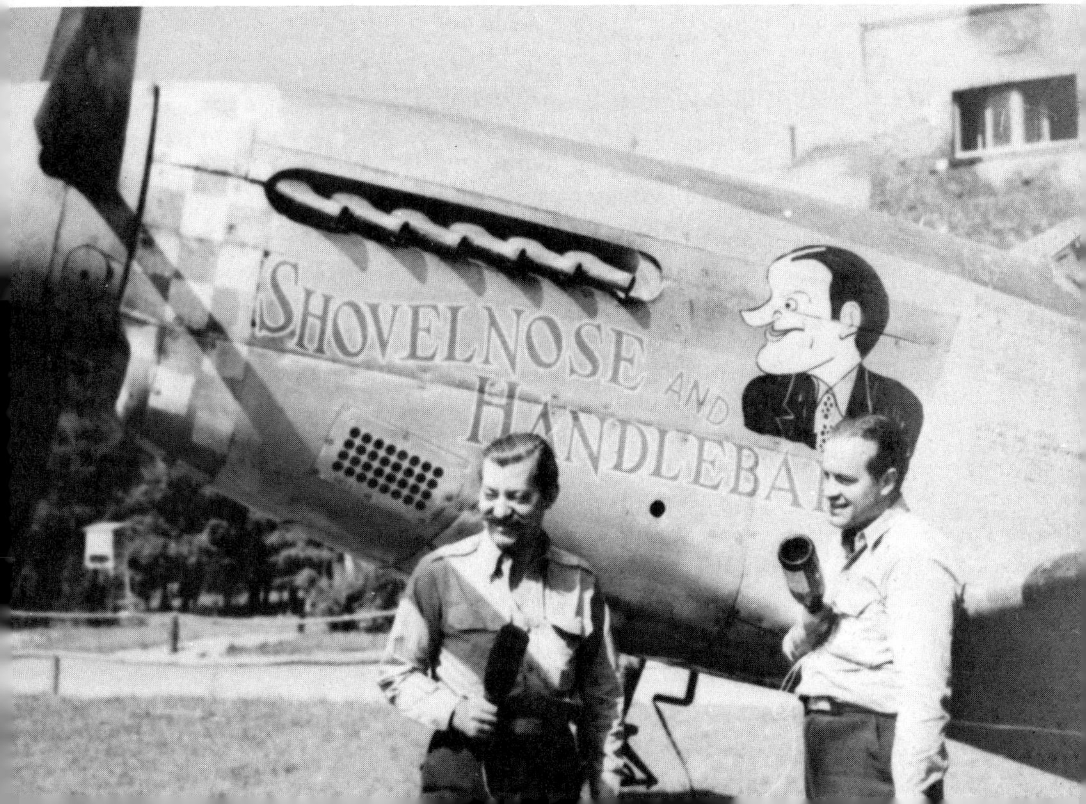

infantry forces broke out in all directions. The 6th Armored, 65th and 80th Infantry Divisions slammed 45 miles northeast to the vicinity of Kassel and in doing so completed the longest and fastest of Third Army breakthroughs—100 miles in less than three days. Simultaneously the 4th Armored and the 90th Infantry Division pushed 25 miles to Hersfeld, and the 11th Armored and 26th Infantry shoved their way to Fulda.

TAC R closed out the month by flying more target seeking missions and met with some success. Lts. Bob Bruce and Bob Little of the 12th TAC R located numerous trains in several marshalling yards in the Hersfeld area, and watched the P-47s prang many of the rail cars they had reported. Lt. "Dusty" Rhoads of the 12th TAC R found targets galore in the Gotha area but could not contact the fighter-bombers to hit the marshalling yard full of flatcars carrying tanks and armored vehicles. Lt. Leland Larson of the 15th TAC R enjoyed better radio contact and saw Thunderbolts pound the concentration of 100 vehicles and 300 troops he had located near Wurzburg.

Perhaps the most unusual incident of the day happened during Captain John Hoefker's mission. He and Lt. Charles White were flying a route recce in the vicinity of Eisnach when he spied a Hs-126 liaison plane that had just taken off and was climbing. Captain Hoefker whipped his P-51 around in a turn in front of the Henschel and when he looked back the plane had crashed, apparently his propwash had flipped the light German aircraft over at low altitude and sent it into the ground. This unique victory extended his score to 8½ confirmed.

April began with Third Army engaged in some hard fighting in its three pronged attack at Fulda, Hersfeld, and Kassel, but by April 4th had captured these cities and opened up a 50 mile wide corridor into eastern Germany. TAC R continued to fly the important recce/fighter-bomber missions in support of Third Army actions. Although the number of targets were fewer and smaller, they exploited every opportunity to destroy them, while the 31st carried out many requests for photo coverage of the breakout area and of usable roads and highways.

Weather on April 1 was poor and observations were limited, but some sections reported movements of vehicles, tanks and personnel, and sighted advance elements of US armor in the vicinity of Aschaffenburg. Lt. Guy Cary of the 15th TAC R found three tanks and thirty motor transports, but when he led fighter-bombers to the attack low clouds hid the enemy and saved them. Lt. Dale Goodermote was able to accomplish a perfect example of air-ground support when he led P-47s to fifteen vehicles and three tanks hidden in some woods near Hilders. As they began their attack an American column was heading right toward the hidden enemy, but by the time the US tanks would have been in range, the fighter-bombers had turned the German position into an inferno. As the section left the area the Shermans were rumbling past the shattered wrecks and on toward their objective.

Little was accomplished during the next two days due to worsening weather, and the 12th and 15th TAC R squadrons used the time to make their move to their new base at Ober-Olm which was just a few miles from Mainz. After the fairly nice accommodations they had enjoyed at Giraumont and Trier, Ober-Olm was a little disappointing since it was a grass field and had neither hangars or buildings to house the squadrons.

TAC R Versus the Luftwaffe

After establishing itself on the 50 mile north/south corridor into eastern Germany, Third Army was ordered to limit its operations so that the First and Ninth Armies could catch up and get on line with it and begin closing the Ruhr pocket. Naturally Patton objected to the slow down and as he predicted, German defense stiffened and they even launched limited counter-attacks. In conjunction with their stiffening defense on the ground, the Luftwaffe was up in strength and several of their aircraft had the misfortune of running into 10th Photo Reconnaissance Group pilots. The series of airbattles began on April 4th when 10th pilots shot down seven enemy planes, and continued for several more days. The 15th TAC R claimed three of these victories, the first of which were scored by Captain Clyde East and Lt. Leland Larson. They were on a railroad recce when they encountered a Ju-188 near Wittenburg and Captain East made the first pass, firing three bursts and hitting the fuselage and left engine which burst into flame. Lt. Larson then attacked from the other side and set the right engine on fire, and as he pulled up saw the big plane go into a gentle glide and explode at 1500 feet. About an hour later the section spotted a FW-190 flying west at 2000 feet, 15 miles south of Leipzig, and East attacked from 6 o'clock and opened fire at 100 yards. His fifties ripped the Focke-Wulf apart and apparently killed the pilot because it just went into a slow roll and dived into the ground and exploded on impact. When weather forced Lt. Bob Shively to abort his mission he compensated for a blank recce report by scoring an economical victory over a Me-109 flying east on the deck. He made a tight diving turn to the right and leveled out right on the 109s tail, but before he could open fire, the German pilot saw him, panicked and bellied his plane in for a crash-landing. Since US troops had been seen in the immediate area, Shively did not strafe.

The 12th TAC R had its biggest day to date in aerial kills with their four, and Lt. Leo Elliott led the day's activities with 1½ kills. The encounter was recalled by Lt. Elliott as follows, "We were halfway through our reconnaissance when I spotted a Ju-88 dead ahead and below us. That was too good to pass up, so with my wingman, Lt. Dan Cartago, following me, I dived on the plane, fired and set his left engine on fire."

"I was going to overshoot him, so I peeled off to the right and my wingman finished him off, shooting at him until he hit the ground. As I peeled off I noticed a Ju-87 off to the right. All my guns but one were jammed, but I used that, following him onto the deck.

"He was going so slow, I started to overshoot just as we came to a high tension wire. I was right above him then and couldn't pull up enough to clear the wire, so I squeezed under it. When I looked back I saw that the German, trying to get away from me, had flown too low and crashed into the ground."

Captain William Winberry caught a Me-109 during his mission over Gotha and peppered it so thoroughly on his first pass that its pilot made a hasty exit rather than face that yellow-nosed Mustang again. The fourth victory of the day was a Fi-56 Storch shared by Lt. Bob Bruce and Bob Gardner, who saw the fragile liaison plane disintegrate from their attack, tumble to the ground and explode.

Missions of April 5th added more Nazi scalps to the 10th's score as its TAC R pilots bagged three more enemy aircraft in aerial combat and one on the ground. Lts. Mingo Logothetis and John Ellis of the 12th TAC R encountered six enemy aircraft, 3 Me-109s and 3 FW-190s, near Gotha and in the ensuing melee each of them destroyed a Focke-Wulf and Logothetis damaged another, but Ellis, whose P-51 was damaged in the initial attack, had to jump from his crippled aircraft when its engine failed two miles from Y-64.

Lt. N. W. Kirkpatrick and Lt. Stewart A. Wilson of the 15th TAC R were in the vicinity of Munchberg checking movement on the Autobahn when Kirkpatrick sighted a Ju-87 flying north at 1000 feet. Pushing his Mustang into a dive, Kirkpatrick closed to within 200 yards and opened fire, then watched as the Stuka dropped off on one wing and went straight into the ground.

In addition to the air action, Lts. Henry Lacey, Haylon Wood, and Bob Shively led fighter-bombers to some juicy targets on the ground. Lt. Lacey began the assault with an attack on two military trains, and Wood found another loaded with motor transport and armor; all of which were clobbered by the Thunderbolts. Lt. Shively led another squadron of P-47s to twenty-five aircraft parked in some woods, the majority of which were Me-109s, and in leading the attack he destroyed one Me-109 himself and saw the Thunderbolts destroy another three before he broke to continue his recce.

While his squadron was preparing its move to Ober-Olm to join the other squadrons, Captain Harold Leuth of the 31st flew one of their more important missions from Trier when he photographed more than 150 miles of Autobahn running east from Eisnach to Dresden to help Third Army prepare for its drive toward Czechoslovakia.

The 15th TAC R dispatched seventeen missions on April 7 and brought in considerable information about rail activity. Lt. A. O. Frick led P-47s to six tanks and over 50 motor transports in the vicinity of Holtzhalloben and Lt. Kirkpatrick observed a tank battle in progress near Effelder. Twelve German and twelve US tanks were slugging it out, and more than thirty vehicles were burning near the American tanks.

While the 15th TAC R was finding its targets on the ground, the 12th TAC R was reducing the Luftwaffe's inventory again. The team of Ellis and Logothetis encountered FW-190s on two occasions near Darmstadt and came out on top both times. At 1850 hours they spotted three FW-190s in formation and knocked one of them out of the sky, and ten minutes later caught a lone Focke-Wulf and saw it crash and explode after they had laced its fuselage and canopy with their fifties.

On the basis of purely reconnaissance work, April 8th would have been an exceptional day but in addition to those results the Group was credited with ten more aerial victories—8 by the 15th TAC R.

Lt. N. A. Thomas scored the 15th's first kill of the day with a vicinity over a FW-190 10 miles southeast of Regensburg, and twenty minutes later Captain Hoefker raised his total to 9½ when he downed a He-111 in the vicinity of Juterburg. At about the same time Captain East and Lt. Larson were raising havoc with a flight of Stukas near Dresden. They sighted a section of three Stukas and attacked with East taking the one on the left and Larson the one on the right. East opened fire at 200 yards and saw white smoke pour back from the stricken bomber which then did a split S and crashed into the ground. Larson attacked his from 6 o'clock and watched it do a wingover and dive into the ground after he had ripped its fuselage and engine apart. The third Stuka began circling the wreck of one of his fallen comrades and East caught it with a three second burst which sent it to a fiery end. A few seconds later the section sighted a He-111 circling a wrecked plane and East attacked from the left and Larson from the right. The Heinkle went down, bounced, hit the ground again, broke apart and burned. An hour later East nailed a FH-104* in the vicinity of Riesa with a three second burst that caused the plane to fold up in mid-air. As its fuselage broke in half and its wings folded, the four man crew of the FH-104 tried to jump but a spinning wing killed two of them outright and collapsed the parachute of a third. The last man made it down safely. With his 3½ victories of the day Captain East raised his total to 12 kills and passed Captain Hoefker as the 10th Photo Reconnaissance Group's top ace.

In the last encounter of the day for the 15th TAC R, a FW-190 jumped Lts. Chuck Rowland and Edmund Maxwell as they were returning to base. The 190 opened fire at Rowland at 700 yards but missed and Lt. Maxwell maneuvered his P-51 into firing position on the German's tail. His fire shattered the canopy, killing the pilot, and demolished the 190's engine. As Lt. Rowland pulled up past the enemy aircraft he saw the pilot slumped in the cockpit and then the 190 slid off on one wing and crashed into a plowed field.

The day's scoring for the 12th TAC R was begun by Lt. Henry Ermatinger who downed a FW-190 near Hof, and completed by Lt. John "Dusty" Rhoads who caught a Me-109 near Gotha. In this engagement the 109 attacked the section but missed and after a 45 second chase Lt. Rhoads sent it down in a spiraling dive and saw it crash into the ground.

The 12th TAC R picked right up where it had left off and scored four more victories on April 9th. Two of the kills were scored by Lts. Bill Davenport and "Dusty" Rhoads, and the events were described by Lt. Davenport as follows, "It was the first mission that I was leading and suddenly these three 190s came in at us out of the sun. We didn't see them until they were firing, but fortunately they overshot us and we were on their tails before they knew it. From then on it was duck soup.

"Two were line abreast, the third higher and in front of the other two. I told Lt. Rhoads to take the one on the left and I'd take the one on the right. My first burst scored hits all over the 190, and he went to pieces, rolled over on his back and just seemed to slip right into the ground. My wingman got his too, and the pilot bailed out. Then we joined up on the third, who hit the deck, and we chased him over the treetops for more than twenty miles. We damaged him alright but weren't doing too much good, and as we'd been finishing our route when we were attacked we were pretty low on gas, so we finally gave it up and came on home."

---

*This was most likely a Siebel 204, since only a prototype FH-104 was ever built.

The other two kills were scored by Lts. Mingo Logothetis and John Ellis near Bayreuth. Their section was headed east at 3500 feet when they were jumped by two FW-190s that came at them from 6 o'clock level. The section broke before the Focke-Wulfs came into range and made a 180 degree turn for a head on pass. As the enemy aircraft broke Logothetis and Ellis selected their respective targets and sent them both down in flames. One German pilot escaped by parachute.

The 15th TAC R sent out nineteen missions during the day and although it had no aerial encounters, they raised a little hell with some targets on the ground. Two of the missions were flown by Captain Clyde East and on each occasion he found some tempting fighter-bomber targets. On his first mission he led them to a train unloading motor transport and armor at a railroad siding, destroyed four trucks himself, and then hung around and watched as the P-47s disposed of the remainder. On his second mission he led the Thunderbolts to 200 vehicles near Erfurt and again went down and pranged three himself and watched while another twenty were sent up in smoke.

Target areas were covered the next day as well as the ground fog and low clouds would permit, but it was the 15th TAC R's day for aerial combat. A FW-190 and a Me-109 jumped Lts. Wayne Patrick and Richard McFadden northeast of Leipzig, and the incident resulted in two enemy aircraft probably destroyed, each man credited with a probable. Over Torgau Lt. Henry Lacey encountered an overzealous Me-110 pilot and sent him crashing into a field and Captain John Hoefker topped off the day with a big report and another victory, number 10½ for him, when a FW-190 made the fatal mistake of jumping his section near Hof.

Lt. Harry S. Utley of the 15th TAC R scored his first aerial victory when a Me-109 jumped his section and then tried to escape by diving. Utley chased him down and shot the 109 down in flames. Lt. Dale Goodermote and his wingman led two squadrons of fighter-bombers to 300 vehicles moving south in the vicinity of Frieburg, and saw at least 150 of them destroyed. Lt. Chuck Rowland continued the assault against ground targets when he led two more P-47 squadrons against a concentration of motor vehicles, tanks and artillery pieces. In this attack more than half of the targets were destroyed.

Finally on April 11th, the leash on Third Army was released and it burst forth toward the east and extended its southern flank to Bayreuth in order to maintain its contact with Seventh Army. Before the day was out the 4th Armored had pushed forty miles and had captured or encircled several towns to include Jena and Weimar and the infamous Buchenwald concentration camp. Another unit was storming Erfurt against heavy resistance. On the 12th Third Army pushed another 35 miles and by late afternoon on April 14th was only 20 miles from Leipzig, 35 miles from Dresden, and only ten miles from the Czechoslovakian border, only to have the leash put back on them by General Eisenhower.

Radio problems and haze affected the missions flown by the 15th TAC R on April 11th, but they still managed to produce some excellent results from some fighter-bomber/recce coordination missions. Lt. Chuck Rowland led them to three targets near Saalfeld, a concentration of thirty vehicles and sixty troops, a marshalling yard loaded with over forty box cars, 20 flat cars and three engines with steam up, and a column of 150 troops and motor transport. Lt. Henry Lacey led a squadron of P-47s to 25 large vehicles towing trailers and the Thunderbolts bombed and strafed the convoy, cut the road and left the road blocked with burning hulks of vehicles. Lt. John Miefert joined the act by leading P-47s against eight 88s which were holding up a US tank column and saw the guns destroyed by direct bomb hits.

In the vicinity of Nuremburg the Luftwaffe was in evidence again and twelve Me-109s bounced Lts. Ron Ricci and Bill Davenport but the section was able to evade their attackers. In the same area Lts. Dan Cartago and Wallace Mitchell were chased by a Me-262 but again the German pilot was not able to bring his guns to bear against them.

Weather worsened on April 13th and forced many of the TAC R missions to abort, but in spite of the elements the 15th TAC R added some more victories to its list. Five miles south of Hof two Me-109s sneaked up on Clyde East and Lt. W. L. Meikle from out of the sun while the section was watching 20 Me-109s flying west at 6000 feet a few miles away. Captain East's Mustang was hit four times with one shell piercing his right gas tank, but he turned into the Me-109 that had fired, jettisoned his wing tanks, climbed and moved in for the kill. After positioning himself on the 109's tail, East opened fire and observed hits on the fuselage and left wing, after which the 109 broke to the right and headed down trailing black smoke and crash-landed. Victory number 13.

The heavy TAC R activity continued on the 15th of April and resulted in more punishment for German ground and air forces. An Me-109 jumped Lts. Bill Davenport and Ron Ricci near Eger from 9 o'clock and fired 90 degree deflection shots at them but missed. The section turned into him and Lt. Davenport opened fire and missed, however Lt. Ricci then fired on it and scored numerous hits in the engine, fuselage and wing. As the 109's engine began to burst into flame, Ricci began to fire again and the enemy pilot jumped.

On the 16th, Lts. A.O. Frick and Harry Utley of the 15th TAC R were attacked by two Me-109s with a FW-190 flying top cover. The enemy aircraft tried to attack from 4 o'clock level, but they pulled up steeply and waited for the 109s to pass under them. Then the two Mustangs dropped down on to the tails of the enemy aircraft and blasted them out of the sky. It was the second victory in two days for Utley.

Lt. Haylon Wood turned in two expert recce missions and located 6 trains, 4 train sections and eight engines in the Roszwein area plus 25 motor transports in the Rhienfriedsdorf area for the fighter-bombers. Lts. Ed Goval and Merlin Reed also of the 15th TAC R found themselves involved in trying to stop P-47s of the 405th Fighter Squadron from strafing US forces north of Plauen. They finally stopped the attack by boxing in one of the "Jugs" and escorting him out of the area and saw the other two fly off. They then determined that the troops below had not laid out the identifying panels of the day and notified the controller so corrections could be made and possibly head off other mistakes.

The 16th of April also became another moving day for the 15th TAC R as its forward elements packed up and began the trip to their new base at Erfurt. The rear echelon continued to operate from Ober-Olm until the 18th and the first light missions of the day were launched there but finished at Erfurt. The remainder of the planes were brought up during the day and a C-47 shuttled back and forth between the two bases bringing up personnel and some of the lighter equipment. In was an amusing and incredible sight that greeted the rear echelon when they alighted from the plane for scrounging expeditions had "requisitioned" a number of automobiles and motorcycles and the perimeter of the base looked like Stateside traffic on a holiday. To top off the festivities, a number of the men wore odds and ends of German uniforms acquired from storerooms and warehouses, providing an ETO version of Barnum & Bailey's Circus.

The Mapping of Bavaria

On April 17th Third Army had received orders to halt their eastward drive and turn south toward Munich. This drastic change called for extensive mapping of the Southern areas of Germany and the "Redoubt" area, which was in Bavaria between Salzburg and Berchtesgaden. It was believed that Hitler had planned for a strong last ditch stand of Nazi Germany here, and it was now Third Army's job to wreck it. In order to assist Third Army preparations for this campaign, the 31st Photo Squadron photographed several thousand square miles of Southern Germany in one week, beginning on April 17. The job was not without opposition and the Luftwaffe came up to try and upset the recce missions daily, and Lt. William Elliott was one of the first who had to untangle himself from an attack by a Me-262. Three days later on April 20, Lt. D.C. Davis must have felt the entire Luftwaffe had singled him out when he was jumped by 22 Me-109s near Nuremburg. Davis spotted the swarm of enemy fighters and climbed to evade them, but an unseen 109 sneaked in and shot his right engine out and his F-5 went into a steep dive trailing smoke and coolant. The enemy pilots apparently thought Davis was done for and didn't bother to follow him down, so he pulled out at low altitude and headed back to base and got to within 10 miles of Y-64 before his F-5 gave out and he had to jump. Lt. Davis' luck continued after hitting the ground when he was picked up almost immediately by an armored column and returned to base. The day did seem to be hexed for the 31st though, as two other F-5s' landing gear collapsed on landing, and a third had serious fuel tank troubles.

In spite of these troubles the 31st Squadron's missions were providing excellent intelligence for Third Army, and a couple of its pilots got real aggressive. On one mission Lt. Stanley Freeth spotted two enemy motor transports on the highway and buzzed them at truck top level, scaring one of the drivers so bad that he wrecked his truck. Claim: one motor transport damaged. The next day Freeth intercepted a lumbering Ju-52 transport on the deck and tried to force him in, but this time the Nazi would not be intimidated.

Bad weather on April 18 tended to limit some of the 15th TAC R's observation reports but it didn't seem to slow down their elimination of German war material. In his usual aggressive manner Clyde East led the attack against a column of motor transport he found for the fighter-bombers, destroying three trucks and a nearby locomotive personally.

At about the same time Henry Lacey was leading another fighter-bomber attack against another railroad siding and got a big bang out of it. The P-47s first hit the locomotive which exploded and set a number of crates afire, which in turn spread to a truck being unloaded and it exploded with such force that it leveled every building within a quarter mile radius, and buffeted all of the attacking aircraft.

While East and Lacey were taking care of the situation on the ground, Lts. Haylon Wood and Bob Jeffrey took care of the aerial chores when they were jumped by four FW-190s. They were at 8000 feet returning to base after weather had aborted their mission when they sighted two 190s at 6 o'clock low, and turned to meet the attack. Two other 190s were approaching as the section broke into firing position on the 190s tails, but they pressed the attack and Wood's fire smashed his target, causing the 190's landing gear to fall down and then the plane went into a steep dive. At this point he had to break off his attack because Lt. Jeffrey called out that his engine was cutting out and a 190 was on his tail. Instantly Wood pulled his Mustang up and on to the tail of Jeffrey's attacker, and when he opened fire at 200 feet, the Focke-Wulf simply broke apart under the impact of 50 caliber fire, spun in and exploded. Seeing this the other two FW-190s which had already been damaged by Lt. Jeffrey's guns turned and ran, freeing Wood and Jeffrey to return to base with a claim of one FW-190 destroyed, one probable, and two damaged, not bad results for an aborted mission.*

Third Army's last campaign began April 21 and was to a great extent a repetition of the battles of previous weeks, resistance at some points and large scale surrenders at other points. The rapid collapse of the German military was graphically illustrated during the first two days when Third Army captured over 24,000 prisoners of war, some of which were Russian and Hungarian troops, and at the same time its own casualty rate declined sharply. Clearly the end was now in sight.

The weather began to turn foul again during April 22 and 23rd and it gave the 10th time to prepare for its next and last wartime move. This time it was to Furth and as in the last two moves, the 15th TAC R led off. On April 24th it took a route that followed the Autobahn most of the way and led through the ruins of Nuremburg. Upon arrival they found a large airfield with more than enough buildings to accommodate the entire Group, and after a large cleanup job, the 15th was comfortably situated.

Also on the 24th, the Group's newly assigned TAC R squadron, the 162nd TAC R, flew its first missions as a part of the 10th Photo Reconnaissance Group. The 162nd had begun operational life as the 382nd Fighter Squadron of the 363rd Fighter Group, but as the need for more TAC R support was recognized the 363rd FG was redesignated as the 363rd Tactical Reconnaissance Group and was placed under the command of Colonel James Smelley who had been Deputy Commander of the 10th PRG. In October 1944, the 162nd was transferred to the Provisional

---

*During an interview with the author in June 1976, H. R. Wood stated that he was convinced that he shot the first 190 down and is somewhat bitter that he was not given credit for a confirmed kill. This controversy was to cost him the title of ace.

Reconnaissance Group of the 1st Tactical Air Force and served with them until joining the 10th. When the 162nd arrived it was commanded by Lt. Colonel Robert Ware who had also previously served with the 10th as a member of the 12th TAC R. Along with LTC. Ware the 10th also welcomed back several other of its former members, to include Captain Joe Waits, who had been with the 15th TAC R, and by now had five and a half victories and achieved ace status.

TAC R was quite busy on April 25th and the 15th TAC R dispatched 17 missions, all of which met with considerable success. Most of their reports concerned highway movement and many large columns were detected. Between Linz and Passau. Lt. Haylon Wood spotted over 800 motor transports and 200 horse drawn transports which he promptly reported to the roving P-47s. The day was not without loss though, as Lt. N. A. Thomas while flying his 96th mission, had to crash-land in German held territory between Kladrau and Bisschofsteinitz. He and Lt. Walsh had received heavy flak from an airfield and ten minutes later Walsh heard Thomas's "Mayday" and that his engine was damaged.

Lt. James Ray of the 12th TAC R evened the score when he clobbered a 109 near Regensburg. He and Lt. Wallace Mitchell were on a route recce when the 109 made a pass at them from 9 o'clock high but scored no hits on either Mustang. Ray quickly followed it into a dive and poured a burst from his fifties into the Messerschmitt's cockpit, then watched as it went into a slow roll and continued its dive into the ground. The pilot did not escape.

The 162nd TAC R was also up and checking airfields in the area, and Lts. Stanley Newman and Edward Panner recorded considerable airfield activity in their respective areas which was promptly reported to the fighter controller.

German aerial activity continued and during the next three days the Group kept adding to its scoreboard. On the 26th, a Me-109 and three FW-190Ds were set to bounce Lts. Charles White and Edmund Maxwell of the 15th TAC R when Maxwell spotted them and the section turned into them. That was enough for the 109 who immediately turned tail and ran, but the 190s kept coming and White gave one of them a long burst from 600 yards to 300 yards and saw pieces begin to fall off. Soon afterward the 190 did a wingover and went straight down trailing a thick column of smoke. Ed Maxwell then attached himself to the tail of another 190, laced the entire length of its fuselage with his guns and watched as it went straight down and exploded on impact.

Above: Lt. William O. Davenport, his crewchief, Sgt. Ernie Weiss and his F-6C. (W.O. Davenport) *Below:* En route to captivity Franz von Papen, Hitler's former vice chancellor and minister to Austria (in knickers) and his son (to his right) step from a C-47 at the 10th PRG's base, late spring 1945. Watching are (l. to r.) Maj. R.T. Simpson, unidentified M.P., Lt. Col. Richard Hibbert, Capt. John Hoefker, unknown and Lt. Col. Rudolph Walters. (J.H. Hoefker)

Officers and pilots of the 12th Tactical Reconnaissance Squadron at Furth, Germany, May 1945. (R. Little) Front row, l. to r.; Lt. W.R. Gardner, Lt. W.R. Koger, Lt. D.R. Lynch, Dr. W. Barone, O'Brien, Lt. E.T. Olson, Capt. E.L. Bishop, Maj. J. Florence (Sqdn. CO), Capt. Gilliam, Lt. D.M. Cartago, Lt. M.G. Strange, Lt. R.C. Little. Second row: Lt. W.O. Davenport, Lt. J.C. Kimler, Capt. Rider, Lt. W.F. Mitchell, Lt. A.C. Reed, F/O Williams, Lt. J.H. Ray, Lt. J.H. Nelson, Capt. R. Repass, Lt. R.E. Bruce, Lt. H.E. Ermatinger, Chapel. Third row: Lt. W.J Koplin, Lt. E.J. Kenny, Lt. H.T. Lefebure, Lt. Cannon, Lt. R. Bleau, Lt. R.K. Marpel, Lt. J.R. Ellis, Lt. G.W. Miller, Lt. R.L. Worrell, Lt. D.H. Shimon, Lt. R.E. Peek, Lt. M.L. Elliott.

Lt. Robert C. Little, 12th TAC R Squadron (above), who scored the last aerial victory in the ETO, May 8, 1945, at 2000 hours, and his Mustang (below). (R. C. Little)

Above: One of three Junkers Ju-87 Stukas that surrendered to the 10th Photo Recon Group at Furth, Germany. This one is coded L; it has a yellow nose band and rudder and must have been used for night missions as it has flame dampers on the exhaust stack. (R. Gaudette) *Below:* Wrecked German aircraft were found at the outskirts of Furth airfield. In the photo are a He-111, two Ju-87 Stukas, three FW-190s, two Bf-109s and a Ju-88. (W.O. Davenport)

Outstanding Mission—Strange Ending

Next day Lts. Bob Ober and Fairfield Goodale continued the scoring when they shared a Messerschmitt 109, but the day's honors went to Lt. Haylon R. Wood who knocked down two Stukas and shared a third with his wingman Lt. Maxwell Chambers. The events of the mission are recalled by Lt. Wood as follows:

"My wingman, Lt. Chambers, and I had been assigned the mission of checking the area south of Munich, a valley leading to the Brenner Pass. Our intelligence had some reason to believe that the Germans were establishing a redoubt in that area. The mission was uneventful until we were emerging from the pass just west of Munich and suddenly a fighter pilot's dream unfolded some 2000 feet to my front at 6000 feet altitude heading in the opposite direction—three Stukas. Two were in close formation and one some 500 feet aside. In great anticipation of 'shooting ducks on the pond' I seemed breathless, but I could hear myself on the radio instructing my wingman, 'pull in close, three Stukas at 12 o'clock low, 2000 feet below us.' As I pushed my Mustang into a dive I was still talking into the RT, 'Take it easy son, just stay tucked in, don't fire until I do, and take dead aim.' I opened fire at 300 yards and the lead Stuka exploded into flame and crashed into the ground. Pulling up from the dive we throttled back, dropped 30 degrees of flaps and started slowing our airspeed to 190 MPH in order to set up for the big kill. Actually I was enraptured by this prospect and possibly a bit incoherent, but this was really something. Although I had shot down two German fighters previously, each one in a rough and tough dogfight, this seemed to be the end of a fighter pilot's dream—that of becoming an ace if I destroyed these three.

"I continued the monologue as we turned in a decreasing speed arc of 180 degrees, 'Easy now Chambers, move out just a little bit, check your gunsights—don't skid—don't get too close—don't panic—this is our day Hoss!!' We leveled out approximately 2000 feet behind them at only slightly overtaking speed, and at approximately 1000 feet with my gunsight centered on the head of the unsuspecting tail-gunner, I pressed the trigger. The stream of tracers from the fifties poured directly into the area in which they were aimed. I recall expressing or thinking a little thanks to the armament crew that adjusted my guns. At 1000 feet all guns were supposed to fire into a one foot circle, providing you weren't slipping. Every bullet was quite obviously finding its mark. Numerous pieces of the canopy were blasted away, and the Stuka appeared to go limp, sliding off in an uncontrolled turn and smashing into the side of a nearby mountain. After breaking off from this encounter, I found the third Stuka diving for the deck and chased him down. After a chase around church steeples, crags etc. which lasted about 10 minutes, I opened fire and saw pieces fall away and it began smoking just as I pulled up. At this point Chambers hit it with a long burst and it began smoking badly, then I hit it with another long burst and just as my guns emptied the crew of the Stuka jettisoned their canopy. Suddenly from an altitude of no more than 100 feet the pilot pulled straight up, and as I side-slipped to avoid hitting him I could almost see the color of the tail-gunner's eyes as he crouched in his seat, about to jump. I thought aloud, 'you poor devil, don't bail out at that altitude.' But bail out they did. One chute opened fully apparently, and I observed its occupant scurry into the nearby woods. The other chute opened only partially, and I'm quite sure the flyer attached to it was killed. A photo taken by my vertical camera later revealed what appeared to be—or obviously was—a chute and a body sprawled on the ground.

"The last Stuka down after a hectic chase, Chambers and I headed homeward. Serene and smug, I was about to suggest that we do three practice slow rolls in preparation for our pre-landing pass over the base. My plans were rather abruptly changed when I noticed considerable smoke in the cockpit. Panic—ask any pilot who has experienced it. I immediately made preparations to bail out, but observing my instruments were all in the green and that my engine was purring like a kitten, I informed Chambers and asked him to move in and around me to observe any evidence of fire. His reply was in the negative, so I cracked open the canopy and the smoke rather quickly disappeared. All appeared normal from there until the landing approach. I had somewhat perfected an approach, peel-off and landing demonstrated to me by Bob Shively, the best P-51 pilot I've ever known—with the exception of John Hoefker. On the approach we dived to a speed of approximately 325 mph, and instantly upon the peel-off break we hit the throttle, gear, and flaps almost simultaneously, racking it on the brink of a high-speed stall, the landing gear went up midway through the small, tight turn. I say up because the position of the plane was almost upside down. The flaps ordinarily came down just prior to the final approach, but on this occasion I quickly realized that I was not slowing down—slipping didn't help—and I zoomed over the strip at approximately 175-200 MPH—landing approach speed was about 125 MPH. I climbed out and checked for gear down, gear was down and locked, but no flaps was confirmed. I made the next approach somewhat like a cautious rookie, and at that, I had to do a considerable jockeying around of breaks and throttle considering the rather short landing strip. What had happened to my hydraulic pressure to cause flap malfunction? The engineers found that the hydraulic slipjoint in the belly of the fuselage had exceeded its limits and practically all of the fluid had been lost. We determined that it happened while I was chasing the Stukas and had come face to face with a pyramid-like formation some 500 feet high and because I was flying on the deck I had to rack it in so tight that I grayed out, narrowly averting a snap-roll and spin at 1000 feet. The abrupt and sustained pullout had literally disfigured the P-51 to the extent that the slip-joint had exceeded its limits and had "hung-up" and failed to return to the normal position. Needless to say it was a hair-raising ending to an exciting mission."*

Weather again limited missions throughout the remainder of April, but Lt. Wood was able to bring back some photos of Moosburg prisoner of war camp and he reported that its inmates were trying to signal him by use of panels. Lts. Tom Davis, Leland Larson, and Merlin Reed of the 15th TAC R also led some successful fighter-bomber attacks on retreating columns of Germans and returned with reports that continued to keep hopes high that the end was in sight. With these hopes in mind, the 15th TAC R historian ended his monthly report with the following: "The month ended on a note of hope and expectancy. The men were fully aware of the significance of the tremendous advances that had been made, saw the end in sight, and awaited with gnawing impatience for the announcement of Germany's unconditional surrender."

May 1945 began with the myth of the "National Redoubt" exploded and Hitler dead, and on May 1st, the Third Army began another three pronged attack. Its northern thrust was toward eastern Germany, its eastward assault was into Czechoslovakia, and its southern spearhead headed into the Austrian Alps. Attacking on a 140 mile wide front Third Army units met some fierce opposition, but poor roads and rough terrain were its main obstacles.

The final collapse of the Wehrmacht began on May 2nd when the Commander-in-Chief of all German forces in Italy surrendered and

---

* Incredibly enough Lt. Haylon Wood was nearly court-martialed for the destruction of these Stukas. Only a few days before the encounter, XIXth TAC Headquarters, becoming upset with the number of encounters that TAC R pilots had become involved in, issued orders that TAC R pilots were not fighter pilots and should avoid combat in order to complete their mission of reconnaissance. Fortunately for Lt. Wood his Group CO, Colonel Russ Berg, was a little more realistic and objective about the matter, and let Wood off with a "reprimand."

gathered momentum on May 3rd and 4th when German troops in Holland and northwest Germany, Denmark and the Frisian Island chain surrendered.

During these operations the 10th's TAC R pilots took the opportunity of getting in a few last punches at its faltering foe and scored both in the air and on the ground. On May 3rd Lts. Henry Lacey and Wayne Patrick were contacted by the pilot of a liaison plane that a four man Panzerfaust and machine-gun team was holding up the advance of a US column, and immediately located and strafed the team, killing all four of the German defenders and allowing the column to resume its advance. Next day F/O Robert Roper and Lt. Glen Gremillion of the 162nd TAC R caught a cream-colored JU-88 eight miles northeast of Linz, Austria, and Gremillion destroyed it without firing a shot. Here is his report:

"On May 4 while running a visual recce in the Linz area I spotted a twin-engined aircraft flying at 2 o'clock at about 1000 feet. I was at 10,000 feet and turned and lost a little altitude to identify the plane. As I came closer I recognized it as a Ju-88. It had black crosses on the wings and a swastika on the tail. Apparently the Ju-88 identified me as enemy because he cut his switches and attempted to belly-land. He crashed in an open field, completely destroying his aircraft, and without a doubt killing the whole crew. The Ju-88 burned for only a short time, and I did not fire at him. I took pictures of the crash. I claim 1 JU-88 destroyed."

On May 5th, Patton's 16th Armored Division liberated Pilsen, Czechoslovakia, home of the famous beer, and requisitioned huge quantities of the golden beverage for the celebration. Also that day they took the surrender of their old foe, the 11th Panzer Division. On May 6th word came down that the new Nazi leader, Admiral Doenitz, was negotiating final surrender, and now about all there was to do was wait.

Roundup in the Sky

May 8th, the final day of the war in Europe, was to become one of the most incredible days in the Group's operational history. Its TAC R pilots spent most of the day as aerial cowboys rounding up surrendering German aircraft and escorting them to Furth. The 15th TAC R's day went like this: Bill Brackett and Floyd Lofland escorted a AR-96 training plane to Ronecken airfield while the German in the back seat waved a white handkerchief. Lts. Dick McFadden and Bob Shively had a field day when they met three FW-190s, 3 Me-109s, a Ju-88 and a Ju-188. They led one of the 190s to a small field where they and the 190 landed, saw to it that the pilot, Sergeant Herbert Skowranek and his passenger who had ridden in the radio compartment were handed over to the Engineer unit on the field, then took off and escorted one more 190 and two bombers to R-43. After seeing these down they escorted the remaining four enemy fighters to Furth.

When Bob Jeffrey and Julian Biniewski tried to escort an Me-109 to the base, it broke into the section and made a pass at Jeffrey, but he countered and scored hits on the 109 with a deflection shot. Then Lt. Biniewski closed and clobbered it with two long bursts.

On the 15th TAC R's last mission of the day Leland Larson and George Schroeder had a similar experience with two FW-190s. This time they managed to destroy both planes without firing a single shot. The section approached the 190s with the intention of escorting them to Furth, but the 190s took hostile action and the section reacted. Lt. Schroeder followed one of them to the deck and chased it until the Focke-Wulf crashed into some trees, and Larson fastened himself on to the tail of the other. The Focke-Wulf dived to 500 feet, made a tight turn to the left—too tight—snapped into a spin and crashed and burned. The only shots fired were those by the FW-190s in their first and only offensive action of the encounter, which scored a single hit on Schroeder's left wing.

The 162nd TAC R's historian recorded the day and his squadron's part in it as follows; "Tuesday, May 8, 1945 was by all means the strangest day in nearly seventeen months. The whole German Air Force went out to return to its old bases and give up to the Yanks, with nearly twenty planes and thirty people landing at R-28 alone, all herded in by the pilots from the 12th, 15th, or 162nd, who found them willing prisoners in most cases. The first, an Me-109 was forced in by Lt. Stanley Newman and Lt. Manuel Geiger about noon. From then on 109s, 190s and Stukas drifted in incessantly, wagging their wings, and swerving off the runway after they were down. There must have been 1000 men on the field, waiting to pick up pistols and get a look at these planes. Our second capture was made by Lt. Ray Conley and Captain Elvin Young, a 190; the third by Lts. Geiger and Stanley Newman, a Siebel 104; and last, another 190 by Lts. George Alm and Frank Seely. This last one was a recalcitrant who first made a fast break which was cut off by a faster pursuit and a few rounds along the German's fuselage; but then, coming in, he pulled up his gear on the runway and settled there, making it necessary for Lt. Alm to wait around in the dark with a low gas tank before the runway was clear. In all this we netted four planes and about a dozen prisoners for the 162nd. Two of the planes, a 109 and a 190, will be turned over to Engineering for keepsakes.

There were three other noteworthy missions, one routine and two special. The first, with Lt. Manuel Geiger and Lt. Stanley Newman (who flew three missions on the 8th) shooting down two FW-190s in Czechloslavkia, each claiming one. They were jumped by the 190s six miles southeast of Bischofteinitz. The section quickly broke into the 190s, who immediately headed for the deck. Lt. Newman and Lt. Geiger followed their respective 190s down, and the enemy planes began rolling back and forth and reversing their turns. Newman fired a four second burst, observed hits all over the 190's tail section and watched as the E/A continued on down and crashlanded. While this encounter was taking place Lt. Geiger bested the second 190 and sent it down. Both downed aircraft were photographed for confirmation.

The two special missions were repeats of missions flown on the 7th over the POW camps at Lienz, Spittal, Klagenfurt, Wulfsburg, and Liebnitz. Lts. Conrad Wright and John Goodrich flew the first and Goodrich was forced to land on a enemy airfield near Graz after his engine was hit by flak. (After he landed at Graz the Germans took away his .45 pistol, but then decided they were doing it all wrong, gave him his own weapon as well as theirs, and he took over. All of them took off to the nearest American unit, and Lt. Goodrich presented the station complement to be interned. He then returned to Furth on May 13th. The second mission, which was flown by Lts. Russell Scara and Ronald Olson, was uneventful and they returned with excellent photos of the camps.

In the spirit of the occasion the pilots of the 12th TAC R escorted in their fair share of the surrendering Luftwaffe too. Lts. Dale Shimon and E.J. O'Brien forced their FW-190 D to land at Linz, Lt. Don Lynch forced another to land at R-28 and Lts. Ed Kenny and Robert Marple forced a third FW-190 into a belly-landing, but the squadron honors of the day went to Lt. Robert C. Little, for it was he who scored the last aerial victory of the European Theatre. He and Lt. Wallace Mitchell were patrolling along the Danube when the section was jumped by five FW-190s. They managed to evade the attack and got in behind the 190s, and Lt. Little lined up on one of them and sent it crashing to earth at 2000 hours, May 8, 1945.

Four hours after Lt. Little's victory it was all over in Europe and the 10th Photo Reconnaissance Group's World War II combat days were over. In its fourteen months of combat operations it established and maintained a record of excellence second to none, and certainly earned its slogan of "FIRST ON D-DAY—LAST ON V.E. DAY."

Appendixes

1. Aircraft and Tactics

TAC R

Tactical Reconnaissance pilots in the 10th Photo Reconnaissance Group operated the photo version of the P-51 Mustang, designated the F-6. The comparative F-6 designation to the fighter version is as follows:

> F-6B—P-51A
> F-6C—P-51B/C
> F-6D—P-51D
> F-6K—P-51K

The basic difference between the fighter and the reconnaissance version was the installation of cameras in the fuselage section. Unlike the unarmed photo version of the P-38, the F-6 retained the full four or six gun armament carried by the P-51. And although he was ordered to avoid combat whenever possible, the TAC R pilot could defend himself against enemy aircraft.

For vertical photography the F-6 normally carried the K-22 camera with a 12-inch cone, which could turn out excellent, finely detailed photos from an altitude of 6,000 feet, or the K-17 with a 6-inch cone, which was used for altitudes of 3,500 feet. The K-17 was later replaced by a 6-inch version of the K-22 that provided a two-second rewind cycle for overlap coverage at low altitude.

For missions that required oblique photography the F-6 carried either the K-24 camera, which had a 7-inch or 14-inch cone, or a K-22 with a 12-inch cone. The K-24 was used for low-altitude oblique coverages of railway runnels, cuts, and bridges. These photos were useful in briefing fighter-bomber pilots for attacking such facilities.

The K-22 camera was used for taking Merton Gridded Oblique Photos. These photos were generally taken at altitudes ranging from 2,500–4,000 feet and from an angle of 12–17 degrees. These gridded photos were quite valuable to both artillery commanders and field commanders in planning barrages or assaults.

TAC R Missions and Tactics

The normal TAC R mission consisted of a two-plane flight called a *section* with the more experienced pilot acting as section leader. The leader or number one pilot was responsible for navigation and for observing or photographing the target zone, while it was the number two man's responsibility to provide protection against air attack and warning against flak. The number two man always flew approximately 200 yards to the immediate flank of the leader and down sun from him so that the leader's tail was always covered toward the sun, from where the German attacks generally came.

For visual recce missions the section usually flew between 3,500 and 6,000 feet, although TAC R photo missions sometimes ran higher. The visual recce was limited to a maximum of 6,000 feet, because beyond that the ground cannot be discerned in sufficient detail. Many times it was necessary to go below 3,500 feet to make specific observations, such as the cargo of a particular train.

Tactical reconnaissance is generally broken down into the following types of missions:

Area Search This type of mission was flown to provide the commanding general of an army area with immediate information on the movement and disposition of troops within its boundaries and along its front. The area covered consisted of all territory within the army boundaries to a depth of approximately 100 miles beyond its front line. Because the area was so large it was usually subdivided into smaller areas of 650 square miles; and an area of this size could be completely covered by one section in an hour. Before the section took off on this type of mission it was thoroughly briefed on the situation by an army ground liaison officer and was given a few specific points to check in addition to the area coverage.

Route Recce This type of mission normally was a visual recce of rail lines and highways to a depth of at least 200 miles behind enemy lines to determine the enemy's supply routes and to note its troop movements.

Artillery Adjustment This mission normally consisted of TAC R pilots adjusting the fire of long range artillery (155mm guns to 8-inch howitzers) in areas where light aircraft such as L-4s or L-5s could not operate safely. These missions were either planned with the use of photos of targets or run at any time by a ground station requesting information from a TAC R aircraft about targets in the area in which it operated.

Merton Oblique Photo Cover These missions were normally flown after a specific request from the artillery commander of a given area, and the gridded photos were used in planning fields of fire for his guns.

Photographic Missions Under certain conditions—such as a 4,000-foot ceiling or a penetration in excess of 150 miles—it was impractical to send the unarmed F-5 to take high altitude photos. TAC R aircraft were used for these missions.

When it operated both of its TAC R squadrons the 10th Photo Reconnaissance Group could complete approximately 30 missions a day. A breakdown of a typical day's operations is as follows:

> 20 Area Searches
> 4 Route Recces
> 2 Merton Obliques
> 4 Artillery Adjustments

Photo Reconnaissance

The Photo Recce squadrons assigned to the 10th PRG used the F-5, which was the camera version of the P-38 Lightning. Unlike the P-51s of the TAC R squadrons the F-5s were not armed, and pilots flying single-plane missions in F-5s had to rely on altitude, speed, or evasive action for protection. The F-5s normally ranged 100–150 miles from their bases, but at times (on airfield coverage for example) they went as deep as 250–275 miles. The comparative F-4/5 designation to the fighter version is as follows:

> F-4—P-38E
> F-4A—P-38F
> F-5A/B—P-38G
> F-5C—P-38H
> F-5E/F—P-38J
> F-5E/G—P-38L

The standard F-5 camera installation consisted of two 24-inch cameras, either the K-17 or the K-22, with a 7° side-lap. Most variations of this were simply the substitution of cameras of longer focal length for extreme high-altitude work, or 12-inch or shorter focal length cameras when the ceiling was too low for the twenty-four inch or when the special dicing mission was being flown.

For the dicing missions, such as those flown over the Normandy area, the F-5s carried a 12-inch focal length nose camera tilted downward at a 10° angle, and two 6-inch focal length oblique cameras, one on each side, aimed slightly forward from right angles to the aircraft's line of flight. This gave an uninterrupted coverage of more than 180°. (See illustration of camera installation on page 180.)

To provide the Army with 1:10,000 scale photographs with a camera of 24-inch lens, the F-5 pilots normally flew at 24,000 feet. At times they operated as high as 35,000 feet using a 40-inch lens. On many high priority missions when weather conditions prohibited high altitude photography, straight-line courses were flown at 6,000 feet using 6-inch cameras that produced 1:12,000 scale photos. Later 12-inch cameras were designed that could be operated as low as 5,000 feet; however, these missions were kept to a minimum since light flak at this altitude was murderous. When photos were extremely urgent or low-level closeups were required, the 10th's F-5 pilots would use the *dicing* technique. For dicing photos they would make a high-speed pass over the target area at about 50 feet and depart before any flak gunners would normally have time to react.

Photo Reconnaissance missions are generally divided into the following types:

Strips and Mosaics These missions involved photographing an entire battle zone and areas of proposed operations, lines of communications, and areas of "no-man's land."

Pinpoints These missions involved photographing specific targets such as airfields, bridges, marshalling yards, roads, gun positions, and command posts.

Front Line Coverage This was the detailed photography of the immediate front line areas to determine enemy defenses, gun positions, priority targets, and the like, and was usually performed daily.

Bomb Damage Assessment These missions involved photographing targets a few minutes after they were bombed in order to determine the extent of damage.

Night Photo Reconnaissance

The 155th Night Photo Reconnaissance Squadron used the F-3, the camera version of the A-20J Havoc, with a crew consisting of pilot, navigator, and aerial gunner. Flown were single-plane missions involving up to 400 miles of flying. At first the F-3s were armed with twin 50-caliber machine guns in the top turret, but these were later replaced by a tail-warning device that rang a bell in the pilot's cockpit if an aircraft approached him from the rear. If a "bogey" approached, the F-3's only defense was violent evasive action.

The biggest problem for the night flying F-3s was navigation, and of all the systems tried, the GEE system was the most successful. Because of the problems of navigation, attack from flak (both German and Allied) and night fighters, night photo missions were a costly effort in terms of both men and equipment. Personnel casualties exceeded 30 percent, and 100 percent of the aircraft used were either damaged or destroyed by the end of the war. But the significance of their work seemed to make the effort worthwhile.

Later in the war Microwave Early Warning was used to check areas for enemy aircraft prior to a mission, and in some incidences the F-3s were escorted by P-61 night fighters. But even with close coordination with Allied antiaircraft batteries the dangers of AA fire and navigation were never completely eliminated.

The F-3s were equipped with one of two different types of camera equipment and flew two different types of missions: pinpoint and strip photo runs.

F-3 s equipped with the D-2 Flash Unit—or the Edgerton Lamp, as it was more commonly called—operated at between 2,000 and 3,000 feet and used a K-19 or a K-29 camera with a 12-inch lens. This camera, which could make 180 exposures, was synchronized with the powerful Edgerton Lamp that discharged a light of 200,000,000 candlepower intensity every three seconds during the photo run and produced photos of excellent quality.

F-3s equipped with the M-46 flash bomb system operated at between 6,000 and 10,000 feet and carried two 12-inch cameras. In this system, the F-3 carried ten M-46 flash bombs that ignited by a set fuse at a given time after release. The 800,000,000-candlepower light generated by the flash bombs tripped the camera through a photoelectric cell.

Dicing Missions

The extremely low-level missions flown by the 10th Photo Reconnaissance Group over the Normandy beaches in May 1944 and later over the Seine and Moselle river areas became known as "Dicing Missions." The term "dicing" is a British slang expression for an extremely dangerous or risky mission, i.e., throwing the dice against death. The name was appropriately applied, since these missions involved quite a bit of risk to the pilots.

Over Normandy's beaches the missions were flown at an average altitude of 25 feet and always during low tide, when the broadest area of the beaches could be seen and the maximum number of German obstacles would be exposed to the camera's eye.

The pilots would fly from Chalgrove, England at minimum altitude to their respective zones of the coastline and turn to make the camera run. Usually the beaches were centered with the land to the pilot's left and the Channel to his right. Then the pilot would push his throttle all the way forward, set the cameras at "run away speed," and head over the beach at approximately 375 miles per hour. With the nose camera and the oblique cameras filming simultaneously with overlapping coverage, broad coverage of the target area could be obtained in one pass.

Shown here is an artist's conception of Lt. G.A. York's "Dicing Mission" that graphically illustrates the above.

Left: This artist's conception shows Lt. G. A. York's dicing mission over the beach at Normandy. (B. Rosen) Below: 5M-M of the 15th TAC R Squadron seen at Furth, Germany with an under-wing camera mounted in a modified drop-tank. (R. Gaudette)

Above left: Vertical photo of a camouflaged German airfield taken by Lt. John F. Miefert, 15th TAC R Squadron. (J. Miefert) *Above right:* Usual location of the oblique camera on the F-6C was just behind the cockpit. (J. Hoefker) *Below:* Later models had an oblique camera located in the rear of the fuselage, as can be seen in the black band under the rear portion of the national insignia. (R. Dawson)

Right: This camera is a vertical 40-inch cone used for large-scale photo reconnaissance pinpoints over strategic targets from as high as 35,000 feet. Pinpoints involved photographing specific targets such as airfields, bridges, marshalling yards, gun positions, and command posts. (Air Force Museum)

Below left: Vertical camera ports on an F-5E. This aircraft is slightly different as it has two camera ports rather than the three used on earlier versions. In the front port is a vertical 6-inch K-16 camera. (Air Force Museum)

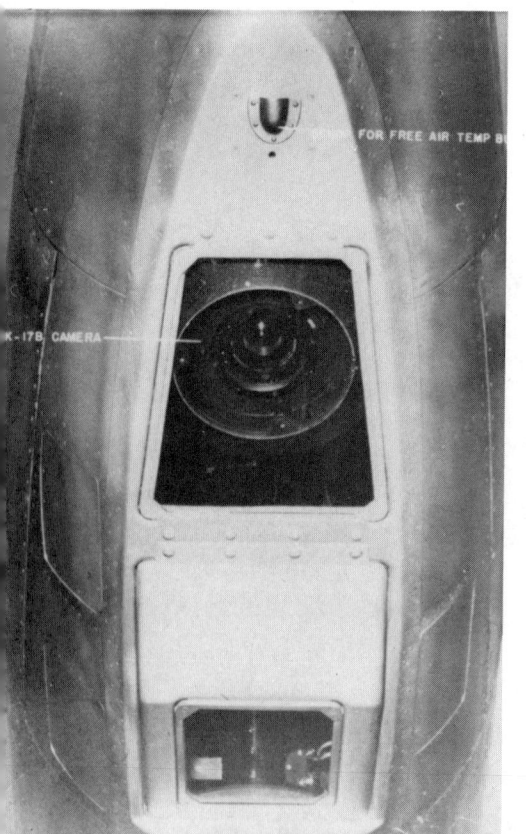

Below: The vertical camera in a Mustang. It was mounted between the tail wheel doors and the rear air scoop. The flap, which is shown in the open position, closes during takeoffs and landings to protect the lens from dust and mud. (Air Force Museum)

Split Vertical Photography in the F-5B.

Typical camera layout in an F-5 outfitted for split vertical photography. The 24" focal length K-22 cameras were mounted in tandem, with the first camera mounted over the number 2 or middle port and the second camera mounted over the number 3 port. The front camera was angled to the right and the second to the left to photograph a wider area.

The cameras as if facing the F-5's nose illustrating how this arrangement greatly increased the coverage of each photo run.

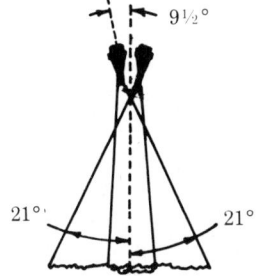

An F-5 modified by the 33rd Photo Squadron for dicing missions. Note "Dicing" camera port in the nose and the oblique camera port on the left side. (USAF via J. Ethell)

Dicing Installation

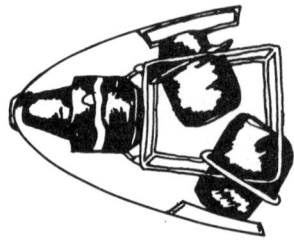

The camera arrangement used on "dicing" missions. It consisted of a 12" focal length nose camera tilted downward at a 10 degree angle and two 6" focal length oblique cameras, one on each side, aimed slightly forward from right angles to the aircraft's line of flight. This gave uninterrupted coverage of more than 180 degrees. Below: An F-5B fuselage showing oblique camera port.

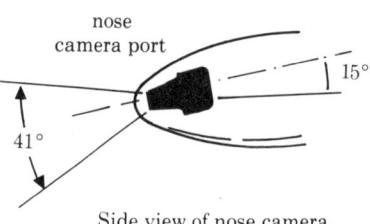

Side view of nose camera.

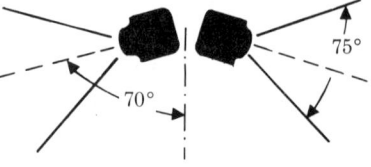

Rear view of the 26" oblique cameras.

An F-5 modified by the 33rd Photo Squadron for dicing missions. Note oblique camera port.

Diagram of night photography using the M-46 flash bomb for illumination of its target.

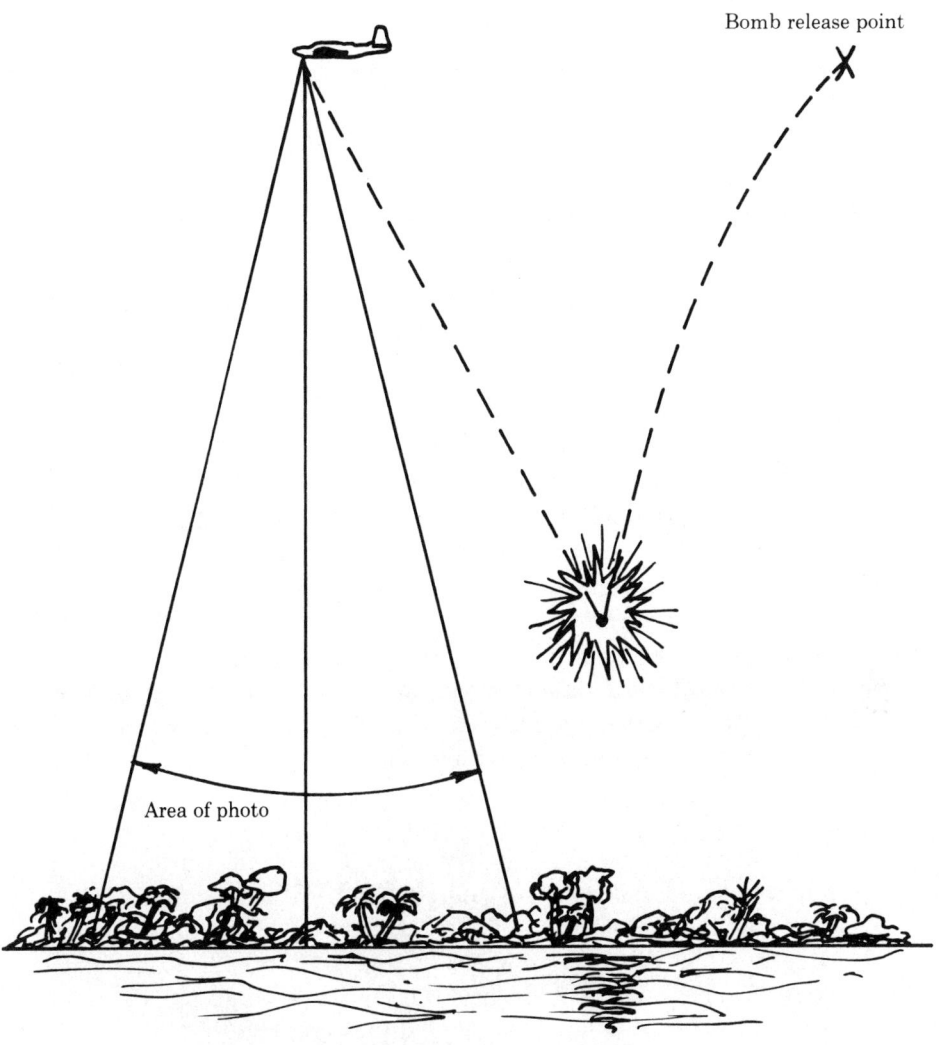

This diagram shows the principle of night photography. The photo-bomb explodes behind the plane and a photo-electric cell works the camera. (K. Gibbs)

2. Low Altitude Flights
Distinguished Unit Citation

HEADQUARTERS
NINTH AIR FORCE

APO 606, US Army
19 Jan 1945
GENERAL ORDERS
NUMBER 13

BATTLE HONORS

Under the provisions of Section IV, Circular No. 333, WD, 1943, the following named unit of the Ninth Air Force is cited for outstanding performance of duty in action against the enemy. The citation reads as follows:

"*The 10th Photographic Reconnaissance Group*. For extraordinary performance of duty in action against the enemy from 6 May to 20 May 1944. *The 10th Photographic Reconnaissance Group* was charged with the heavy responsibility of furnishing vitally important photographs of the beaches on the Continent upon which the Allied Forces subsequently landed on 6 June 1944. In order to insure that the requisite photographs were of such quality and scale that beach and shore defenses could be studied minutely for the briefing and training of assault troops it was necessary that the extremely low level oblique photographs be obtained at minimum altitude. Employing specially modified equipment installed in unarmed P-38 type aircraft, the intrepid pilots of the *10th Photographic Reconnaissance Group* gallantly undertook the most hazardous missions. Flying unarmed and unescorted at an altitude as low as twenty-five feet, they fearlessly piloted their aircraft over the difficult photographic runs in the face of intense fire from some of the strongest antiaircraft installations in Western Europe. Despite the great difficulties and dangers involved in the execution of these missions of the highest priority, *the 10th Photographic Reconnaissance Group* was successful in obtaining excellent photographs of the coastal defenses from Blankenbergne to Dunkerque and from Le Touquet to St. Vaast la Hougue. The extraordinary skill, fortitude, and gallant devotion to duty demonstrated by the airmen of *the 10th Photographic Reconnaissance Group* in the brilliant

discharge of this exacting assignment reflects the highest credit upon the organization and are in keeping with the finest traditions of the Army Air Forces."
By command of Major General Vandenburg
W.W. Milliard
Colonel, GSC
C of S
OFFICIAL

Group Pilots Making Low-Altitude Missions, May 6–May 20, 1945

30th Photo Reconnaissance Squadron:

Capt. William D. Mitchell	May 7
1st Lt. Donald F. Thompson	May 19
1st Lt. Joseph E. Smith	May 20

31st Photo Reconnaissance Squadron:

1st Lt. Merritt G. Garner	May 19
1st Lt. Rufus Woody	May 19
1st Lt. Fred F. Hayes	May 7
(KIA on his dicing mission)	
1st Lt. James M. Poole	May 20
1st Lt. Robert M. Holbury	May 20
2nd Lt. Albert Lanker	May 6

34th Photo Reconnaissance Squadron:

2nd Lt. Garland A. York	May 19
2nd Lt. Allen R. Keith	May 20

3. Group Organizational Changes

September 1941
73rd Observation Group
Headquarters activated

November 1941
HQ 73rd Observation Group
HQ & HQ Squadron
12th Observation Squadron
16th Observation Squadron
22nd Observation Squadron
91st Observation Squadron

3. Group Organizational Changes (cont'd.)

January 1942
HQ 73rd Observation Group
HQ & HQ Squadron
16th Observation Squadron
22nd Observation Squadron
91st Observation Squadron

July 1942
HQ 73rd Observation Group
15th Observation Squadron
28th Observation Squadron
91st Observation Squadron

April 1943
HQ 73rd Reconnaissance Group
14th Liaison Squadron
15th Reconnaissance Squadron (Fighter)
28th Reconnaissance Squadron (Bomber)
91st Reconnaissance Squadron (Fighter)

August 1943
HQ 73rd Tactical Reconnaissance Group
15th Tactical Reconnaissance Squadron
28th Tactical Reconnaissance Squadron
152nd Tactical Reconnaissance Squadron

November 1943
HQ 73rd Tactical Reconnaissance Group
15th Tactical Reconnaissance Squadron

December 1943
73rd TAC Reconnaissance Group
redesignated as
HQ 10th Photo Group (Recon)

February 1944
HQ 10th Photo Reconnaissance Group
30th Photo Squadron

March 1944
HQ 10th Photo Reconnaissance Group
30th Photo Squadron
31st Photo Squadron
34th Photo Squadron

3. Group Organizational Changes (cont'd.)

April 1944
HQ 10th Photo Reconnaissance Group
30th Photo Squadron
31st Photo Squadron
33rd Photo Squadron
34th Photo Squadron

June 1944 (late)
31st Photo Squadron
33rd Photo Squadron
34th Photo Squadron
155th Night Photo Squadron
15th Tactical Reconnaissance Squadron
12th TAC R Squadron (detached)

August 1944
HQ 10th Photo Reconnaissance Group
12th TAC R Squadron
15th TAC R Squadron
31st Photo Squadron
34th Photo Squadron
155th Night Photo Squadron

October 1944
HQ 10th Photo Reconnaissance Squadron
12th TAC R Squadron
15th TAC R Squadron
31st Photo Squadron
155th Night Photo Squadron

February 1945
HQ 10th Photo Reconnaissance Group
12th TAC R Squadron
15th TAC R Squadron
31st Photo Squadron

April 1945
HQ 10th Photo Reconnaissance Group
12th TAC R Squadron
15th TAC R Squadron
162nd TAC R Squadron
31st Photo Squadron

4. Group Aces

Capt. Clyde B. East, 15th Tactical Reconnaissance Squadron—13
    June 6, 1944—1 FW-190
    Dec. 17, 1944—1 Me-109
    March 15, 1945—1 Me-109
    March 24, 1945—2 Me-109
    March 27, 1945—2 Me-109
    April 4, 1945—1½ (1 Me-109, ½ Ju-188
            shared with L.A. Larson)
    April 8, 1945—3½ (2 Ju-87, 1 FH-104,
            ½ He-111 shared with L.A. Larson)
    April 13, 1945—1 Me-109

Capt. John H. Hoefker, 15th Tactical Reconnaissance Squadron—10½
    June 7, 1944—1 Me-109
    June 20, 1944—1 Me-109
    June 29, 1944—1 Me-109
    Nov. 19, 1944—1 FW-190
    Dec. 17, 1944—3½ (2 Me-109, 1 FW-190,
            ½ Ju-188 shared with C.D. White)
    March 31, 1945—1 HS-126
    April 8, 1945—1 He-111
    April 10, 1945—1 FW-190

Lt. Leland A. Larson, 15th Tactical Reconnaissance Squadron—6
    March 21, 1945—1 FW-190
    March 24, 1945—1 Me-109
    March 27, 1945— ½ Me-109 (shared with W. Patrick)
    March 28, 1945—½ Me-109 (shared with R. Landers)
    April 4, 1945—½ Ju-188 (shared with C.B. East)
    April 8, 1945—1½ (1 Ju-87, ½ He-111 shared with C.B. East
    May 8, 1945—1 FW-190

Capt. Joe Waits, 162nd Tactical Reconnaissance Squadron—5½
    July 15, 1944—2 Me-109 (scored with 15th TAC R Sqdn)
    March 18, 1945—2 Me-109
    March 19, 1945—1 Me-109
    April 11, 1945—½ U/I S/E trainer (possible AT-6)
            (shared with R. Knudson)

Aces of the 10th Photo Reconnaissance Group here and following page. Above: Capt. Clyde B. East, 15th TAC R Squadron and his F-6D "Lil Margaret" (insert) at Furth. With thirteen victories, East was the top-ranked recce ace in the ETO (H.E. Lewis) Below: Capt. John H. Hoefker, 15th TAC R Squadron, ten and one-half victories was recce's number two ace in the ETO. (J.H. Hoefker)

Aces of the 10th Photo Reconnaissance Group, continued. Right: Lt. Leland A. Larson, 15th TAC R Squadron, six victories. (L. Larson via W. Hess) Below: Capt. Joe Waits, 162nd TAC R Squadron, five and a half victories. Two of Waits's victories were scored while he was with the 15th TAC R Squadron. (J. Williams)

5. Aerial Victories by Group TAC R Squadrons*

12th TAC R Victories

Pilot	Destroyed	Probable	Damaged
Lt. Mingo V. Logothetis	4	0	3
Lt. Ronald R. Ricci	3	0	½
Lt. John R. Ellis	3	0	0
Lt. M. Leo Elliott	1½	0	0
Lt. Leon Canady	1½	0	0
Lt. Robert Bruce	1½	0	1
Lt. William Lacey	1	0	0
Lt. H.W. Dieckman	1	0	0
Lt. William R. Gardner	1	0	0
Lt. William Winberry	1	0	0
Lt. Henry Ermatinger	1	0	0
Lt. William O. Davenport	1	0	½
Lt. J.K. Rhodes	1	0	0
Lt. J.H. Ray	1	0	0
Lt. Jacob Piatt	1	0	0
Lt. Robert C. Little	1	0	0
Lt. M.E. Strange	½	0	0
Lt. J.C. Kimber	½	0	0
Lt. D. M. Cartago	½	0	0
Lt. John Tillett	0	1	0
Lt. L.R. Leonard	0	1	0
Lt. William Enneis	0	0	1
Totals	26	2	6

Note: 10th Photo Recon Group Headquarters records indicate the 12th's unofficial record as 26—3—10. However, Squadron records were sketchy and the author could not document the missing scores.

15th TAC R Victories

Pilot	Destroyed	Probable	Damaged
Clyde B. East	13	0	0
John H. Hoefker	10½	0	1
Leland A. Larson	6	0	2
Haylon R. Wood	3½	1	0
Henry E. Lacey	3	0	0
Norbourn A. Thomas	2½	1	1

*Unofficial lists

15th TAC R Victories (cont'd.)

Pilot	Destroyed	Probable	Damaged
James McCormick	2	1	0
Joe Waits	2	0	0
Harry S. Utley	2	0	0
Ernest Schonard	1½	1	0
John L. Murtha	1½	0	0
Theodore Trulson	1½	1	1
Alfred O. Frick	1½	0	0
George T. Walker	1½	0	0
William J. Boyle	1½	0	0
Charles D. White	1½	0	0
Joseph Conklin	1	0	0
Thomas Milner	1	0	0
Jackson A. Marshall	1	½	0
William M. Brackett	1	½	0
Guy F. Cary	1	1	1
Robert W. Shively	1	0	0
Charles R. Rowland	1	0	0
Edmund F. Maxwell	1	0	0
Julian Biniewski	1	0	0
George R. Schroeder	1	0	0
Fred J. Trenner	1	0	0
Frank Khare	½	1	0
J. Harrison	½	0	0
Hubert H. Hughes	½	0	0
Dale N. Goodermote	½	1	0
Charles D. Johnson	½	0	0
Wayne S. Patrick	½	1	0
Robert C. Landers	½	0	0
Robert H. Ober	½	0	0
Fairfield Goodale	½	0	0
Maxwell E. Chambers	½	0	0
Henry A. Hansen	0	1	0
Richard C. McFadden	0	1	0
Robert A. Jeffrey	0	0	2
Norbert W. Kirkpatrick	0	0	1
F.B. Boyden	0	0	1
Totals	71	12	10

162nd TAC R Victories

Pilot	Destroyed	Probable	Damaged
Joe Waits	5½	0	1
Robert A. Perry	3½	0	0
William I. Williams	2½	0	1
Perry Reavis	2	2	3
Manuel W. Geiger	1	1	0
Earl B. Scott	1	0	2
Roland M. Kollar	1	0	1
Glenn B. Gremillion	1	0	0
Stanley Newman	1	0	0
Clarence Louden	1	0	0
William Wardle	½	0	0
Arthur Oemcke	½	0	0
Robert F. Knudson	½	0	0
Walter P. Simpson	0	0	5
Robert Rumbaugh	0	0	2
William Yarborough	0	0	1
Totals	21	3	16

6. Colors and Markings of Group Aircraft

During its training days from November 1941 to December 1943, the 10th Photo Reconnaissance Group was equipped with a number of types of aircraft. From November 1941 into 1942 many of its aircraft were still obsolete observation planes such as the Douglas O-46, the North American O-47, and the Curtiss O-52. But as time went on—and especially after American air action in North Africa—the need for more modern types of aircraft and tactics became readily evident, and the Group began using P-39s, P-40Ns, P-51As, A-20s, and some L-4 and L-5 Liaison aircraft.

These were usually painted in the standard olive drab and gray scheme. But there were some exceptions to the rule: a number of the A-20 Havocs were in RAF dark earth and green camouflage with sky undersurfaces and RAF serial numbers. Most of the aircraft carried their squadron insignias on the fuselage along with the standard national insignia markings and serial numbers. The fighter aircraft carried three-digit aircraft numbers in white on each side of the nose and propeller spinners were painted in the squadron color. The 15th Tactical Reconnaissance Squadron P-39s and P-40s had the aircraft numbers and spinners painted in yellow, the squadron color.

In August 1943 the Group was composed of the 15th, 28th, and 152nd Tactical Reconnaissance Squadrons. Their aircraft had the spinners painted in the squadron colors: yellow for the 15th, white for the 28th, and blue for the 152nd. Most of the aircraft still carried their squadron insignias, and many carried art work or names. During the fall 1943 maneuvers in Tennessee the Group's aircraft were split between the opposing ground forces, and a color movie film taken at the time shows various temporary markings on the aircraft. In the film were 28th Tactical Recon P-39s with red-orange bands on the outer wings and rear fuselage and spinners overpainted in this color. The 152nd Tactical Recon P-40Ns were painted with a broad white fuselage band just aft of the cockpit section. Some 15th Tactical Recon P-40s were seen with no special markings while others had the broad white fuselage band as seen on the aircraft of the 152nd. At this time the aircraft numbers carried on the nose had been changed from a three-digit number to a two-digit number and a letter. For example, one 28th Tactical Recon P-39 was numbered 33E. National markings on the aircraft at the time of the fall maneuvers were the star-and-bar type with a red surround. The Squadron commander's aircraft still carried the twin fuselage band identification marking.

When the 10th Photo Recon Group arrived in England to set up operations at Chalgrove in February 1944, many of its initial issue of F-5 Lightnings were painted in olive drab and gray, but this scheme quickly gave way to photo recon colors. The finish applied initially was azure blue overall with yellow serial numbers and aircraft numbers. Some of the F-5s were stripped of all paint and flown in a bare metal finish. This was especially true for some of the aircraft used for the May 1944 dicing missions; these had not only the paint but some equipment removed as well to lighten the aircraft, and many seams were filled and polished to help increase its speed. Later models of the F-5 received by the Group came in photo recon blue paint overall or in a natural metal finish. The serial numbers and aircraft numbers applied to the aircraft painted Photo Reconnaissance Blue were in black on some planes and in yellow on others; however, some F-5s were seen with black serial numbers and the aircraft number in yellow. The squadron code letters applied to Photo Reconnaissance Blue aircraft were in white. The bare metal F-5s had all aircraft serial numbers, aircraft numbers, and code letters in black. The aircraft number assigned to each plane was the last three digits of its serial number and was in eight-inch letters. This number was painted on both sides of the nose on some aircraft and on the outer engine cowlings on others. About the only consistency to these markings on F-5s was their inconsistency.

The placement of Squadron codes on the F-5s was not standardized, either. The 30th Photo Squadron, which was the first assigned to the 10th, followed the example of other Lightning units in Europe. The Squadron code was placed on the rear portion of the boom and the individual aircraft letter was placed on the radiator scoop. Following the arrival of the 30th Photo Squadron at Chalgrove in February 1944 came the 31st and 34th Photo Squadrons in March and the 33rd Photo Squadron in April 1944. These squadrons did not carry individual aircraft letters on their F-5s, and the Squadron code was placed on the radiator scoop. By October 1944 the 30th, 33rd, and 34th Photo Squadron had departed the 10th for their new assignments; this left the 31st Photo Squadron as the only F-5 squadron in the 10th Photo Reconnaissance Group. The 31st then began using individual aircraft letters along with the squadron codes on its Lightnings.

The codes assigned to the F-5 squadrons while they were assigned to the 10th Photo Reconnaissance Group were as follows:

30th Photo Squadron	I6
32st Photo Squadron	8V
33rd Photo Squadron	SW
34th Photo Squadron	S9

The last type of unit marking applied to the F-5s of the 31st Photo Squadron was the blue and white checkerboard that became the 10th Group's marking during the last months of the war.

The Tactical Reconnaissance Mustangs assigned to the Group were painted and marked very much like the Mustang fighters of the 8th and 9th Air Forces. The first F-6Cs (P51Bs and Cs) received by the 12th and 15th Tactical Reconnaissance Squadrons were olive drab and gray and carried the white wing bands, white nose band, and white spinner. The olive drab F-6Cs had yellow serial numbers and white squadron codes. Before D-Day, however, both squadrons had already received a number of natural metal-finished F-6Cs, and all later F-6D and F-6K Mustangs were received in natural metal. These F-6s carried the standard black wing and tail bands, but the noses and spinners began to reflect the squadron colors: yellow for the 12th TAC R and dark blue for the 15th. (Many of the olive drab Mustangs still serving with these units at the time also had their spinners and nose bands repainted in the squadron color. Squadron codes and serial numbers for these natural metal aircraft were in black.

As mentioned, the 10th adopted a Group marking during the last months of the war: a blue and white checkerboard on the upper portion of the rudder and vertical tail surfaces. The F-6s also carried the squadron colors similarly on the nose. Their spinners were painted in the Squadron color, and the 12 inch nose band was checkerboarded to correspond: yellow and white for the 12th TAC R and blue and white for the 15th TAC R. When the 162nd TAC R joined the Group in April 1945, it carried red spinners and a red and white checkerboard. Since applying these checkerboards was time-consuming all of the Group's aircraft did not receive these markings before the war's end. The Squadron codes for the 10th PRG's Mustang squadrons were as follows:

12th Tactical Reconnaissance Squadron	ZM
15th Tactical Reconnaissance Squadron	5M
162nd Tactical Reconnaissance Squadron	IX

The 155th Night Photo Squadron flew Douglas F-3s, the photo version of the A-20J bomber. Most of its aircraft were finished in standard olive drab and gray finish with yellow serial numbers, and some had olive drab upper surfaces and black undersurfaces. A few were painted all black. This squadron carried no unit codes or markings.

All these types of aircraft carried a variety of art or names. They ranged from a basic stenciled name to elaborate artwork. The mission symbols of the 10th were varied. The unarmed F-5 Lightnings displayed the outline of a camera, a swastika, or a camera inside of the swastika. The symbols used on the F-6 Mustangs were a pair of binoculars to represent visual recon mission or a camera for photo missions. The Mustangs also displayed swastikas or German crosses to represent enemy aircraft destroyed in aerial combat. Unlike the 8th Air Force, pilots of the 9th Air Force were not given credit for enemy aircraft destroyed on the ground. The F-3s (A-20Js) of the 155th Night Photo Squadron carried a winged camera to represent their missions.

10TH PHOTO RECON GROUP, 15TH TAC RECON SQUADRON, 9TH AIR FORCE
F-6C- SERIAL No. 43-12479

10TH PHOTO RECON GROUP, 34TH PHOTO RECON SQUADRON, 9TH AIR FORCE
F-5A-3LO SERIAL No. 43-12786

10TH PHOTO RECON GROUP, 162ND TAC RECON SQUADRON, 9TH AIR FORCE
F-6C SERIAL No. 42-103213 (PILOT-LT. STANLEY F. NEWMAN)

Index

A

A-13 (Tour-en-Bessin), 54
Aachen, 95, 100
Abbeville, 43
Adams, Lt. Frazier, 81
Aerschot, 27
Ahr River, 137
Aisne-River, 66, 67
Alberty, Lt., 27
Alencon, 41
Algesheim, 105
Allen, Lt. Charles M., 17
Allen, John, 1
Allied Expeditionary Air Force, 9
Alm, Lt. George, 169
"Alma", 134
Alzev, 141
Amiens, 43, 51
Anderson, Lt. C.G., 35, 39, 72, 95, 99
Anderson, Sgt. Robert, 118
Ansbach, 114
Anzio, 21, 26
Ardennes Forest, 109
Argenten, 59
Argonne Forest, 67
Arnhem, 71
Arnold, General Henry H., 19
Arras, 50
Ashaffenburg, 129, 130, 144
Autobahn, 141
Avranches, 49, 51
"'Azel", 136
  Boomerang, 148

B

Babbington-Smith, Constance, 6
Bad Krevznach, 78, 139, 141
Bad Nauhem, 107
Bagley K-3 Camera, 5
Balachowski, Lt. Eugene F., 60, 89, 105, 133, 137
Bar-Le-Duc, 66
Barnes, Lt. Neal J., 59, 99
Barone, Dr. William, 162
Barron, Sgt. Charles, 64
Bastogne, 105, 107, 109, 113, 114, 115, 116, 120
Bayreuth, 155
Beachy Head, 41
Beaumont-Le-Roger, 23
Becker, Lt. Walter G., 73
Beckingen, 73
Belfort Gap, 68
Belleme, 41
Berchtesgaden, 157
Berck-Sur-Mer, 26
Berg, Col. Russell A., 37, 54, 68, 84, 94, 126, 131, 167
Berlin, 125
Bernay, 41, 42
Best, Lt. Thair W., 125
Bielinski, Lt. Edward H., 72, 73, 108, 117, 120
"Big Week", 20
Bingen, 73, 78, 105, 139, 140
Biniewski, Lt. Julian, 169
Bishop, Capt. Edward L., 56, 72, 108, 122, 124, 140, 162
Bisschofsteinitz, 160, 170
Bitburg, 123, 130, 131, 132, 133, 137

Bleau, Lt. R., 162
Bone, Lt., 23
Bonn, 132
Bosworth, Lt., 30
Boulogne, 32
Bowling Green, Kentucky, 14
Boyden, Lt. F.B., 138
Boyle, Lt. William J., 28, 59
Brackett, Lt. William M., 85, 94, 125, 137, 168
Bradley, General Omar, 36, 48-49, 108, 131-132, 144
Brady, Matthew, 2
Brandt, Lt. Karl, 66, 105
Brest Peninsula, 38, 50, 56, 62, 66
Bruce, Lt. Robert, 132, 150, 152, 162
Breisach, 72
Brighton, 36
Brittany Peninsula, 50
Brown, Capt. Harvey C. Jr., 6
Buchenwald, 155-156
Bunker, Lt. F.B., 137
Burdick, Lt. William, 82
Burkhalter, Lt. Max, 87-88, 93, 102, 116
Butler, Lt. Harry J., 85
Butler, Lt. James F., 107

C

Caen, 48
Cambrai, 50
Cameron, Lt., 25
Camp Campbell, Kentucky, 14
Canady, Lt. Leon, 116, 131
Canner, Lt. Stephen, 48
Cannon, Lt. 162
Cartago, Lt. Daniel, 152, 156, 162
Cary, Lt. Guy, 140, 150
Cash, Lt. Earston H., 28
Caumont, 48
Chalgrove, 17, 20, 23, 25, 27, 35, 48, 50
Chalons, 60, 66
Chambers, Lt. Maxwell, 165-166
Chambliss, Capt. C.C., 95
Charmes, 73
Chateaudun, 65, 66, 68, 101
Chateau Salines, 81
Chateau-Thierry, 66, 67
Chateau-Villaine, 68
Chateauroux-Issodun-Fourages, 68
Cherbourg Peninsula, 20, 24, 25, 27, 35, 36, 37, 43
Cherisy, 50
Chinn, Lt. Arthur, 65
Clark, Capt. James, 41-42
Clasters, 51
COBRA, OPERATION, 49
Cochen, 105
Cohn, Lt., 39
Cologne, 95, 130
Combined Bomber Offensive, 19
Commercy, 88
Conflans, 87
Conklin, Lt. Joseph E., 28, 34, 38
Conley, Lt. Raymond, 169
Cotentin Peninsula, 49
Countelle, Col. Jean-Marie, 1
Coutances, 36, 49
Crawford, Lt. H.C., 52
Creil, 23
CROSSBOW, OPERATION, 20
Culbertson, Lt. Robert E., 28, 75

D

Danube River, 170
Darmstadt, 95, 140, 144, 153
Dasburn, 125-126
Davenport, Lt. William O., 98, 139, 141, 143, 154, 156, 161, 162
Davis, Lt. Daniel, 132, 158
Davis, Maj. Lyon L., 28, 85, 148
Davis, Lt. Robert, 131
Davis, Lt. Thomas P., 139, 167
Dawson, Capt. Robert E., 28, 119, 132, 133
D-Day, 35, 36, 38, 69
Delem, 99
Denby, Lt. Col. George M., 2
De Ridder Army Air Base, Louisiana, 10
Dicing, 25-26, 33, 121, 125
Dieckman, Lt. E.W., 54, 75, 78
Dieuze, 70, 75, 76, 85-87
  Etang De Lindre Dam, bombing of 85-87
Dijon-Besancon Gap, 62
Dijon, 85
Dillengen, 88
Dingle, Col. Jack, 17, 21, 25-26, 133
Doenitz, Adm. Karl, 168
Doolittle, Gen. James H., 20
Dowell, Lt. Donald, 105, 114, 133
Dreux, 38, 50, 56
Dresden, 153, 156
Dungeness, 26

E

East, Capt. Clyde B., 28, 38, 94, 106, 108, 123, 125, 129, 132, 133, 135, 143, 144, 146, 148, 151, 153-154, 155, 156, 157, 187
Echternach, 73, 133
Edgerton, Dr. Harold, 15, 57, 84, 89
Edgerton Lamp, 15, 33, 35-36, 37
Effelder, 153
Eger, 156
Eifel, 127
Eighth Air Force, 20, 49, 54
Eisenhower, Gen. Dwight D., 19, 25, 32, 36, 68, 71, 108, 129, 156
Eisman, Capt. Paul, 84
Eisnach, 144, 150, 153
Elliott, Lt. M. Leo, 152, 162
Elliott, Lt. William, 158
Ellis, Lt. John, 98, 131, 152, 153, 155, 162
Elster, Gen. Botho, 72
Enneis, Lt. William, 100
Erfurt, 155, 156, 157
Ermatinger, Lt. Henry, 154, 162
Euskirchen, 113
Evereux, 42

F

Falaise Gap, 54, 56, 59, 126
FE Camp, 32
Florence, Maj. John, 123-125, 140, 141, 162
Fluhr, Lt. William, 64, 68
Fort Driant, 75
Fort Jean D'Arc, 101
Fort Knox, Kentucky, 10, 12, 14
Fort Monroe, 1
Foulois, Lt. Benjamin, 2
Frankfurt-Am-Main, 73, 94, 95, 99, 106, 140, 141, 144, 147
Franklin, Lt. Claude, 78, 96, 123, 131, 143
Freeth, Lt. Stanley, 158
French, Capt. D.R., 54
Freudstadt, 75, 78
Frick, Lt. Albert O., 28, 51, 78, 136, 145, 153, 157

Frieburg, 155
Fulda, 131, 150
Furth, 136, 168, 170

G

Gardner, Lt. William R., 152, 162
Garner, Maj. Merritt G., 27, 29, 36, 55, 73, 102
Garr, Lt., 65
Geiger, Lt. Manuel, 56, 169-170
Giessen, 94, 106, 131, 141
Gilbert Islands, 6
Gillespie, Maj. Joe, 59, 88, 120
Gilliam, Capt., 162
Giraumont, 99, 101
  A-94, 101, 111, 118, 151
Goddard, Dr. George W., 5, 6
Godman Field, Kentucky, 10, 12
Goodale, Lt. Fairfield, 148, 165
Goodermote, Lt. Dale, 66, 81, 90, 93-94, 105, 108, 130, 138-139, 150, 155
Goodrich, Lt. John, 170
Gotha, 150, 152, 154
Goval, Lt. Edward, 81, 102, 123, 129, 157
Graz, 170
Gremillion, F/O Glen, 168
Grisham, Lt. Lonnie, 75, 82

H

Hadden, Capt. Howard "Buzz," 42
Halle, 78
Hammelburg, 146
Hampton Roads, Virginia, 1
Hanau, 106, 129, 131, 140
Hansen, Lt. Henry, 28, 42, 81, 82
Hardy, Lt. Douglas, 39
Haslup, Lt., 27
Haun, Maj. James, 54
Hayes, Maj. Donald, 21, 25
Hayes, Lt. Fred, 27
Haywood, Lt. William, 25
"Heaven Can Wait," 48
Heilbron, 80
HERMANN, OPERATION, 120
Hersfeld, 150
Heugueville, 32
Hibbert, Col. Richard B., 25, 84, 161
Hickman, Lt. John F., 30
Hilders, 150
Hitler, Adolph, 167
Hodges, Gen. Courtney, 49, 144
Hoefker, Capt. John H., 28, 38, 41, 82, 94, 97, 99, 106-107, 108, 111, 113, 115, 116, 133, 139, 150, 153, 155, 161, 187
Hof, 154, 155, 156
Hohner, Capt. William, 114
Holbury, Capt. Robert J., 27, 32, 80, 104, 121-122, 124
Holtzhalloben, 153
Homburg, 95, 137
Hooke, Lt., 75
Houffalize, 122
Hoy, Lt. Charles, 68
Hughes, Lt. H.H., 65
Huggins, Lt. Nelson, 39, 95
Hulse, Lt. Gordon, 88
Hunsruck Mountains, 138
Hunt, Lt. Phillip, 95, 148

I

Idstein, 146
Immeldorf, 140

Isigney, 37

J

Jackson, Lt. Wendell, 36
Jarny, 101
Jarrard, Maj. Newton E., 11, 17
Jarrell, Capt., 30
Jeffrey, Lt. Robert, 158-159, 169
Jena, 155
Johnson, Lt. Charles, 78, 90, 93, 148
Johnson, Lt. M.F., 28
Johnston, Capt. William, 141
Julich, 95
Juterburg, 153

K

Kaden, Capt. James, 14, 21
KaisersLautern, 78, 80, 99, 139, 141
Kassel, 102, 150
Keith, Lt. Allen R., 32
Kennedy, Lt. Col. John C., 10
Kenny, Lt. Edward, 131, 162, 170
Key Field, Mississippi, 15
Kezziah, Lt. John, 117
Khare, Lt. Frank C., 28, 42, 81, 87, 100-101
Kieffer, Lt. Ward, 94
Kimler, Lt. John, 94, 162
King, Lt. J., 131
Kinyon, Lt. Charles, 73, 82
Kirchberg, 140
Kirch-Kons, 93, 94, 106
Kirkpatrick, Lt. N.W., 123, 133, 137, 140, 152, 153
"Kitten," 136
Kladrau, 160
Klagenfurt, 170
Kluge, Field Marshall Guenther (German) 49
Knickerbocker, Lt., 27
Knoebel, Lt. Ralph E., 28
Koblenz, 75, 102, 114, 122, 130, 137, 138, 140
Koger, Lt. W.R., 162
Koplin, Lt. W.J., 162
Krone, Lt. Ray, 125
Kulak, F/O Stanley, 37

L

Lacey, Lt. Henry, 106, 108, 137, 138-139, 145, 146, 147, 148, 152, 155, 156, 158, 168
Lacey, Lt. William, 49, 55
Lachen-Speyerdorf, 95
Laigle, 41
Lake Placid, New York, 11
Lamstein, 105
La Mountain, John, 1
Landers, Lt. Robert, 147
Lanker, Lt. Albert, 18, 26, 30, 36, 115
Larson, Lt. Leland A., 143, 144-145, 146, 147, 148, 150, 151, 153-154, 167, 169, 188
Lassudat, Col. Aime, 1
Laughlin, Col. Joseph, 86
Lawson Field, Georgia, 10
Leavenworth, Lt. William, 88
Lee, Col. Robert M., 11
Lefebure, Lt. Henri, 141, 147, 162
Leghorn, Capt. Richard, 20
Le Havre, 23, 41
Leigh-Mallory, Air Marshall Sir Trafford, 9
Leipzig, 151, 155, 156
Le Loupe, 59
Le Mans, 54
Le Molay, 48

Lentscher, Lt. Edward, 35, 36, 39
Leonard, Lt. Lawrence, 81, 106
Le Treport, 26
Leuth, Capt. Harold, 153
Lewis, Lt. Henry, 82, 86, 138-139, 147
Liebnitz, 170
Lienz, 170
Lille, 50
Limburg, 95, 102, 144, 145
Linz, 160, 168
Little, Lt. Robert C., 150, 162, 163, 170
Liseaux, 42
Lofland, Lt. Floyd, 133, 168
Logothetis, Lt. Mingo V., 81, 93, 98, 102, 115, 123, 143, 152, 153, 155
Loing River, 60
Loire River, 43, 44-47, 50, 55, 61-62, 68
Loomis, Lt., 117
Lorient, 50
Lowe, Thaddeus S.C., 2
Ludwigshafen, 143
Luke, Lt. Frank, 3
Luneville, 72
Luxembourg, 94, 114, 126, 140
Lynch, Lt. Donald, 73, 87-88, 116, 140, 147, 149, 162, 170

M

MacArthur, Gen. Douglas, 5
McClendon, Lt. W.C., 95
McCook Field, Ohio, 5
McCurdy, Maj. Leon H., 25, 32
McCormick, Lt. James, 28, 56
McCotter, Lt. Douglas, 98
McFadden, Lt. Richard C., 133, 146, 155, 168
Machern, 99
McKeon, Lt. William, 39
Mackie, Lt. Clifford "Joe," 35, 39, 88
Maher, Lt. (363 TRG), 114
Mainz, 73, 93, 143, 151
Mannheim, 80, 102, 139, 143
Marnt River, 59, 66, 67, 79
Marple, Lt. Robert, 141, 162, 170
Marshall, Lt. Jackson A., 94
Martin, Lt., 23
Matthews, Lt. James, 60
Mauberge, 1
Maupertus, 20, 24, 25
Maxfield, Lt. Col. Joseph E., 2
Maxwell, Lt. Edmund, 128, 134, 154, 160
"Mazie, Me and Monk," 111, 142
Mecca, Lt. Salvatore A., 45, 47-48
Meikle, Lt. William L., 156
Meltzer, Lt., 117
Merhausen, 107
Merl, 140
Merzig, 93, 112, 120, 121, 124, 131
Metz, 72, 73, 74, 75, 80, 81, 82, 87-88, 91, 92, 93, 99
Meuse River, 59, 67, 69, 105
MEW (Microwave Early Warning), 82, 89
Meyer, Lt. Arnold, 110, 132
Miefert, Lt. John F., 28, 44, 46, 47, 50, 156, 177
Miller, Lt. G.W., 162
Miller, Lt., 23
Milner, Lt. Thomas H., 28, 66
Mitchell, Lt. Wallace, 133, 134, 156, 160, 162, 170
Mitchell, Capt. William, 23, 27
Montes, Lt. Raymond, 128, 134

Montgomery, Field Marshall Sir Bernard L., 71, 130, 131-132
Montgomery, Lt. George, 88
Mortagne, 48
Moselle River, 73, 91, 120, 121, 123
Mowery, Lt., 75
Muelheim, 95
Munchberg, 152
Munich, 80, 165
Murtha, Lt. John L., 28, 62
Mykyten, Lt. Russell, 80, 102, 141

N

Nahe River, 141
Nancy, 72, 87
Nantes, 61
Nelson, Lt. J.H., 162
Nelson, Pvt. T.G., 95
Neunkirchen, 123
Neustadt, 144, 147
Neweid, 131
Newman, Lt., 109
Newman, Lt. Stanley, 136, 149, 160, 169-170
Nicklas, Lt. Gilbert, 133, 134
Nichols, Capt. Howard, 95, 102, 110, 123, 125, 126, 132, 140
Nijmegan, 71
Ninth Air Force, 17, 19, 36, 37, 49, 79, 89
XIXth (US) Tactical Air Command 37, 53, 61, 62, 66, 67, 68, 72, 87, 91, 92, 125, 133, 138, 139, 147
Norman, Lt. (363rd TRG), 114
Nuremburg, 156, 158, 159

O

Ober, Lt. Robert, 148, 165
Ober-Olm, 151, 153
O'Brien, Lt. E.J., 170
Octeville, 20
O'Dowd, Pvt. Frank, 81
Olson, Lt. Elmer, 131, 147. 162
Olson, Lt. Ronald, 170
Oppenheim, 130, 144
Orleans, 56, 61, 62
Ostend, 43
Oswald, Lt. Bernard, 98
Ouistreham, 27
Overlord, 9
Oxford, 38

P

Palatinate, 138, 140, 144
Palko, T/Sgt. John, 39
Panner, Lt. Edward, 160
Papen, Franz von, 161
Paris, 56, 60, 61, 66
Passau, 160
Patrick, Lt. Wayne S., 129, 146, 147, 148, 155, 168
Patton, Gen. George S. Jr., 49, 51, 60, 67, 69, 71, 99, 108, 112, 120, 125, 127, 131-132, 138, 140, 144
Pearl Harbor, 6, 10, 60
Peek, Lt. R.E., 162
Pershing, Gen. John J., 2
Peterson, Lt., 30
Pettigrew, T/Sgt. John, 9
"Phantom Gun," 87
Piatt, Lt. Jacob, 49, 55
Pilson, 168
Pirmasons, 73, 78
Pitts, Martin, 81
Plauen, 157
Pleujean, 32

Poe, Lt. Col. Edgar A. "Jack," 17, 24, 112
POINTBLANK, OPERATION, 9, 20, 24
Polifka, Col. Karl, 25
Pont-a-Mousson, 86, 92
Poole, Lt. James M., 32, 68, 95, 113-114
Porter, Lt., 117
Posey, Lt., 59
Pratt, Adm. William, 5
Prum, 123, 126, 130, 131-132, 133, 137
"Skyline Drive," 126
"Puff," 77

Q

Querqueville, 20, 24, 25
Quinn, T/Sgt. Jack, 96

R

Rastatt, 75, 78
Rau, Lt. Joseph, 64
Ray, Lt. Earl A., 73, 102, 139
Ray, Lt. James, 160, 162
Raymond, Capt. Robert L., 28, 51, 60, 94, 99
Read, Lt. C.I., 28
Red, Lt. Vernon, 39
Reed, Lt. Alfred, 147, 162
Reed, Lt. Merlin, 105, 148, 157, 167
Reed, Col. William B., 9, 15, 17, 20, 25, 37
Reeves, Lt., 117
Reger, Lt. Theodore E., 28, 48, 73
Regensburg, 153
Remagen, 137, 145
Remick, 73
Rennes, 50, 54, 55, 56
Renton, Lt. Elliott R., 99
Repass, Capt. Robert, 162
Rhienfriedsdorf, 157
Rhine River, 67, 93, 133, 137, 138, 141, 143, 144
Rhoads, Lt. John, 98, 115, 143, 150, 154
Rhone Valley, 62
Ricci, Lt. Ronald R., 81, 98, 106, 115, 141, 156
von Richthofen, Baron Manfred, 3
Rider, Capt., 162
Riesa, 154
Ristau, Lt. Frank, 28, 50
Roosevelt, Col. Elliott, 57
Roper, Lt. Robert, 168
Rose, Capt. James L., 55
Rosen, Cpl. Ben, 96
Rowland, Lt. Charles, 75, 86, 99, 144, 154, 155, 156
Royal Air Force, 6, 54, 114
Rozwein, 157
Rudel, Lt., 23
Ruhr, 151
Ruschberg, 78
Rusten, Capt. A.M., 48

S

St. Dizier, 67, 89, 94, 97, 99, 101, 77, 84, 98
St. Lo, 37, 48, 56, 59
St. Malo, 50
St. Mihiel, 67
St. Quentin, 50
St. Vaast-La Hogue, 27
St. Valery, 32
St. Vith, 105, 116, 117, 123, 125, 126
St. Wendell, 93, 140
Saalfeld, 156
Saar River, 102, 120, 121
Salzburg, 157
Samur, 44

199

San Juan Hill, Battle of, 2
Sarrebrucken, 73, 81, 82, 102, 115, 122, 123
Sarreburg, 85, 95
Sarrelautern, 93
Sarvik, Lt. 23
Scara, Lt. Russell, 170
Scattergood, Maj. Edgar, 9
Schonard, Lt. Ernest M. "Bud," 28, 38, 41, 43, 44, 48, 50, 56, 65, 82, 85
Schroeder, Lt. George, 169
Schweinfurt, 75
Sedan, 115
Seeley, Lt. Frank, 169
Seine River, 43, 54, 59
Shaeffer, Lt. George, 78
SHEAF, 129
Shimon, Lt. Dale, 73, 162, 170
Shively, Lt. Robert, 139, 151, 152, 168
Siegfried Line, 73, 101, 138
Siek, Lt., 30
"Silver," Capt., 74
Simpson, Lt. 23
Simpson, Lt. Col. Robert T. IV, 28, 45, 74, 84, 131, 161
Skowranek, Sgt. Herbert, 168
"Sleepy Time Gal," 64
Smelley (now Shelley) Col. James M., 17, 159
Smiley, Lt., 66
Smith, Lt. Joseph H., 32
Sobernheim, 105
Sonne, Fred, 6
Spearman, Lt. 30
Spencer, Lt., 24
Spittal, 170
Stapp, Louis, 10
"Starize," 83
Starmont, Lt. Thomas, 35, 39
Staup, Capt. Glenn, 28, 92
Stelle, Lt. Russell E., 28, 48
Strange, Lt. Melvin, 140, 162
Strasbourg, 120
Stuttgart, 80, 123

T

Tackis, T/Sgt. Jack, 39
Taylor, Gen. Maxwell D., 116
Tennessee Maneuvers, 14-15
Tenny, Lt. A.R., 114
Tessy-sur-Vire, 49
Thionville, 94, 95
Thirwall, Lt. J.C., 52
Thomas, Lt. Norborne, 81, 132, 140, 153, 160
Thompson, Lt. Donald F., 23, 27
Tichemont Chateau, 101, 111
Tiefield, PFC Roy, 96
Tillett, Lt. John, 73, 100, 123
Torgau, 155
Tourchon, Gaspard F., 1
Tours, 44, 59, 61
Travis, Capt. E.B. "Blackie," 109, 111
Trenner, Lt. Fred J., 28, 38, 41, 43, 44, 50, 59, 61, 65, 70, 75, 76, 85, 100-101
Trier, 73, 94, 95, 102, 112, 122, 123, 129, 132, 135, 137, 138, 151, 152
  Trier-Evren Y-57, 137, 147
Trulson, Lt. Theodore M., 28, 51, 66, 82

U

Utley, Lt. Harry S., 155, 157

V

Val D'Enhue, 49

Vandenburg, Gen. Hoyt, 117
Verdun, 67, 108
VERITABLE, OPERATION, 130
Verket, Lt. Lloyd, 68, 72, 73
Vianden, 125
Vienzon, 59
Villa, Poncho, 2
Villediev, 36
Villeroche, 59
Vire, 37
Vitry-Le-Francois, 67
VonRunstedt, Field Marshall Gerd, 103
Von Tempsky, Lt. Robert, 68

W

Waits, Lt. Joe, 28, 41, 160, 188
Walker, Lt. Col. George T., 28, 38, 56, 68, 7 85
Walker, Lt. Robert, 81
Wallaert, Lt. Henry J., 23, 24
Walsh, Lt. Charles, 160
Walters, Lt., 75
Walters, Lt. Col. Rudolph, 23, 55, 84, 161
Ward, Lt. Russell A., 80
Ware, Lt. Col. Robert, 160
Warenskjold, Lt. James (pronounced "Var Shaw"), 28, 48, 75
Warren, Lt. Byrne, 138
Warren, Capt. Lloyd, 8, 21
Wassom, Lt. John J., 80
Webb, Lt. James, 145, 146
Weimar, 155
Weisbaden, 73, 95, 100, 106-107, 130, 144 147
Wetzler, 146
Weyland, Gen. O.P., 60, 72, 117
Wheeler-Sack Field, Pine Camp, New York, 10
White, Lt. Charles D., 106-107, 113, 130, 150, 160
Whiteman, S/Sgt. C.H., 88-89
Williams, F/O, 96, 162
Williams, Lt. James E., 52, 57, 88, 100, 120
Williams, Maj. Samuel, 84
Willis, Sgt. James, 39
Will Rogers Field, Oklahoma, 17
Wilson, Lt. Stewart A., 133, 152
Winberry, Capt. William, 75, 82, 105, 116, 131, 152
Wise, John, 1
Wittenburg, 151
Wolcott, Capt. Roger, 115
Wolfe, Lt. W.A., 123
Wood, Lt. Haylon R., 130, 133, 137, 144, 146, 152, 157, 158-159, 160, 165-167
Wood, Lt. Thomas J., 54
Wood, Lt. Thomas L., 59
Woodrow, Lt. Col. Gordon L., 54
Woody, Col. Rufus, 27, 73, 103, 114-115
Worms, 82, 93, 94, 102, 137, 139, 140, 143
Worrell, Lt. R.L., 162
Wright, Lt., 24
Wright, Lt. Conrad, 170
Wulfsburg, 170
Wurzburg, 95, 150

Y

York, Lt. Garland A., 22, 27, 30, 176
Young, Capt. Elvin, 169
Youll, Lt. Richard "Doc," 28, 50, 61, 99

Z

Zondlo, Lt. Steve A., 59, 81, 132
Zweibrucken, 88, 102